CONFLICT NARRATIVES IN MIDDLE CHILDHOOD

Conflict Narratives in Middle Childhood presents evidence from twenty years of research, examining nearly 3,000 narratives from 1,600 children in eight settings in two countries about their own experiences with interpersonal conflict. Close readings, combined with systematic analysis of dozens of features of the stories, reveal that when children are invited to write or talk about their own conflicts, they produce accounts that are often charming and sometimes heartbreaking, and that always bring to light their social, emotional, and moral development. Children's personal stories about conflict reveal how they create and maintain friendships, how they understand and react to the social aggression that threatens those friendships, and how they understand and cope with physical aggression ranging from the pushing and poking of peers to criminal violence in their neighborhoods or families. Sometimes children describe the efforts of adults to influence their conflicts – efforts they sometimes welcome and sometimes resist. Their stories show them 'taking on' gender and other cultural commitments. We are not just watching children become more and more like us as they move through the elementary school years, we are watching them become the architects of a future we will only see to the extent that we understand their way of making sense.

Marsha D. Walton is the Winton C. Blount Chair in Social Science at Rhodes College. She completed her doctoral work in developmental psychology in 1979 at the University of North Carolina at Chapel Hill. She has supervised many bright and committed undergraduates on a Child Narrative Research Team, forty-five of whom have gone on to take doctorates in psychology or related fields.

Alice J. Davidson is an Associate Professor of Psychology and a Cornell Distinguished Faculty member at Rollins College. She holds a PhD in Human Development and Family Studies from The Pennsylvania State University. She teaches community engagement courses in child and adolescent development and studies peer relations in middle childhood.

CONFLICT NARRATIVES IN MIDDLE CHILDHOOD

The Social, Emotional, and Moral Significance of Story-Sharing

Marsha D. Walton and
Alice J. Davidson

Routledge
Taylor & Francis Group

NEW YORK AND LONDON

First published 2017
by Routledge
711 Third Avenue, New York, NY 10017

and by Routledge
2 Park Square, Milton Park, Abingdon, Oxon, OX14 4RN

Routledge is an imprint of the Taylor & Francis Group, an informa business

Library of Congress Cataloging in Publication Data
A catalog record for this book has been requested

ISBN: 978-1-138-67074-7 (hbk)
ISBN: 978-1-138-67075-4 (pbk)
ISBN: 978-1-351-86601-9 (ebk)

Typeset in Bembo
by Swales & Willis Ltd, Exeter, Devon, UK

To my parents, Jesslyn Austin Walton and Granderson Field Walton. They made a home rich with stories – about every hurricane that hit Hatteras Island, about youthful adventures and inventiveness, about injustice observed and endured, and about finding meaning in each adversity and laughter in most.

– *Marsha D. Walton*

To my father, Nelson Marvin Davidson, Jr. ("Mike"), a masterful story-teller, whose tales (most of which were situated in the Texas Hill Country) got better with every telling. His own life, which included contracting polio at the age of four and dying at the young age of sixty-six after forty-two years of marriage to his best friend, my wonderful mother, Barbara, was a beautiful story of loss and resilience.

– *Alice J. Davidson*

CONTENTS

ACKNOWLEDGMENTS

Our research is unusual in its utter reliance on the work of thoughtful and committed undergraduate researchers, and we've done our best to name as many of these as we can. Many of these students have gone on to take doctorates in psychology or in related disciplines, and we look forward to the contributions they will make to our understanding of human development.

Exceptional conceptual work and/or indispensable assistance with every phase of the research from data collection to writing was contributed by Christy Brewer-Boyd, Angela Fox, Darcy Gist, Alexis Harris, Eliza Hendrix, Regan Humphrey, Bhavna Kansal, Sandra Keller, Jiawen Li, Janna Miller, Kelly Parry, Anna Stagg, Stephanie Wilson, and Annika Wuerfel. Many of these individuals continued to be a part of our interpretive community well past their own graduation, orienting a next generation of team members, and/or publishing with us.

Besides this, our work could not have been accomplished without the following students helping with data collection and transcription; attending weekly team meetings to establish coding systems and achieve inter-coder reliability, and contributing their interpretations and understandings of individual stories: Stephany Albury, Brandy Alexander, Brittany Alexander, Ellen Alpaugh, Laura Atkinson, Heather Banks, Caitlin Campbell, Theresa Cannon, Brandy Cantrell Cook, Katie Castile, Dara Chestnut, Tara Connors, Jessica Dunn, Megan Etz, Rachel Farley, Kim Farmer, Sybil Fortner, Elyssa Geer, Elyse Gilbert, Liz Giraud, Angela Gooden, Meredith Guillot, Cara Guthrie, Jennifer Hansen Staub, Nicole Jones, Emily Jordan, Heidi Kane Ottman, Laura Lyons, Abby May, Lorin McGuire, Paige Mossman, John Nichols, Perry Person, Lin Qiu, Amy Reid Alford, Kaitlyn Reynolds, Rebecca Robertson, Lisa Schum Pascoli, Lucy Shores, Michelle Staley, Katherine Stewart, Jessica Struby, and Natasha Westrich.

Many students over twenty years in advanced methods classes or in senior seminars have worked with subsets of these stories for a single semester, or sometimes for two semesters. Some of their literature reviews or data coding became important for our further work, and we would like to acknowledge their contributions: Brooke Bierdtz, Virginia Brady, Rebecca Brewster, Molly Buck, Kyle Capstick, Priscilla Chancy, Elizabeth Collins, Natalie Darar, Andrea Davis, John Del Rossi, Katie DuBose, Chigozie Emelue, Darcy Emerson, Sara Ellen Erde, Brittany Erwin, Sarah Finney, Talia Flantzman, Ellie Frame, Alexandra Friedman, Jenny Frierson, Jessica Gatewood, Paige Goemaere, Yan Guo, Kryseanna Harper, Marian Hill, Cuyler Hines, Kristina Holland, Marian Howorth, Julia Humphrey, Josie Kisalus, Celeste Lake, Taylor LaPort, Ashley Luthy, Adele Malpert, Alessandra Mayo, Sheena McKinney, Allison Miller, Joseph Naranjo, Danielle Parrott, Katelyn Profaca, Christina Rodriguez-Feraro, Marissa Scales, Trent Schill, Kelly Schricker, Lena Seiferling, Lauren Shames, Jasdev Singh, Tierney Sisk, Destiny Smith, Lyndsay Solomine, Kathryn South, Jessica Sprenkel, Anna Stratton-Brook, Madison Tallant, Rebecca Thompson, Rupa Vachaspati, Emily Weiner, and Ellie Wiggins.

Besides this critical support from our students, many of whom have become colleagues, we owe much to many other colleagues who have shared their expertise and good judgment over the years. Robert Cohen, and members of the University of Memphis Peer Interaction Group, have assisted with data collection and consistently given critical and supportive feedback about preliminary results and interpretations. The following people who have reviewed selected chapters of this book for us can be credited with meaningful improvements to the manuscript: Shannon Audley, Barbara Austin, Gabrielle Gipson Banks, Sarah Elaine Barnes, Whitney Chatterjee, Erin Cue, Jan Horn, Corissa Raymond, Robert Strandburg, Ryland Testa, Allyson Kelsey Topps, Jenny Walton-Wetzel, Chris Wetzel, Yeh Hsueh, and Hui Zhang. We are grateful for guidance given by anonymous reviewers on early drafts of several chapters. Anna Peacher-Ryan patiently worked behind us, verifying references, checking for style inconsistencies, and finding our errors.

We are especially indebted to Jiawen Li, Hui Zhang, Yeh Hsueh, Jin Zuo, Zhaochang Peng, and Lin Qiu, who spent much time helping us understand various aspects of childhood in China and helped us interpret stories by children in Shenzhen, despite our own language limitations.

Loving support from family and friends has sustained us both as we sometimes gave attention to this project that we might have given to those relationships instead. From Marsha, thanks to husband and daughter and sometime collaborators Chris and Jenny, to soul-mate Beth, parents Jesslyn and Granderson, sister Barb, and an amazing group of women who gather for breakfast every Wednesday. From Alice, thanks to my parents, Mike and Barbara, to Sarah and Andrew who always make me laugh and have taught me much about dealing with conflict, and to my favorite travel companions and loves, Eric and Norah.

We are deeply grateful to the administrators and staff who welcomed us into their schools and community centers and to the teachers who opened their class-room doors to us and gave away precious class time to allow us to collect stories from their students.

Our most profound gratitude, expressed throughout this book, is to the 1,600 children who shared stories with us for the eight studies we included in this book, and to several thousand more who have participated in weekly story-sharing circles that were not a part of a research project, but were an important part of shaping our understanding of "what it is like to be a kid these days." It is our deepest hope that they like what we have done with their stories.

INTRODUCTION: "WHAT I'VE BEEN IN IS A LOT OF CONFLICTS"

Story-Sharing and Making Sense of Conflict in Middle Childhood

Holding one's own in the sometimes brutal world of middle childhood means navigating a social universe full of gossip, teasing, daring, and telling secrets. The childhoods we like to remember as simple and carefree were also characterized by competing demands for resources, competing bids for social standing, shifting loyalties, and child-sized betrayals that, at the time, felt crushing. The successful negotiation of the social universe of an elementary school requires the development of impressive skills in understanding the motives and experiences of self and other. Consider the account in Example 0.1 by Daria, a fifth-grade girl who was asked to "write a true story about a conflict that really happened to you."

EXAMPLE 0.1   DARIA, FIFTH-GRADE GIRL, MAGNOLIA SPRINGS ELEMENTARY, ORLANDO

"I'll kick you in your face talk to me that way"! I was yelling my head of to this stuck up no good girl. Who thougt she was the big bad wolf all of this day at the day cares playgound. She walked and she talked and she got knocked right in the face by the bigger wolf in town me! But it all started when she told my bff that I was useing her an that she needed not be my friend any more then the whole day care spreded the romer and she stop being my friend and. Told me what that toe jam said So I confronted her about it then she went bleasick! And acted like she was going to hit me but of stad of her hitting me I pounched her and made her nose bleed then I looked at my fit and realied what I had just done. Then I realy wasent the cool Kid in day care and to think I would had even done it over not having to just ask to tell the troth to my X bff then doing what I did. And at the end of it all I was the one who got in the boialing hot water with my mom and the towlets mother. But that is the old me and now I look back and say wow I did something So mean and sien then I have not been in nother fit! And that was 4 years ago![1]

Write a story about a conflict with another
kid that really happened to you. Think
about a fight, an argument or some kind of
misunderstanding. Write everything that
happened from the beginning to the end.

"I'll kick you in your face talk to
me that way!" I was yelling my head of
to this stuck up no good girl. who
thought she was the big bad wolf all
of this day at the daycares playground.
She walked and she talked and she
got knocked right in the face by the
bigger wolf in town me! But it all
started when she told my bff that
I was useing her an that she needed
not be my friend any more then the
whole daycare spreded the rumer and
She stop being my friend and. Told me

what that toe jam said so I
confronted her about it then she went
beasick! And acted like she was going
to hit me, but of stad of her hitting me
I pounched her and made her nose
bleed then I looked at my fit and
realized what I had just done. Then
I realy wasent the cool kid in day
care and to think I would had
even done it over not having to
just ask her to tell the troth to
my x bff then doing what I did.
And at the end of it all I was the
one who got in the boialing hot water
with my mom and the toilets mother.
    But that is the old me and
now I look back and say wow I
did something so mean and sian then
I have not been in a nother fit!
And that was 4 years ago!

EXAMPLE 0.1 Daria, fifth-grade girl, Magnolia Springs Elementary, Orlando

This conflict story involves many of the peer relational challenges that we expect as part of the experience of an elementary school girl; but just consider what Daria's narrative reveals. Her antagonist has convinced Daria's best friend (the bff) that Daria is "just using her." (Note that Daria is recounting what her antagonist made another child believe about Daria's own motives here. Note also that she has at least a nascent grasp of the idea that friendship requires a respect for agency that is violated if one person is "using" the other.) Even worse, the whole day care spread this rumor so Daria's friendship was ruined. She reports that her first reaction was to confront the antagonist, but the situation escalated to physical violence, resulting in bloodshed. This provokes a self-evaluative realization by the author. She makes a clear distinction between her younger self and her current self, explaining how she came to the understanding that her earlier behavior was not "cool" and was "so mean." She now believes that her antagonist's offense did not warrant the violent response, and she proposes an alternate response she might have made (just ask the offender to tell the truth to the former best friend). Daria got in trouble (boiling hot water), but this is not presented as the source of the moral evaluative insight in the story – before there was punishment, the author had looked at her hand and realized what she had done.

What we have here is an account of a very ordinary elementary school conflict (social aggression, rumors, lost friendship, physical violence, punishment) – but what extraordinary analysis accompanies this account! Multiple layers of perspective-taking (reports about efforts of one person to manipulate the belief of another person about the self) accompany sophisticated moral analysis (self-recriminations and lessons learned). Daria contrasts the authorial self with a former self ("the old me") to produce a child-sized version of a redemption narrative, and to make her account compelling, this fifth grader appropriates a cultural trope (e.g., "the big bad wolf" who ultimately "gets into boiling hot water"). Is it ordinary for children this young to do so much analysis and interpretation of their own experiences?

In 1999, when the nation was reeling after two high school boys in a suburban neighborhood in Colorado wrote in journals about their painful experiences with peer rejection, and then expressed their rage by planting ninety-nine explosive devices and shooting thirty-seven classmates, killing thirteen, we were in the second semester of a study asking what children have to say about their own conflicts. We invited children to tell true stories about their arguments, fights, and misunderstandings. They told us about conflicts with peers and siblings, conflicts with parents and teachers, and even conflicts with the very institutions of our society. Sometimes their insights astounded us; sometimes their naïveté delighted us. Sometimes we could not contain our laughter; sometimes their stories made us cry. Nearly twenty years and over 3,000 stories later, we continue to be fascinated by the work children do to make their own experiences meaningful.

This book is about children's conflicts, and it is about children's narrative sense-making. We argue that narrative accounts of interpersonal conflict in middle childhood are the site of critical social, emotional, and moral development. We manage conflict in human relationships largely by explaining our actions to one another in terms that make our behaviors understandable as compatible with culturally shared values. The primary way we do this is by telling stories. When conflicts erupt between individuals, we often make sense of them by assigning roles (such as aggressor and victim), and we recognize culturally commonplace ways of responding (such as retaliating, protesting, apologizing). During the elementary school years, this work is especially naked, as children are learning to negotiate new complexities of peer relationships and as they are first trying their hand at proposing accounts of their conflicts that will 'work' in their social worlds. A close examination of the stories children tell about their experiences promises to help us understand peer conflict and the development of peer relationships. It also promises to offer insights about important moral and emotional development during a period of childhood that has been slighted by developmental psychologists who have tended to be more fascinated by infancy, early childhood, and adolescence. But even more than promising insight about social, emotional, and moral development, we are increasingly convinced that the study of children's accounts of their own conflict offers us a glimpse into the future. As children come to be more full-fledged participants in the discursive practice of sharing stories, they come to appropriate bits and pieces of the cultural world that is in play around them. They find the metaphors and myths, the character types, and the explanatory frames that work for them. They blend the discursive ingredients offered to them in fairy tales and music videos and courtroom dramas and Sunday School lessons. What they collectively produce with this blend will alter the way we talk about and the way the next generation will come to understand human conflict. We are not just watching children become more and more like us as they move through the elementary school years; we are watching them become the architects of a future we will only see to the extent that we understand their way of making sense.

This book is divided into three parts. In Part I, we present the theoretical and methodological ground on which we stand. We explain why we decided that our curiosity about children's conflicts could best be satisfied by listening to how children describe their conflicts in their own words. We explore Jerome Bruner's writing about the role of narrative in bringing children into culture and in the creation of a 'folk psychology' that makes human experience meaningful. Part I also describes our data and our method of analysis. We draw on approximately 3,000 stories collected in two cities in the southern United States and one city in southeastern China. The stories were collected over a period of eighteen years for a variety of different studies. Chapter 2 describes the young authors who contributed these stories and presents a description of the corpora. Our analysis is largely descriptive, and this is unusual. Most of the analytic methods used by developmental psychologists have been designed to test hypotheses. Our approach has appropriated some of these methods and has used them in conversation with more qualitative, close readings of our data. We have been systematic and disciplined in our approach, and we make this work transparent in Chapter 2.

In Part II we present the bulk of our descriptive work. What do children say when they describe their personal conflicts? What is the source of conflict, from their point of view? How do they describe it and how do they interpret it? In each of these chapters we briefly summarize what previous research has led us to understand, and we show how children talk about the matter in their own words. Sometimes their accounts corroborate the work of researchers who have relied on surveys or observational methods; often we get a richer and more nuanced view of the world of middle childhood when we listen to children's own descriptions.

Much of the previous research on middle childhood has focused on the development of peer relationships. Even the most casual observations of children in this age range are sufficient in convincing us that making (and losing) friends is of critical importance for their well-being and adjustment. Our work has corroborated such casual observations. When children wrote about their own conflict, many of their stories focused on their struggles to fit in in a social universe where there is danger of rejection and where the obligations and privileges of friendship are under constant negotiation. Chapter 3 looks at what children had to say when they wrote about these matters. We compare what they said in their own words to what researchers have said about their peer relationships, identifying the qualities of friendship that the children regularly featured in their stories, and the 'trouble' between friends that they most frequently reported when they told us about conflicts with people they identified as friends or best friends. Our analyses of these stories led us to three insights that have not often been emphasized in previous research on friendships in middle childhood. These include (1) a clearer picture of friendship as a cultural practice that is established and maintained by negotiation between children, (2) a recognition of friendship development as uniquely child-guided (rather than adult-directed), and (3) an appreciation and deep respect for the struggles required to accomplish friendship in middle childhood, and for the courage and creativity of the children who undertake the struggle.

Another prominent focus of previous research on elementary school children has been a study of aggression. Middle childhood appears to be an important time for the development of skills that allow children to manage their own and others' aggressive urges. When we asked children to talk about their conflicts, we certainly found them accusing one another (and themselves) of aggressive action. We saw a notable difference in how children described aggression that threatened a developing sense of self or social belonging as compared to physical violence that threatened the body. Chapter 4 describes what we learned from close readings of stories about social aggression, and in Chapter 5 we examine stories about physical aggression.

Children's descriptions of psychological and social aggression fell into three main categories: name-calling and face-to-face insults, behind-the-back aggression, and rejection or exclusion. When we looked closely at young authors' recounting of these acts of aggression, we came to see how the children were aligning themselves with selected cultural norms. We saw them adopting and defending or resisting culturally ascribed identities and we saw interesting ways that the identity work of middle childhood is shaped within cultural communities. In Chapter 4 we discuss interesting differences across our samples in the kinds of insults children endured and in their moral evaluations of direct, compared to behind-the-back, aggression. We saw that rejection and exclusion was a form of aggression more difficult for children to describe and to evaluate than name-calling or behind-the-back aggression, and we discuss the implications of this for children who experience peer difficulty and for our efforts to create more inclusive classrooms.

Our interest in children's stories about conflict began with an effort to understand how they construe acts of violence and how we might prevent violence in schools. Much concern has focused on children's exposure to violence and on their participation in violent activities. When we asked children to tell us about conflict, we were not surprised to find many descriptions of hitting, pushing, bumping, and general 'fighting' in stories children wrote or told. We were not even surprised that these reports sometimes included descriptions of bloody noses or black eyes or other child-inflicted injury. We were more surprised to find that nearly 10% of 2,883 stories included descriptions of criminal or life-threatening violence. In Chapter 5 we examine reports of physical aggression in conflicts between children, documenting astute moral analysis and psychological mindedness by the authors of such stories. Children who wrote about mild or moderate physical aggression by other children reported their own motives and speculated about the motives of their antagonists. They did the evaluative work that brings them into the moral discourse of their cultural community, positioning themselves as moral authorities, with an authorial responsibility to evaluate what has happened and to specify what should have happened instead. By contrast, we show that stories about severe violence, those describing violence in the child's own family, and those describing criminal violence in the child's neighborhood tended to be reported with little attention to the thoughts or feelings of the characters and with very little moral evaluation. We argue that the development of a strong narrative voice is especially critical in contexts that include violent conflict, and exposure to criminal or traumatic violence.

Peers certainly become the central actors in the stories of middle childhood, but this does not mean that the adults relinquish their roles as socializing agents. In Chapter 6, we ask how the adults fit in. What do children have to say about the grown-ups who sometimes enter their stories? We compare stories of conflict in which children report adult intervention to those in which they do not mention any adult involvement. We look closely at stories in which children position the adults as enforcers of rules and standards, exercising coercive control or administering punishment, and we compare these to stories in which the adults are positioned as consultants, offering advice or comfort. We suggest that children's own moral analysis is suppressed when they describe punishment, and especially so when they describe corporal punishment. Stories of corporal punishment constituted a minority of stories in each of the eight communities in which we collected data, and we did not find differences in the ways children in different cultural communities presented this kind of adult violence. Children rarely criticized adults when they administered corporal punishment, but they also did no critical evaluative work at all when they told stories about these events.

As children work to find a place among peers and to establish satisfying relationships in their schools and neighborhoods, they are also beginning the work of finding a way to fit in with a larger cultural community. Although we usually think of adolescence as the dawning of gender and sexuality, there are expectations for gendered behaviors in middle childhood in most cultural communities. In Chapter 7, we raise two questions: What can children's stories about conflict tell us about how they are taking on (in the sense of adopting) gender? What can their stories tell us about how they might take on (in the sense of resisting) the gender system? We begin by asking how stories by girl and boy authors differed from each other, and although we found some differences in some of our samples, it became clear that the really interesting differences were in the ways that girl and boy characters were described in stories by *both* girl and boy authors.

The most interesting questions about gender in our stories concerned what children *did* with gender – how the conflicts they described either enforced or resisted cultural expectations for masculinity and femininity. Boys, but not girls, made gendered identity claims, and boys were often called on to defend their masculinity in a way that girls never had to with their femininity. Gendered insults and name-calling, in fact, almost always defamed femininity, so that being called a 'girl' was always an insult to a boy and was sometimes an insult even when addressed to a girl. Children described insults that made gender nonconformity socially risky, and they sometimes described efforts to resist these enforcements of the gender system. Some boys tried to align themselves with a kinder, gentler masculinity, claiming to "be the better man," and some girls demanded that they be taken seriously "in the real world." When children wrote stories about romantic interests and romantic teasing, we saw a groundswell of resistance to culturally stereotypical notions of agentive, desiring males and passive, objectified females. Both girls and boys tended to prioritize same-sex friendship over romance, and girls wrote about romance in ways that affirmed their own agency and desire. Although most stories that featured gender as a source of conflict seemed to support or enforce gender roles, we saw enough stories of resistance to fuel an abiding curiosity about how this next generation will change gender roles.

Gender is not the only cultural category children 'take on' in middle childhood. By Chapter 8, we will have seen children positioning themselves as particular types of persons in their own stories: loyal friends or remorseful ex-friends, victims or aggressors, heroes or peacemakers. They sometimes claim age or race or ethnicity or other group memberships as they negotiate to make places for themselves in their various cultural communities. In Chapter 8 we examine the ways children borrow freely from the voices they hear around them. They bolster their own claims to authority with the language of the criminal justice system, or school or state or church, sometimes changing things up in surprising ways and making them their own. We challenge the inclination to think of identity development as the developmental task of adolescence. While elementary-aged children's identity is very much in the early stages of development, we become convinced that the cognitive and socio-cultural struggles to achieve a sense of identity begin well before adolescence. Elementary children will grow into teenagers who are famously critical of the flaws they diligently find in the values built into the worlds they inherit. Many researchers have theorized and studied this inclination of teens to become social critics. We argue that at least some of the resistance to socialization we see in elementary school children is not just the untamed behavior of the immature. We believe that we see in these young authors the beginnings of a thoughtful and justifiable resistance to injustice and ineffectiveness in the social systems they are preparing to join – preparing to join and to change.

Part III of this book takes stock of what we have learned about children's own construal of conflict – what we have learned and what we may be able to do with it. We consider the implications for educational practice. In Chapter 9, we describe an oral story-sharing practice we call KidsTalk in which children in small groups take turns sharing stories. Our work has shown that over time, children who participate in these sessions come to produce stories that become more complex, and more psychologically sophisticated. We also find that over time, KidsTalk nurtures a story-sharing culture that has a positive impact, even on the children who have not participated. We see how the regular sharing of stories creates local culture – culture writ small – in which ideas and themes and literary tropes are propagated through friendship groups. We see that children come to share interpretive repertoires and explanatory systems – some of them aligned with the cultural communities familiar to their grown-ups and some of them quite distinct from anything that the grown-ups in their world would use or recognize. We end this chapter with a set of recommendations for implementing oral story-sharing as a regular classroom practice in a way that supports the important academic aims of the school.

In two of our eight data collection sites, children shared stories orally, but most of the stories we examined were written. In Chapter 10, we consider the importance of a narrative writing practice, arguing that this allows teachers to use the oral story-sharing traditions of their students' families to serve as a springboard to literacy while supporting social, emotional, and moral well-being in the classroom. How can we convince classroom teachers, justifiably reluctant to divert attention from the learning objectives that will be assessed in high-stakes tests, that they should devote class time to having children write and share stories about their personal experiences? Our effort to make this case takes us to the Common Core, a set of educational standards adopted in many U.S. school districts. We present evidence that the classroom practices we recommend can support the educational aims that are the basis for funding and for teacher evaluation in many U.S. schools. Following this, we review research evidence for the benefits of a writing practice that includes personal narratives, especially narratives about interpersonal conflict or other difficult experiences, arguing that such a practice can support children's social, emotional, and moral development while simultaneously supporting academic goals and mandates.

In our final chapter, Chapter 11, we review our claims that telling or writing stories about personal conflict is important to the social, emotional, and moral development of children in the elementary school years. Relying again on Jerome Bruner's analysis of narrative form and function, we consider the mechanisms by which story-sharing promotes development in these three domains. In the end, we come back to our assertion that the study of children's narrative accounts of their own experience gives us a glimpse into a future world. However much of human history is shaped by economic and political forces, no real change happens until the next generation takes up some of the truths, values, and realities offered by their grown-ups and rejects the truths, values, and realities that do not work for them. The process accelerates in middle childhood when narrators make sense of the fact that somebody got excluded, when they negotiate with their peers about which behaviors count as 'mean,' which are justifiable retaliations, and which are legitimate assertions of individual rights. If we pay attention to the way children talk about their conflicts, we have a chance to see where they appropriate themes and adopt discourses from popular culture and when they call on the authority of church or state. We see when they align the self with authority and when they position the self as outlaw. We see the first steps that a new generation is taking toward establishing the interpretive repertoires that will make the future make sense. When we watch children in middle childhood sharing stories of their own experience, we lose any illusions that children 'receive' culture in any passive or straightforward way. We see the process of culture being recreated, not simply passed down.

Note

1 Here, and throughout, we have used pseudonyms and have transcribed stories from the children's handwriting, without correcting spelling, punctuation, or grammar.

PART I

Listening to Children's Stories About Their Own Conflicts

1

WHY CONFLICT? WHY NARRATIVE?

A Theoretical Framework for the Study of Peer Conflict Narratives in Middle Childhood

> In human beings, with their astonishing narrative gift, one of the principal forms of peacekeeping is the human gift for presenting, dramatizing, and explicating the mitigating circumstances surrounding conflict-threatening breaches in the ordinariness of life.
>
> *Jerome Bruner, 1990, p. 95*

This book is about the stories children tell about their own conflicts. We are asking questions about both the role of narrative in development and the nature of middle childhood conflicts. In this chapter, we present theory that grounds our thinking about narrative and theory that grounds our thinking about peer conflict. We find critical overlaps in support of our argument that many of the skills involved in managing the conflicts of middle childhood are fundamentally narrative.

Why Narrative?

When William James (1890) set about the business of delineating a field of psychology, he noted that there are two quite distinct modes of thought, which he labeled narrative and paradigmatic. Narrative thought can give us a good story, and its highest form is great literature; paradigmatic thought can give us a good argument, and its highest form is philosophy and mathematics. Narrative thinking is motivated by an effort to explain a particular experience, usually in terms of human intentions and reasons, with close attention to a rich context; paradigmatic thinking is motivated by a search for general principles, usually in terms of physical causes, with the vagaries of contextual variations under scientific control. Narrative thought is concerned with life-likeness and meaningfulness;

paradigmatic thought is concerned with truthfulness and accuracy. Children make impressive leaps in their paradigmatic thinking skills during middle childhood, especially if they are given experiences with formal education, and developmental scientists have made impressive progress toward describing and explaining these leaps. Maybe it is not surprising that those scientists, having so finely honed their own paradigmatic thinking skills, have devoted much more time and energy and journal pages to understanding the development of logic and reasoning skills than to the development of narrative thought.

In 1990, with the publication of *Acts of Meaning*, Jerome Bruner took a backward look at his own first fifty years of critical conversations about and seminal contributions to the study of cognitive development. He noted the serious neglect of narrative thinking, and made a powerful argument that this neglect had tragically isolated the field of psychology from important conversations with scholars in anthropology, philosophy, and literary criticism. This, Bruner argued, has encouraged theory and research in psychology that ignores the fundamental truth that humans are cultural animals. Narrative thinking, according to Bruner, structures and is structured by human culture. A deep understanding of narrative thinking requires us to recognize ourselves as fundamentally cultural, because the same qualities of thought that structure narrative also structure language and most other human cultural practices. *Acts of Meaning* offered a deep critique of a cognitive science that had given a great deal of attention to how people process information without considering how they use that information to make sense of things – to make their lives meaningful. It also contributed a blueprint for the construction of a developmental science in which meaning-making practices are crucial.

Narrative thinking gives us stories, and story-sharing practices are a critical feature of most human settings that include children. We surround children with stories – didactic stories and fables with morals, fiction designed to entertain, and ordinary accounts about the experiences of daily life. Dozens of studies have now documented both the pervasiveness of stories in children's lives and the importance of these stories to socialization and education (e.g., Miller & Mehler, 1994). Inspired by Vivian Paley's (1990; 1997; 2004) beautiful descriptions and interpretations of the narrative quality of children's play, researchers have considered the role of stories in a variety of classroom endeavors (e.g., Nicolopoulou, 2002). Robyn Fivush and her colleagues working in the Family Narratives Lab at Emory University have listened in on family dinners and other family interactions, seeking to understand the development of autobiographical memory, and incidentally coming to see the transmission of values and gender stereotypes across generations (Bohanek, Fivush, Zaman, Lepore, Merchant, & Duke, 2009). Shirley Brice Heath's ethnographies in North Carolina and Peggy Miller's research with colleagues at the University of Illinois have looked at similarities and differences in the narrative worlds of children in cultural communities that differ in socioeconomic and educational opportunities and in ethnicity, finding notably rich narrative skills among children who are likely to be described as disadvantaged (Heath, 1983; Wiley, Rose, Burger, & Miller, 1998). Inspired by a discursive turn in psychology, Michael Bamberg and his colleagues at Clark University have observed the small stories that children share in casual interaction, noting how children banter and chatter about the events of their daily lives to position the self as a certain kind of a person (Bamberg, 2004). Cecilia Wainryb and her colleagues at the University of Utah examined similarities and distinctions in the conflict narratives told by victims and perpetrators, noting that children's accounts of conflict situations in which they had been the perpetrators were less coherent and less self-focused than in stories about victim experiences, and children's moral judgments varied by perspective (Wainryb, Brehl, & Matwin, 2005). All of this work and much more that has been done since the publication of *Acts of Meaning* has made a convincing case that the world of childhood is a storied universe.

Bruner asserted that it is in telling stories and encouraging children to tell their own stories that we do the primary work of bringing children into culture. This is because the stories we tell our children instantiate what Bruner calls 'folk psychology.' This is a set of loosely defined and sometimes contested beliefs about what makes people tick. For example, our cultural communities include students and colleagues who sometimes present their own behavior as sub-standard, and excuse this with such explanations as "I was so tired," or "I was so stressed out," or "My roommate broke up with her boyfriend last night." These will sometimes work fairly well to maintain the respect of peers and professors in the face of poor performance. The excuse "a devil tugged at my spirit all night" would be considerably less effective in our circles, although it might function quite well in some other communities. A folk psychology is a collection of beliefs (about which members of a cultural community will sometimes negotiate) about what kinds of people there are in the world (e.g., children and adults, nobles and commoners, introverts and extroverts), about what might motivate them (greed, anger, altruism) to engage in what kinds of behaviors (playing, studying, taking up arms). Members of a cultural community share a sometimes contested folk psychology that makes sense of their experiences.

Most people would be hard-pressed to articulate the various features of the 'common sense' that guides their meaning-making, and there is rarely explicit instruction in folk psychology. Children (and other individuals just joining a cultural community) will 'pick it up.' According to Bruner, this uptake is largely accomplished because of a fundamental quality of story-telling that Bruner describes as a dual landscape. At one level, the landscape of action, a story will describe the 'who, what, where, and when' of the matter. Events and behaviors will be recounted with attention to their sequence, so that causality may be established or inferred. This kind of reporting creates a stark, 'just the facts, Ma'am' story that is recognizably unsatisfying unless it is elaborated upon and enriched by what Bruner called the "landscape of consciousness."

A good story, according to Bruner, is peopled by characters who have motives and flaws. It is more likely to focus on reasons than on causes, and a good story-teller will be managing the listener's inferences about why the protagonists behaved as they did. The landscape of consciousness fills out the action of the story with all the meaning-making work that motivates humans to tell stories in the first place. We want to know what happened, but, more importantly, we want to know why it happened. We want to know who did it, what motivated them to do it, and how they felt about it. We want to know who was responsible, who were the good guys and the bad guys, what were the mitigating circumstances, and what are the lessons to be learned. The landscape of consciousness, described in our stories, is the closest we get to the articulation of our folk psychology.

Stories bring children into culture and teach them our folk psychologies because they function to get us into each other's heads. We felt the terror of the three little pigs as the big bad wolf promised to huff and puff and blow the house down. Our understanding of jealousy was fundamentally shaped by Snow White's stepmother. When the little red hen believed that the sky was falling in, but we knew that only an acorn had fallen on her head, we got a glimpse of the power of false belief, and we delighted in the experience of our own knowing. Stories are about what happened, about how those happenings were experienced, and about what those experiences mean. As children listen to stories, and especially as they begin to be called upon to tell their own stories about their own experience, they come to share with other members of their communities a basic understanding about 'what counts.' They come to share this, and they also get a chance to contest it. Authoring your own story means you get to make at least the first draft of an account that makes sense of your own experience in light of the common sense of the people around you. This is, in large part, what it means to be a member of a human community. According to Bruner, it is fundamentally what it means to be human.

In the years since Bruner published *Acts of Meaning*, researchers in cultural psychology have collaborated with educators, clinicians, and social activists to take on the challenge of attending to the stories shared in our cultural communities – stories that celebrate and problematize a wide variety of human plights faced by a wide variety of human characters. These stories, the ones children hear and the ones they create in their families, classrooms, and neighborhoods, prepare them for their own experiences with a host of conflicts.

Why Conflict?

A defining feature of middle childhood development is surely the broadening and deepening of peer relationships, and it is not surprising that peer conflict is a prominent feature of children's social experience during this time. The establishment and maintenance of new relationships and new kinds of relationships requires new skills, and the practice of those skills is sure to involve awkward missteps.

In 1953, Harry Stack Sullivan wrote convincingly about the developments that change the fairly simple and unstable playmate preferences of early childhood into the 'chumships' of the elementary school years. Friendships, during this time of middle childhood, entail a set of obligations and privileges that must be negotiated and renegotiated in the context of painful rejections and betrayals. According to Sullivan, a drive for intimacy with age-mates motivates the important work children do during these years to achieve a more realistic sense of self, a keener ability to take the perspective of others, and to match one's own needs and resources with those of another person to form satisfying reciprocity. Interpersonal conflicts are puddles or hills on the course that run toward the development of those satisfying relationships. Children discover that their goals are running counter to the goals of a valued playmate. Their desires are opposed, their efforts are thwarted, and conflicts erupt. The preservation of relationships in the face of these conflicts requires an impressive set of newly emerging skills – skills that require deepening understanding of self and other, and skills that require communication and negotiation.

Even before Sullivan's important work, Piaget's (1932/65) theory addressed the developmental significance of the emergence of peer relationships in middle childhood, and he gave a good bit of attention to the conflicts that children experience in these relationships. Social interaction with peers provokes conflicts that promote moral development. The spats and tussles that wrinkle family life are typically resolved by an appeal to authority and by the superior power of the parent or older sibling. By contrast, the conflicts that arise between peers set the stage for negotiation among equals. When a parent or teacher lays down the law of the land, there is little impetus to consider the reason for the rule; the child has only to learn what behaviors constitute compliance and violation. The laws of the playground, on the other hand, are imminently disputable, and these disputes invite argument (and reasoning) both about the reason for the rule and about which behaviors constitute violation. With no adjudicating grown-up nearby, children must practice emerging communication and perspective-taking skills. They'll need to persuade their playmates to take their own view of the situation, and they will be urged to consider interpretations that differ from their own. They will get better at understanding what motivated the behavior of their antagonists, and they will get better at getting their antagonists to understand the reasons for their own behavior. Peer conflicts will play an important role in helping children see connections between intentionality of actors and their culpability for outcomes. The interpersonal conflicts that interrupt the ongoing activities of middle childhood are not unfortunate diversions from a path toward maturity; those conflicts are the bridges and tunnels on the road children must traverse.

As children negotiate conflict episodes, they choose to stand up for themselves and others, to back down when their own and others' goals collide, to assume a conciliatory or a hostile stance, to avoid or endure the provocations of another child or to instigate conflictual interactions with others. These choices are informed by the child's assessments of the thoughts and emotions, motives and dispositions of self and other, and by the child's understanding of the norms and interpretive frames that operate in the immediate cultural context. Children enter the conflict arena of their specific cultural communities and are socialized to handle conflict, drawing on various behavioral and interpretive skills depending on the norms, values, and practices of their school and neighborhood communities.

Barbara Rogoff (2003) has made convincing arguments for the importance of attending to the particularities of the cultural communities that surround children. As they come to be more full-fledged participants in these communities, children will sometimes adopt and sometimes resist the expectations of their elders and peers. They will take up some of the discourses and explanatory frames, the metaphors and idioms, the proverbs and folk wisdom that are a part of what Bruner called a 'cultural toolkit.' In the context of peer conflict we see children practicing (clumsily at first) the use of these tools. Marjorie Goodwin's (1990) detailed descriptions of 'he-said-she-said' disputes among Philadelphian children, William Labov's (1972) careful linguistic analysis of the insult games played by pre-teens on the streets of Harlem, and our own work describing conflict narratives of children in four different inner-city schools (Davidson, Walton, & Cohen, 2013; Humphrey, Walton, & Davidson, 2014; Walton, Harris, & Davidson, 2009) all underline Rogoff's imperative that we frame our observation of children's conflict with a sensitive analysis of the cultural context that gives rise to them.

Why Conflict Narratives?

We argue that many of the skills involved in managing the conflicts of middle childhood are fundamentally narrative. This is partly because the skillful presentation of one's own side of the story is so critical to the peaceful resolution of conflicts. It is also because the same skills involved in making a good story are critical to the understanding and management of human relationships. Three features of narrative, described by Bruner, explain how narrative functions in middle childhood to support developments that undergird conflict management skills. Each of these raises interesting questions both about the role of narrative in child development and about the important role of conflict in promoting development. Making a narrative account requires a story-maker to take a cultural stance, a moral stance, and an epistemic stance. We will discuss each of these below.

Report-Worthiness and the Recognition of Non-Canonicality: Taking a Cultural Stance

People share stories when something report-worthy happens – something unexpected in a cultural context (Labov & Fanshell, 1977). We can imagine that every single thing that happens must be unexpected to a newborn, who will only gradually come to see some features of a social world as routine. Part of what it means to be child-like, indeed part of what is most charming and endearing about children, is an inclination to see perfectly ordinary things as wondrous. Gradually, as children are exposed to and participate in the story-sharing practices of their families and schools, they come to share with members of their cultural communities a 'common sense' about what is ordinary and what requires explanation. Bruner argued that this development is achieved in the context of a variety of story-sharing practices. Children notice what behaviors and situations provoke narrative accounts from parents and teachers and book-writers. They find themselves called upon to make accounts for their own behavior when it fails the test of ordinariness for their family and friends. For these accounts to be successful, an author must provide a 'take' on his or her own behavior that makes it understandable in light of culturally shared beliefs and values. Consider the work of this sixth-grade boy, Jake, who has had an extraordinary day on the basketball court:

EXAMPLE 1.1 Jake, sixth-grade boy, College Elementary, Memphis

EXAMPLE 1.1 JAKE, SIXTH-GRADE BOY, COLLEGE ELEMENTARY, MEMPHIS

Every day almost every boy plays basketball during recess. I always play it along with some other boys. Almost every day is an average day for everyone. But sometimes players have their season highs. They score many points in one day and sometimes in another day they score even more points than the day before. Also, players make assists so that other players can score and players earn rebounds, blocks, and steals that can lead to points. That day was just an average day and I scored 10 points, 5 rebounds, 5 assists, 3 blocks, and 2 steals. It was probably my luckiest day, but it was also my most skillful day. That day I must have been luckier than other days but for some reason I also put the most effort. That day I made all types of shots: 3 pointers, mid-shot jumpshots, lay ups and low range jumpshots. It was the best day I ever had for recess and I will remember it for the rest of the school year and next school year too. Other people will remember it, too the people that were with me, but I will remember it the most.

Jake begins his story with a discourse on canonicality. What happens every day (or "almost every day")? What can we expect of "every" boy (or "almost every boy")? He informs us of the 'almost everydayness' of 'average' performance (for everyone) and contrasts this with the 'sometimes-ness' of season high performances. He recognizes a need to account for the exception of his own performance on this "average day," and he is able to appropriate three culturally prominent explanatory discourses to account for his performance: a discourse of luck, a discourse of skill, and a discourse of effort. It is doubtful that Jake has read Carol Dweck (2006) or the other educational psychologists and attribution theorists whose research on effort/skill/luck fills academic journals and scholarly books. (He is also likely unaware of the research on human memory that would corroborate his prediction that his own memory for this event will be more enduring than that of his classmates.) We can only hope that this sixth grader will grow up to be a psychologist or a sportscaster!

Departures from the ordinary inspire story-telling, and stories have the power to foreground circumstances and events that are potentially problematic for the smooth operation of social life. In middle childhood, especially when children interact with age-mates, the matter of ordinariness is under constant negotiation. "I was just sharpening my pencil," claims the girl whose 'ordinary behavior' has been mistaken for an attempt to break in the water-fountain line. The management of conflict requires that antagonists agree about what is 'background context' and what is noteworthy, and this 'common sense' that is shared by members of cultural communities is accomplished by story-sharing. 'Culture writ large' and 'culture writ small' come into being and are continuously recreated in this process of negotiating about what is ordinary and what will count as an explanation for behaviors that are not expected. In the

Introduction, we saw the author of the 'big bad wolf' story appropriate fairy tales and also such street slang as "the toe-jam" insult. Children take a cultural stance when they give narrative accounts, using bits and pieces of literature, popular media, holy scriptures, school textbooks, campaign slogans – a truly amazing assortment of cultural products are taken up by children and put to use in their negotiations about what is and is not to be expected in their social world (Humphrey, Walton, & Davidson, 2014). This is not a simple matter of learning a cultural canon, however, because narrative accounts have to work in very local cultural contexts. What counts as an account at home ("My momma says somebody hit me I hit them back") may not work at school, where there are different expectations that establish ordinariness and different explanatory systems that will work to account for violations of those expectations ("I decided to use my words").

As children listen to the dozens of narrative accounts that fill their days, they come to share a common-sense notion of what does and does not need to be explained in their social world. As children become story-tellers, they claim the power to focus the attention of others on those events they have experienced as out of the ordinary and report-worthy. This gives them a voice in a negotiation about what their own behaviors and the behaviors of others will mean in their social context. In elementary school, we open for children a new compartment in a cultural toolkit as we teach them to write. With the addition of literacy to their cultural practices, they will be able to extend their audience over time and enjoy some freedom from the immediacy of live interaction. With the leisure of time to consider how they will construct their account, they will expand an expressive vocabulary and mobilize a host of literary devices (e.g., metaphor, hyperbole, caricature) that increase their power to become creators as well as consumers of culture (Humphrey, Walton, & Davidson, 2014).

Agency and Evaluation: Taking a Moral Stance

We rarely experience unexpected events as neutral, and when we narrate our experience, we are compelled to take an evaluative stance vis-à-vis the non-ordinary circumstances that inspire our stories (Bruner, 1990). This second feature of narrative makes story-telling a critical discourse practice for establishing the self as a moral actor (Bamberg & Damrad-Frye, 1991; Walton & Brewer, 2001). When children create narrative accounts of their own experience, they seek to convince others about the moral justifiability of their own and others' behaviors. Stories have good guys and bad guys. Characters make mistakes and learn lessons. Non-violent conflict resolution is possible when actors are able to tell a story that explains their behavior in ways that allow others to continue to see them as cooperative companions with acceptable motives.

Narrative practice requires children to understand what will count as an acceptable excuse or justification for their own and others' behavior (Tappan, 1991).

Competent story-tellers are able to attribute their own questionable behaviors to culturally valued motives, and to position the self as a 'hero' or a 'hapless dupe' or a contrite actor who has learned a lesson (Bamberg, 1997; Walton & Brewer, 2001). Negotiating non-violent resolutions to conflict generally requires that participants come to share an understanding of the cultural context that allows them to agree about what rules apply and what behaviors constitute violations of those rules. In this sense, story-telling is a fundamentally moral activity. Consider the moral work accomplished in the story below by a fifth-grade boy, Warren.

EXAMPLE 1.2   WARREN, FIFTH-GRADE BOY, IRONWOOD ELEMENTARY, MEMPHIS

One day when I was on the blacktop playing basketball a boy took my basketball and kicked it. I was already having a bad morning so I called him a punk. As a comeback he checked my mother. So I checked his whole family twice. He was ticked off then so he tried to dislocate my jaw. I let myself go then I mean I went ballistic on him. We were to toe to toe for about a minute. My friends pulled me away right when he kicked me. After I had a chance to consider what I had done, I got angrier because I had loss. I though about the boy and myself. I compared him to me, and really he isn't such a bad guy. When I really thought about it we were both wrong. I decided to be the better man and apologize about checking his family. When I went over there I heard him bragging about he could grind me into meat.[1],[2]

Warren's recounting of "a conflict that really happened to you" is full of explanation, interpretation, evaluation, and moral deliberation. He recognizes that calling someone a punk requires an explanation and he expects his reader to understand that "having a bad morning" might account for this violation of propriety. Warren labels his antagonist's response as "a comeback," calling on a culturally shared notion that retaliation can count as an explanation for the boy's insult against Warren's mother. Escalation ensues, with the result that the antagonist is "ticked off." Anger counts as an explanation for violence. In response to the violence our author reports that he "let himself go." This fifth grader is calling on a conception of selfhood that involves effortful control. He is claiming moral agency and taking responsibility for a decision to relinquish control of a violent self. From here, the moral analysis gets even more sophisticated. Once the violence is stopped, Warren reports that he "had a chance to consider" what he had done. His first response was to be angry, but he reports that he "thought about the boy and myself." Upon comparison, he decided that the other boy is not "such a bad guy." Even more thought leads Warren to the conclusion that both actors in this story were morally culpable. Now he decides that an apology is in order and in deciding to make an apology, he positions himself as "the better man." The last sentence leaves the reader uncertain about whether this intended apology actually got delivered, but Warren leaves us with his claim to the moral high ground. So much moral analysis and so much moral deliberation in a 150-word story about a child-sized conflict!

Establishing Truth and Making Sense: Taking an Epistemic Stance

The author of a story has the first shot at establishing the epistemic status of the account. Did the events recounted 'really happen' or did they originate in the author's imagination? Which features of the story are reported with certainty, which are acknowledged to be under dispute, and which are presented as speculation? When we tell a story, we are obliged to distinguish those assertions we know first-hand from our own experience, those we know second-hand from another source, and those about which we are uncertain. Sometimes, especially in the creation of fiction, the author takes an epistemic stance of omniscience. If we create characters from our imagination, we are allowed to say with authority what each of them thinks and feels at each point in the story. Narrative accounts of personal experience, on the other hand, generally afford the author much less power. Reports about the thoughts or feelings or motives of the protagonists are up for negotiation. What can we presume to know about other minds? As story-makers are called upon to make culturally understandable accounts of their own behaviors and the behaviors of others, and as they offer their own moral evaluation of the events they recount, they are confronted with serious epistemic concerns. They must distinguish knowledge from belief and this requires a consideration of the kind of evidence that can support belief or certainty. Consider sixth grader Robin's story below.

EXAMPLE 1.3 ROBIN, SIXTH-GRADE GIRL, CONNORS ELEMENTARY, MEMPHIS

one day I was sitting in connors elementary school in my desk minding my own business it was about 1:52 and the students was reading and so was I, so anyway it was this weird kind of nouse and my teacher Ms. Jones though it was me but it was not me. Ms. Jones said Robin Corina quite making that nouse and I said that's not me, Ms. Jones said whoever that is will do it again and they did. Ms. Jones said get out Robin then I said what did I do she said you know what you did by making that strange kind of nouse. Then everybody in the class starts to laugh, then some of the class said that Rose not Robin. Ms. Jones said I must have a misunderstanding sorry Robin.

Robin begins her story with a report of her own attentional state ("minding my own business") and she reports (with all the authority of authorship) what her teacher thought ("Ms. Jones thought it was me"). Robin's challenge to the teacher's accusation is made in the form of an ostensible question ("What did I do?"). The author knows that she is not guilty of making the offending noise, and she probably knows that the teacher's expulsion order is based on a false belief that Robin made the noise. But instead of making an outright denial, she poses a question designed to elicit from the teacher a clarification of the teacher's 'take' on the situation. The teacher's response to this is "you know what you did." Notice that Robin is reporting here about her teacher's false assertion about Robin's own epistemological state. The whole story turns on Ms. Jones' false belief, and indeed the 'misunderstanding' of the grown-up is a source of delight (everybody in the class starts to laugh). It is amusing when the adult, designated as the source of authority in the classroom, is shown to be wrong, labels her own misperception as a 'misunderstanding,' and makes an apology to a child.

A good story often turns on who knew what when, and a good story-teller must keep in mind what each character in the story knows at each point in the story. Moreover, a skillful author is always mindful of what his or her audience knows, both about the events of the story and about what the various protagonists know, feel, and believe. The requirement that the teller of a tale keep up with what the listener knows about what the story characters know pushes the author into a meta-narrative awareness. The author comes to be aware of the self as an author, aware of the impact the story is having on the mind of the listener. Story-sharing is an impressive feat of other-mindedness.

Conclusions

Both peer conflict and narrative accounts are provoked when something unexpected or out of the ordinary transpires. Both peer conflict and narrative accounting put children in positions of moral authority and require them to take a moral, evaluative stance. Both peer conflict and narratives occur when there is epistemic puzzlement or an uncertainty about what really happened and what it means. Peer conflicts and the stories children create to describe them offer us a rich opportunity to increase our understanding of human development during the elementary school years. In this book we consider how research and theory about children's developing ability to manage peer relationships can help us understand their narrative accounts of conflict experiences. We also show how research and theory about narrative development can orient us in useful ways to the study of peer conflict.

Notes

1 As we explain in Chapter 2, stories were transcribed and coded without correcting the authors' spelling or punctuation.
2 "Checking" is a word that Memphis children use to refer to name-calling. The practice is discussed in Chapter 4.

References

Bamberg, M. (1997). Positioning between structure and performance. *Journal of Narrative and Life History*, *7*, 335–342.

Bamberg, M. (2004). Talk, small stories, and adolescent identities. *Human Development*, *47*, 366–369.

Bamberg, M., & Damrad-Frye, R. (1991). On the ability to provide evaluative comments: Further explorations of children's narrative competencies. *Journal of Child Language*, *18*(3), 689–710. doi:10.1017/s0305000900011314.

Bohanek, J. G., Fivush, R., Zaman, W., Lepore, C. E., Merchant, S., & Duke, M. P. (2009). Narrative interaction in family dinnertime conversations. *Merrill-Palmer Quarterly*, *55*(4), 488–515.

Bruner, J. S. (1990). *Acts of meaning*. Cambridge, MA: Harvard University Press.

Davidson, A. J., Walton, M. D., & Cohen, R. (2013). Patterns of conflict experience that emerge in peer reports and personal narratives during middle childhood. *Journal of Applied Developmental Science*, *17*(3), 109–122.

Dweck, C. S. (2006). *Mindset: The new psychology of success*. New York, NY: Random House.

Goodwin, M. H. (1990). *He-said-she-said: Talk as social organization among black children*. Bloomington, IN: Indiana University Press.

Heath, S. B. (1983). *Ways with words: Language, life, and work in communities and classrooms*. Cambridge: Cambridge University Press.

Humphrey, R., Walton, M. D., & Davidson, A. J. (2014). "Im gonna tell you all about it": Authorial voice and conventional skills in writing assessment and educational practice. *Journal of Educational Research*, *107*(2), 111–122.

James, W. (1980). *The principles of psychology* (Vol. 1–2). New York, NY: Dover Publications.

Labov, W. (1972). *Language in the inner city: Studies in the black English vernacular*. Philadelphia, PA: University of Pennsylvania Press.

Labov, W., & Fanshell, D. (1977). *Therapeutic discourse: Psychotherapy as conversation*. New York, NY: Academic Press.

Miller, P. J., & Mehler, R. A. (1994). The power of personal story-telling in families and kindergartens. In A. Dyson & C. Genishi (Eds.), *The need for story: Cultural diversity in classroom and community* (pp. 38–54). Urbana, IL: National Council of Teachers of English.

Nicolopoulou, A. (2002). Peer-group culture and narrative development. In S. Blum-Kulka & C. E. Snow (Eds.), *Talking to adults* (pp. 117–152). Mahwah, NJ: Erlbaum.

Paley, V. G. (1990). *The boy who would be a helicopter: The uses of story-telling in the classroom*. Cambridge, MA: Harvard University Press.

Paley, V. G. (1997). *The girl with the brown crayon*. Cambridge, MA: Harvard University Press.

Paley, V. G. (2004). *A child's work: The importance of fantasy play*. Chicago, IL: University of Chicago Press.

Piaget, J. (1932/65). *The moral judgment of the child*. New York, NY: Free Press.

Rogoff, B. (2003). *The cultural nature of human development*. New York, NY: Oxford University Press.

Sullivan, H. S. (1953). *The interpersonal theory of psychiatry*. New York, NY: Norton.

Tappan, M. (1991). Narrative, language, and moral experience. *Journal of Moral Education*, *20*, 243–256.

Wainryb, C., Brehl, B., & Matwin, S. (2005). Being hurt and hurting others: Children's narrative accounts and moral judgments of their own interpersonal conflicts. *Monographs of the Society for Research in Child Development*, 70(Serial No. 281), 1–122.

Walton, M. D., & Brewer, C. L. (2001). The role of personal narrative in bringing children into the moral discourse of their culture. *Narrative Inquiry*, *11*(2), 1–28.

Walton, M. D., Harris, A. R., & Davidson, A. J. (2009). "It makes me a man from the beating I took": Gender and aggression in children's narratives about conflict. *Sex Roles*, *61*, 383–398.

Wiley, A. R., Rose, A. J., Burger, L. K., & Miller, P. J. (1998). Constructing autonomous selves through narrative practices: A comparative study of working-class and middle-class families. *Child Development*, *69*, 833–847. doi:10.1111/j.1467-8624.1998.tb06246.x.

2

"WHAT ARE YOU GOING TO DO WITH OUR STORIES?"

Collaborating With Children to Understand Peer Conflict

Do you have to write a paper about us? To turn in?

Mitch, fifth-grade FLASH camper, Memphis

In many ways the prospect of learning about children's lives by asking them to tell us about their lives is very appealing, especially if we are primarily eager to know how they understand the social world. We like the idea of hearing about their experience as they construe it. It may be a little disingenuous to talk about children as research collaborators; they have only an elementary understanding of the nature of our research questions, and they have virtually no say in how we choose to represent them – in how we interpret the experiences they tell us about for an audience of adults. But we do seek to honor a partnership we have established with the children who agreed to tell us their stories. We told them that we want to learn about "what it is like to be your age nowadays," or "what it's like to be a kid in your grade," and we encouraged them to tell us what they want grown-ups to know about this. We have tried to keep the partnership in mind as we seek to understand what it is they wanted us to learn. In the sections below, we tell the story of our research, explaining how we came to hear over 3,000 stories by elementary school children and how we have approached the task of representing their voices.

The Research Story

In 1997, in Memphis, Tennessee, a coalition of twelve community organizations, convened by the MidSouth Peace and Justice Center, began meeting to discuss ways to support the city schools in reducing violence and disruptive conduct.

Participating organizations included the National Civil Rights Museum, three local colleges and universities, and several community service and religious organizations. After a year of fact-finding efforts that included a review of scholarly research as well as conversations with parents, teachers, and administrators in the schools, members of the coalition came to believe that efforts to suppress conflict among school children would be misguided. Instead, we should seek to give voice to children's experiences with interpersonal conflict, and to help children develop the skills that support their ability to describe their own experiences. What would they have to say about the kinds of behaviors and situations that provoked conflict? How would they describe the insults and accusations they endured and perpetrated? What responses to these provocations would they report? What would they see as legitimate justifications? What would count as evidence of blame-worthiness or innocence? What accounts would they give of reconciliation? We started asking children to tell us about their conflicts because we were curious about these matters, and because we believed that skills in constructing accounts of their own conflicts would help them develop strategies for resolving conflict without violence.

The stories we collected in the 1998–99 school year from Memphis school children gave us a glimpse of how much we have to learn by really listening to children and by respecting the validity of their 'take' on the society they are joining. In the fifteen years that followed, we collected over 3,000 stories from over 1,000 children in six elementary schools, one summer camp, and one after-school care setting in three cities. Some children contributed one story; a few gave us up to thirty stories over a two-year period. Some children lived in neighborhoods experiencing serious problems with poverty and crime, and attended schools the state came to designate as 'failing.' Some lived in historic districts on graceful, tree-lined streets, and attended well-resourced schools. Some attended racially and ethnically homogenous schools (nearly 100% Han Chinese, or nearly 100% African American). Some of our story-tellers attended schools with notable ethnic diversity, serving children whose families spoke different languages at home and families with differing socioeconomic conditions. Table 2.1 lists the eight corpora with a brief description of each, and Appendix A provides a full description of each data-collection site, with demographic information about the children and details about the collection procedures.

Dozens of undergraduate researchers have been able to work with subsets of these stories, gaining experience in formulating research questions, identifying features of children's narratives worthy of close examination, and learning research strategies and skills as they contributed to our exploration of these corpora. Sixteen of these students have gone on to do doctoral work in psychology and eleven have taken advanced degrees in related fields. Several of these former students have occasionally met at conferences and a few have continued to collaborate, finding new questions we want to address and new ways to study the stories we continued to collect. We have regularly noted that

TABLE 2.1 Overview of corpora

Collection site	Ethnicity	Economic resources★	Years of data collection	Grades	Number of children	Number of stories	Number of stories about conflict
Connors Elementary, Memphis, TN	97% African American 3% other ethnicities	87.6% economically disadvantaged	Fall 1998 Spring 1999 Spring 2000	4–6	179	387	387
Ironwood Elementary, Memphis, TN	65% African American 30% European American 5% other ethnicities	51% economically disadvantaged	Fall 1998 Spring 1999 Spring 2000	4–6	351	726	726
Winterton Elementary, Memphis, TN	79% African American 20% European American 1% other ethnicities	60% economically disadvantaged	Fall 1996	3–5	345	345	151
Community Wellness, Memphis, TN	87% African American 7% European American 6% other ethnicities	All working families with no health insurance, living in central city neighborhoods	Summer 2006 Fall 2006	1–6	69	370	250
College Elementary School, Memphis, TN	64% European American 27% African American	19% economically disadvantaged	Spring 2010 Spring 2011	3–6	364	1162	804

(continued)

TABLE 2.1 *(continued)*

Collection site	Ethnicity	Economic resources ★	Years of data collection	Grades	Number of children	Number of stories	Number of stories about conflict
Magnolia Spring Elementary, Orlando, FL	36% African American 32% European American 19% Hispanic Americans 8% multi-ethnic 3% Asian American 2% other ethnicities	82% economically disadvantaged 20–25% homeless	Fall 2009 Spring 2010	3–5	114	183	183
ChunTian Primary, Shenzhen, China	Over 95% Han Chinese Approximately 5% other Chinese ethnicities	All children came from a middle-class, urban neighborhood	Spring 2012	4–6	152	152	152
FLASH Summer Camp, Memphis, TN	81% European American 7% African American 12% mixed or other ethnicities	All children came from middle-class suburban neighborhoods	Summer 2014	1–6	26	317	158
					1600	3642	2811

Note: ★ Economic disadvantage was determined by eligibility for free lunch and breakfast at school.

the child development literature is lacking in the study of children's personal conflict narratives – most studies that explore child conflict do not get the children's take on the subject. Always, these meetings stimulated more ideas and richer insights about how to work with the stories we have and they often provoked us to collect more data – to hear children in different contexts. Finally, it became clear that we needed to do something to bring together our years of work with our nearly 3,000 stories. This book is that something.

How Did We Get Children to Tell Their Stories?

We just asked them! In central-city Memphis schools, or in Shenzhen, China, children living in homeless shelters and the children of university professors, children being treated for hyperactivity and children referred for obesity, children working on books they plan to self-publish with Amazon, and children who are barely literate – almost all of the children we asked to tell us about their own experience with conflict were happy to do so. Third-grader Paige, below, is a good example.

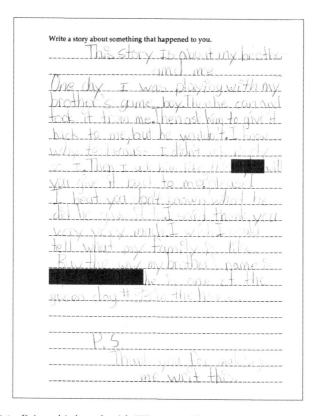

EXAMPLE 2.1 Paige, third-grade girl, Winterton Elementary, Memphis

EXAMPLE 2.1 PAIGE, THIRD-GRADE GIRL, WINTERTON ELEMENTARY, MEMPHIS

This story is about my brother and me. One day I was playing with my brother's game boy. Then he can and took it from me. Then ask him to give it back to me, but he wouldn't. I know why to because I didn't ask nicely. So I then I ask him like this. Kyle will you give it back to me? Please! I beat you don't known what he did he gave it to. I said thank you very very much. I wish I could tell what my family is like. Buy the way my brother's name is Kyle Dickerson he is one of th green dog #33 in the house.

P.S. Thank you for making me writ this

Paige seems to recognize the impossibility of fully communicating the richness of her own experience, but she longs to be able to do it: "I wish I could tell what my family is like," and she recognizes that there is value for her in the exercise of trying to explain, so she thanks us.

When we asked children to write stories for us, we told them that we are researchers who are "trying to learn what it is like to be your age nowadays." With few exceptions, they were eager to tell us. The only children who declined to give us stories were a few of the children in the university-affiliated school – and those children participated in multiple research studies each year, so their lack of enthusiasm is understandable. Even in the summer camp and after-school facilities, where children chose between coming to our story circle rather than participating in such other activities as computer games or water slides, even in those situations where we competed with very attractive alternatives, there were very few children who never chose to come and contribute a story about their own experience. On occasions where we were not able to get signed consent from parents, we generally let the children tell their stories, even though we did not transcribe them or include them in our study, because the children felt so bad about being left out. One fourth-grader from a school that served children from a nearby homeless shelter expressed his distress at not being able to find his parental consent form, with "But I want MY voice to be heard, too!" It is not difficult to get children to share their stories, and we take their eagerness to share as evidence that we really ought to listen.

How We Listened to Children's Stories

This is the hard part. Once we have children's stories about their own experience, full of child-sized insights and also child-invented spelling and grammar, what do we do with them? Can we, *should* we wrestle these little literary oeuvres into something we are accustomed to calling data? Over the years we have spent working with these stories, we have identified hundreds of features we found worthy of study. We have found interesting ways to categorize the stories; we have rated them on various dimensions, and have counted dozens of features that have been inter-correlated and organized into factor structures. We have broken our stories down into words, into sentences, into parts of the narrative so that they could be dissected and analyzed. And always, as we have performed these surgery-like procedures, we have been aware that the real wealth in our data can only be realized when we keep all the parts together and listen for the voice of that child who exclaimed, "I want my voice to be heard!"

Our first data preparation task involved transcribing stories and removing identifying information. In electronic files, we organized the stories line-by-line using subject-predicate units, which facilitated some of our analyses. Some of the children's stories are so unique and so specific that anyone who knows the child might recognize the incident. We did not attempt to obscure details of the story (and we discuss the ethics of this decision in Chapter 5), but we did change all person and place names. We did this with an effort to preserve any social information in the name. The names we chose preserved ethnic identity, so that Carlos might become Juan, LaQuitra might become Kenisha. We selected names that matched in formality, so that Kathryn might become Elizabeth but Kathy would be Lizzie. Biblical names were substituted for children who had Biblical names. Children named after flowers or virtues were given names of different flowers or virtues. We chose rare names when the children wrote about people with rare names. When children wrote their stories, we preserved their spelling and punctuation; when they spoke their stories, we preserved their grammar, but did not phonetically transcribe their pronunciation unless it was pertinent to the meaning of the story.

Stories that were collected in Shenzhen were written in Mandarin, and these were coded by two members of our research team for whom Mandarin was their first language. These student researchers achieved reliability with other members of our team, coding stories in English. Translations were made of these stories so that we could discuss them with team members who do not speak Mandarin, but we did not attempt to code the stories in translation because the nuances of language use are important to us. These translations were made independently by two of our team members and then checked by a third Mandarin speaker not on our research team.

We have taken an 'ever-which-way' approach to studying the stories contributed by our authors – borrowing shamelessly from analytic approaches developed by grounded theory sociologists, discursive psychologists, phenomenological philosophers, linguistic anthropologists, cognitive linguists, and literary theorists. Besides this, we have exploited many statistical procedures that were designed for hypothesis testing, using them to explore our data and to detect relationships between variables. Our data analysis proceeded in iterative steps involving multiple readings of our stories by members of our research team. We began with open coding that identified common categories and recurring themes. We flagged and performed close readings of the narratives that seemed prototypical as well as those that stood out as atypical. Briggs (1992) called this kind of close reading a micro-analysis, and he described it as "following the interpretive footsteps of the child." Such readings helped us to hone the categories we had already defined as well as create additional categories our initial coding had not captured.

We did exploratory statistical analyses of the co-occurrence of the features we had coded for, determining which combinations of features were of particular interest for further close reading. When we found qualitatively interesting features in the stories, we were prompted to ask questions about frequencies and co-occurrence of those features. Interesting or surprising quantitative results, on the other hand, sent us back to the stories for more nuanced qualitative readings of the features we had seen in the first place. Our understandings emerged as a weaving together of the results of our close interpretive work and our statistical explorations. Essential to both the 'qualitative' and 'quantitative' analyses was the development of what Niobe Way (2001) called an interpretive community. In weekly meetings we raised questions, expressed doubts, and shared insights about features of the stories and about the classification systems we were developing. Part of this process involved the important role of undergraduate honors students and recent graduates who mentored and trained younger students joining the team to preserve these insights and continue the conversation across the years.

Both the interpretive work and the quantitative work were guided by three overarching questions: How did children describe conflict? How did they describe themselves and the other characters in their stories? How did they appropriate a cultural toolkit of narrative forms and cultural discourses to accomplish these descriptions?

How Did Child Authors Construe Their Conflict Experience?

Among our first questions as we began reading our stories was a concern for what children identified as a conflict. What accusations did children make against their antagonists? Which behaviors or situations were described as provoking conflict? In multiple passes through our data, we made exhaustive lists of accusations. We identified instances of blaming, and instances of excusing or justifying. We identified those conflict situations that recurred frequently, and we noted those stories that were singular or strikingly unlike the others. In early passes through the data, we grouped stories together when the source of the conflict seemed very similar. "She decided to play with Ella so I didn't have nobody," was grouped with "He sat by Jadon for the whole fieldtrip." As these groupings began to coalesce, we asked two important questions: (1) did the sources of conflict described by our child authors fall neatly (or roughly) into the categories described in previous research on peer conflict, and (2) could independent readers of the stories reliably classify the stories into these categories? Much of the work we describe in Part II of this book reports on how our data did and did not corroborate previous research in this way.

As our work proceeded, we found that our efforts to assess inter-coder reliability folded into our efforts to establish clear and valid categories. When two coders disagreed about how a story should be classified, we found that those disagreements could themselves be classified in three categories. Some of our coding misses were clear mistakes. One coder or the other was just inattentive, and as soon as the miss was identified, all members of the research team knew which coder was in error. Some of our coding misses happened because the situation was genuinely ambiguous or unclear. This happened sometimes when children with minimal literacy skills were writing, rather than telling their stories. Sometimes these misses seemed to stem from the genuine confusion of the author. We took these misses to be inevitable. A third kind of miss, however, occurred when there was legitimate disagreement between the coders about how the category should be defined. When these misses happened, they prompted us to bring the story to the team and to reconsider our category definitions. Our work of category development continued until two independent coders working with a set of stories achieved statistically acceptable reliability, and when none of the misses fell into the third category.

We classified dozens of sources of conflict in the stories and combined those dozens into larger categories. For example, moving out of turn in a game and 'butting in line' were combined with other instances of 'taking unfair advantages,' and later with other instances of 'cheating' in a game or 'copying' schoolwork. Later still, these were combined with instances of 'lying,' to form a broad category of 'dishonesty.' Always, we retained the subcategories, so that we regularly moved back and forth between more fine-grained analysis and a consideration of broader categories. This fine-grained analysis allowed us to respect the ambiguity and the multiplicity of meanings that are often built into narrative sense-making. For example, a group of stories that included accusations of 'lying' included some stories of lying to gain advantage or to avoid responsibility, some stories of 'lying on' someone, which were acts of social aggression, and some stories in which the function of the lie was unclear. Our system of coding always allowed us to go back to these distinctions.

We classified the sources of conflict and we also identified categories of responses children reported. When an antagonist hit someone or lied or betrayed a secret, did the author report that the wronged individual retaliated? Did the author describe communication about the misstep? Was the assistance of an adult sought? Using the same category-development procedures described above, we identified and reliably coded responses to conflict events described in the stories. Sometimes children ended their stories with a clear description of a reconciliation or resolution to the conflict (e.g., "We held our hands and said loudly, 'Best friends forever!'"). In these cases, we classified the paths to reconciliation described. Sometimes children noted the failure to reconcile (e.g., "and to this day I never trusted him again"). In some stories, the reader is left completely in the dark about whether or how the problem got resolved.

Always, as we sought to answer the question, 'How did child authors construe their conflict experience?' we were looking at what features of their experiences our young authors chose to report. Always, we tried to keep in mind that these were the aspects of 'what it is like to be a kid nowadays' that our research participants wanted the grown-ups to know.

Who Were the Characters in Children's Stories About Conflict?

A major focus of narrative psychology has been on the role of narrative in self-making (Fivush & Haden, 2003). When we tell stories about our own experience, when we become a character in our own story, we must decide what kind of a character to be – or more precisely, what kind of character we want our audience to take us to be. We have been very curious to see how children position themselves and others in their stories about their own conflict, and this coding proceeded differently than did the category development described above, because we formulated our categories in advance of our coding. We asked specific questions about how authors positioned themselves and other characters in a moral universe, in a social-relational world, and as psychological beings.

Story Characters Positioned in a Moral Order

When children describe acts of aggression, do they describe the self as a victim, an aggressor, both, or neither? Unlike the categories described above for types of conflict, in which a single story could include conflicts that fell into several different categories, here we have a mutually exclusive and exhaustive category system, and independent coders were able to place every story into one of these groups with kappa statistics assessing their agreement, usually in the .90s.

Things got more complicated when we asked how the author evaluated the self and the other characters in the story. Some authors made clear excuses and justifications for their own behaviors and clear accusations against their antagonists, taking a position of a morally good actor in the face of wrongdoing by others. There were, however, many variations and complications here. Some authors critiqued their own behavior at the beginning of the story, coming to recognize the error of their ways, and ending on a moral high ground. Occasionally, an author would unabashedly present the self as the 'bad guy' in his own story, but these stories were rare. More often, the author was a hero or a hapless dupe or a minimally involved reporter, but not morally culpable. These positions were sometimes explicitly stated in the story (e.g., "but I was not the guilty one") but many times there was moral evaluative ambiguity (e.g., "I knew it was right but I thought it was not right").

Finding it impossible to classify stories neatly into categories based on a single moral position assigned to self and other actors, we developed a rating system for assessing moral voice. Appendix B includes the coding manual for this variable. We asked four questions of each story: How explicitly did the author make a positive evaluation or a moral justification of the self? How explicitly did the author make a positive evaluation or moral justification of another character in the story? How explicitly did the author negatively evaluate or make a moral critique of the self? How explicitly did the author negatively evaluate or make a negative critique of another character in the story? Independent coders were able to make reliable explicitness judgments on a three-point scale: zero indicated no moral evaluation at all, one indicated an implied evaluation, and two indicated a clearly articulated moral stance. These ratings gave us four moral voice scores for each story, so that we could compare stories by the children who made moral critiques of both self and other, to those who made critiques of the other and justifications of the self, to those who were critical of both self and other, and so on. This rating system also allowed us to compare stories in which children tended to be explicit about their moral judgments to children whose evaluations had to be inferred by the reader, to children who included no moral evaluation in their stories.

Story Characters Positioned in a Relational World

Our children's stories were peopled by all kinds of characters, and young authors were generally aware of an expectation that the actors in their stories be assigned positions in a social universe. Straightforward content analyses allowed us to identify where our authors labeled the characters in their stories as friends (or best friends, or bffs, or frenemies, or "my former friend"), as siblings or other family members, or as members of other groups or social categories (e.g., "those boys from the projects," "a third grader"). We were able to count how often children positioned themselves and the others in their stories as family members, as students, and as members of other social groups, and how often they marked the gender, age, or race of their characters. These last three membership categories used by our children were especially interesting and productive for our analyses.

Story Characters Positioned as Psychological Selves

We described in Chapter 1 how one of the functions of narrative is to allow us to get into one another's heads, and we have seen how Bruner's (1990) landscape of consciousness is critical to fleshing out a good story. As we looked at how children positioned self and other in their stories, we found them showing considerable awareness of a psychological self and other – of protagonists with thoughts, emotions, motives, and traits. Our content analyses included counts for each instance of the use of mental state verbs (e.g., think, know, wonder, suppose) attributed to self, other, or to self and other (e.g., "we misunderstood each other"). We identified all emotional states attributed to self, other, or 'we,' and added up the number of such reports in each story. Children sometimes attributed enduring traits to self and others, and these could be classified as physical traits (e.g., tall, pretty), cognitive traits (e.g., smart, good at math), or personality traits (e.g., bossy, nice). A count of trait terms attributed to self and other gave us another assessment of the psychological mindedness or the attention to a landscape of consciousness in the children's stories. Finally, we were interested in seeing how attentive children were to reporting the motives of the characters in their stories. When they report about a character's behavior, did they recognize a need to report what that person was trying to do? Did they offer reasons for the actions of self and other in their stories? Independent coders were able to identify reasons and motives that were offered to explain behavior in the stories with good reliabilities, so each story had a count of the number of motives attributed to self, other, and we. For some of our analyses, we summed the authors' reports of thoughts, emotions, traits, and motives to create a psychological-mindedness score. This score was summed separately for reports about self, other, and we, so that we were able to select stories in which authors gave greater and lesser attention to the internal states of self and other. Appendix C is a coding manual for the psychological mindedness variables.

How Did Children Make Use of a Cultural Toolkit to Describe Their Conflicts?

As we read through hundreds of stories by elementary school children, we were struck by wide differences in narrative skill. Some of our story-tellers had a clear command of narrative form, impressive literacy skills, and a strong authorial voice. Some were dreadfully behind grade level in spelling and punctuation, but had an engaging and charming narrative style. Some produced narratives so confusing that we could not discern who had done what or why it was important to the author. Our efforts to explore and understand these variations took us down three frequently intersecting paths. Below we describe first our efforts to assess coherence. After this, we describe our efforts to look closely at the ways children appropriated (and sometimes resisted) many cultural discourses in their stories. Finally, we show how we endeavored to assess the development in our young authors of an authorial voice, a personal narrative style.

Telling a Coherent Story

Narrative form differs in interesting ways across cultural communities, with some traditions valuing a straightforward reportorial form and others valuing a 'garden path' interweaving of narrative components, with some traditions valuing loquaciousness and some laconicity (Miller, Koven, & Lin, 2011). Despite many cultural differences, most children learn to tell stories that provide an interpretable sequence of events located in space and time. They come to take into account the needs of the audience for elaborations or clarifications that give their stories coherence. They come to recognize what events are report-worthy in their cultural communities, and they get better at providing culturally reasonable explanations for those. Many approaches to narrative coherence have been proposed. Clinical and personality psychologists have focused on narrative promoting self-understanding or reflecting organizing principles of the psyche (Fiese & Sameroff, 1999; McAdams, 2006). Cognitive and cognitive developmental psychologists have focused on narrative structuring of memory and thought (McCabe & Pederson, 1991; Stein & Albro, 1997). Linguists and literary critics have focused on narrative as genre (Labov & Waletzky, 1997). Discursive psychologists have focused on story-telling exchanges, with coherence created in interaction (Edwards & Potter, 1992). Our early attempts to find a way to measure coherence borrowed liberally from these approaches. We identified components of narratives (e.g., introduction of setting and characters, introduction of trouble and resolution), and we rated narratives for clarity.

In 2007, Baker-Ward and several collaborators developed a three-dimensional model for assessing coherence (the Narrative Coherence Coding Scheme or NaCC) that incorporated linguistic and cognitive developmental approaches. The system considers three components of coherence, the first two related to Bruner's landscape of action and assessing the author's ability to recount a chronology and a context that establishes the who, what, where, and when of a story. The third component of narrative coherence assesses attention to a landscape of consciousness, attending to authors' elaboration about motives, meanings, and evaluations of the events of the story. We have used this method of assessing narrative coherence, and we will see in subsequent chapters that it helps us predict several aspects of children's academic and peer adjustment across school years.

Although our efforts to examine narrative structure and to assess coherence helped us see children appropriating the forms and complying with the sense-making demands that operated in their environments, they did not fully capture our sense that children were becoming more active participants in their cultural communities as they created narratives of their experience. Getting a handle on this required additional ways of assessing the stories.

Developing a Cultural Voice

As we read stories contributed by children from different settings, we often had the strong impression that we could identify a narrative style that located an author in a cultural community. The child who said "We go together like sock with shoe, like chip with dip, like koolade with the flavor!" was an African American drawing on a rich oral tradition. The child who said "We should cherish our friendship because it is the most beautiful thing in the world!" was a fourth-grade Chinese national, drawing on a rich Confucian tradition. The child who said, "She thinks she's all that because her clothes are old navy," was a middle-class European American, developing a voice of resistance to a kind of materialism that threatens to define her community. This sense that we could hear a cultural voice in children's stories led us to look for ways to assess what Mikhail Bakhtin (1981) called a polyphony of voices. We attempted to identify children's appropriation of (and with more difficulty, their resistance to) the voices they heard around them.

Sometimes children were very clear about whose voice was included in the story. To investigate this, we identified all occasions of direct quotation (e.g., "My mother said, 'no, silly'"), indirect quotation (e.g. "he asked me why I did that"), and reports of speech acts (e.g., "We discussed it out"). These reports were coded according to whose speech was brought into the story. Children quoted parents, teachers, and other adults, sometimes to lend authority to their argument ("Coach said I was the best dancer"), sometimes to document their resistance to adult authority ("She told me I couldn't go to the park but I went to the park anyway"). They quoted other children and they quoted themselves. An examination of how children talked about talking in their stories was an important part of our analysis of a developing authorial voice and a developing sense of self.

Like adult authors, our children did not always make clear attributions when they were borrowing from a variety of cultural sources. We would have expected to encounter literary allusions in the stories of college students, but we were surprised and delighted to see how freely children borrowed from literature and mythology ("his nose was just growing and growing"), from holy scriptures or liturgy ("let those who have ears, hear"), from courtroom discourse ("the truth and nothing but the truth") and even from popular psychology ("he is the most anger management class needed kid in the whole school"). Some of the language we read in children's stories was identifiably 'school language' ("I used my walking feet"), and could be easily contrasted with 'street language' ("I was knocking him upside his head"). When children borrowed phrases from TV commercials, movies, or popular songs (e.g., "I tried to do the matrix on my bike"), they were placing themselves in historical time and geographic place and aligning themselves with a cultural community. These features of children's stories underlined for us the extent to which children were beginning to claim an identity and to make a place for themselves in a social world as they made accounts of their own experience. They were coming to claim their own voice.

Authorial Voice and a Personal Narrative Style

As children develop proficiency with the narrative structures that are valued in their cultural communities, and as they learn to orchestrate a polyphony of voices, they simultaneously develop their unique sense of what stories should be told and begin to develop a personal narrative style. This development happens in conversation with all the people who listen to the child's stories. It happens as the child tries out a wide variety of communicative devices, metaphors, and tropes, and bits and pieces of the various discourses available in the cultural toolkit opened up in deliberate lessons designed for the child (e.g., children's literature, children's television, school lessons, religious teachings) and also from the wide range of adult conversations and cultural practices overheard (newscasts and political arguments, televised drama and advertisement – all the multiple meanings we call 'popular culture'). We offer our children an enormous array of meaning-making devices from which they can select those that work for them as they recount their own experiences. What an accomplishment to pull this together to create a personal narrative voice!

Sometimes, as we read a child's story, it was impossible to escape the impression that we can hear a ten-year-old voice speaking the story aloud as we read. Our efforts to get a handle on this feature of children's narratives led us to think about an authorial voice that seemed much easier to recognize than to define. We found that independent raters could reliably rate stories for this feature we might call 'style,' 'flair,' or 'expressiveness,' or just that 'je ne sais quoi.' But even when we were able to identify it reliably, we were hard-pressed to come to a precise description of the features that made us know it was there. Our efforts to pin down this quality we call voice set us to counting emphasis markers, hyperbole, repetition, onomato-poeia, rhetorical questions, metaphor, and simile – all literary devices that Regan Humphrey (2013) identified as an "author's tool kit." Appendix D includes a coding manual for the variables that contributed to our assessment of authorial voice.

A critical feature of the quality we identified as authorial voice was an inclination to 'go meta.' "In case you don't know," one of our authors from an inner-city school explained to the researchers from a college he knew to be predominately white, "checking is saying bad about his momma." Our authors interrupted their stories to make parenthetical comments for the benefit of the researchers only occasionally, but this was enough to remind us and to reassure us that our participants were indeed telling us what they wanted us to know about what their lives are like (e.g., "and I punched him in his face and the techer don't know yet. p.s don't let her read it"). Some of these meta-narrative comments functioned to inform us of what our authors thought of us, or of what they thought we believed about them. "You won't believe this," a sixth-grade boy wrote, "but we never fought again." This boy, on the cusp of adolescence, imagines that adult researchers are not likely to believe that he could find a nonviolent solution to his problems. Sometimes meta-narrative remarks were made not so much to explain things to the readers as to affirm or encourage a relationship with them – to provoke our engagement. "Guess what happened next," an author urges. "You should never make this mistake," we are warned. Sometimes meta-narratives identified components of the narrative, making sure we know where we were in the story ("Here is the beginning of my story." "Now I'm going tell you what she did." "The moral of this true is: You don't allways get what you whant, even if you try really hard … PS. Crying won't help either"). These are especially revealing for us because they let us know what the author knows explicitly about narrative as narrative. When story-tellers recognized themselves as the narrator or addressed the reader as a listener, when we got to see an explicitly self-conscious author, we were given a glimpse of the child's understanding of the nature of narrative communication.

Our attention to cultural voice (the ways young authors incorporated discourses and devices to create coherence) was consistently braided together with our examination of children's representation of character (the ways they described themselves and the various protagonists in their stories as relational, psychological, and moral actors) and with our analysis of their construal of conflict (the ways they ascribed roles and recounted resolutions) into a strand that inevitably led us back to look at whole stories.

Taking Stories Apart and Keeping Stories Together

As we worked to identify scores of features in our stories that could be counted, to develop dozens of ways the stories could be classified or rated, and to examine associations between these story features and other measures of children's adjustment, we were keenly aware of our responsibility to listen to the whole story, trying to hear what the authors wanted us to know. The story excerpted in Example 2.2 is a good illustration of what we gain by considering whole stories, not just a set of counts and classifications. It was written by a fifth-grader we have named Li Na, in Shenzhen, China, in response to a request to "Write a true story about a conflict that really happened to you. Think about an argument, a fight, or some kind of misunderstanding. Tell everything you can remember from the beginning to the end."

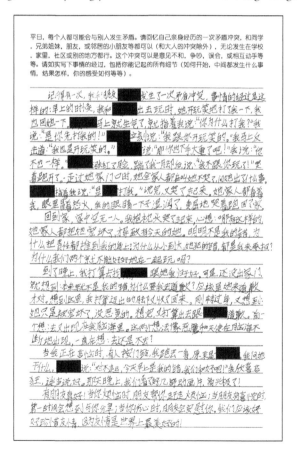

EXAMPLE 2.2   Li Na, fifth-grade girl, ChunTian Primary School, Shenzhen

EXAMPLE 2.2 LI NA, FIFTH-GRADE GIRL, CHUNTIAN PRIMARY SCHOOL, SHENZHEN

1. I planned to make up with Hu Jia-Li at night.
2. But before I left home, it occurred to me that it was not my fault in the first place,
3. why should I apologize to her?
4. She should apologize to me.
5. I stepped back.
6. As I turned around, I thought: well, she is just spoiled.
7. She meant no harm.
8. As I was thinking about apologizing to her, the previous thought emerged in my head again.
9. These two thoughts were like angel and demon competing in my head.
10. I kept thinking: should I go or not?
11. As I was wondering, I heard someone ring the bell.
12. It was Hu Jia-Li.
13. I asked what she was doing here.
14. She said "sorry,
15. it was my fault this morning,
16. let's be friends again!"
17. I was thrilled, approving such a good idea.
18. At night, we watched many cartoons.
19. We were exhilarated!
20. It is so good to have friend!
21. Friends dispel your trouble, share your joy and comfort your sadness.
22. We should cherish our friendship
23. because it is the most beautiful thing in the world!

When we look at the profile of scores for this story, we are pleased to see that they construct a picture of a sophisticated and thoughtful young author. Her story is classified with those that present a clear resolution and that describe apology as a resolution strategy, and with those stories that express moral puzzlement or ambivalence and with those that provide an explicit moral summary (on lines 20–23). She scores high on all the moral voice explicitness ratings, with explicit critiques and justifications of self and other. The story includes four deontic auxiliaries (on lines 3, 4, 10, and 22), and this is high for stories of this length. Her scores on the relational/social role variables are quite low, since the only membership category she ascribes to any characters is gender, and this is ascribed only by the use of gendered pronouns on lines 3, 4, 6, 7, 13, and 14. Her psychological mindedness, on the other hand, is exceptionally high. She reports on her own mental states eight times (on lines 2, 6, 8, 9, 10, 11, and 17), and additionally reports on her own motive in line 1 and her own emotional state in line 17. To her antagonist she attributes thoughts in line 7, an emotion in line 14, a motive in line 7, and a trait in line 6. Overall, the psychological-mindedness score for this story is 15, which was in the 90th percentile for this measure. The story rates well on coherence, with the highest rating on chronology, context, and theme. Our scoring procedures identify the use of six literary devices: rhetorical questions (on line 3), dialogue (on lines 13–16), internal dialogue (on lines 3, 4, 6–8, 10), metaphor or simile (on lines 5, 6, 9), intensifiers (on lines 17, 18, 20), and emphasis markers (on lines 16, 19, 23). The story gets our highest expressiveness/authorial voice rating. We are satisfied that all of our scoring and counting captures critical features of Li Na's story and allows us to make reasonable comparisons with the other thousands of stories in our various corpora. However, we do not see it as a substitute for reading closely and doing an interpretive analysis, as we do below.

Li Na has given us a story about an internal conflict that is waged between the 'angel and demon' in her own head (described on line 9). She begins with a report on line 1 about her own plan to "make up," and she tells us how this plan was interrupted by the debate she had with herself about culpability. Our author is clear that "it was not my fault in the first place" (an explicit justification of the self in line 2), but she is also not sure that Hu Jia-Li should be held entirely blameworthy. "She is just spoiled." Here, Li Na may be calling on a popular discourse in her community, reflecting a concern in China's emerging middle class that a generation of only children may be 'spoiled little emperors.' The blame, then, would not fall on Hu Jia-Li. Li Na also recognizes that ill intentions are required for assigning blame, and her antagonist "meant no harm." Li Na describes her consideration about whether to apologize as an internal dialogue, which she reports with direct and indirect quotation of her own thoughts on lines 3, 4, 6, 7, 8, and 10. This internal voice is distinguished from Hu Jia-Li's voice, which is marked by quotation marks on lines 14–16. This author's attention to the landscape of consciousness is noteworthy, especially in her reports about her own mental states. On lines 2, 6, 8, 11, and 17, we learn that the author is thinking and wondering. Things occur to her and thoughts emerge and then compete in her head. Later, in line 17, she reports being thrilled at her antagonist's "good idea," and in line 19 she attributes to both herself and Hu Jia-Li an emotional state, "we were exhilarated." Li Na ends her story with a moral, a 'lesson to be learned,' a familiar narrative device that lends coherence to her narrative and aligns the author with Confucian ideals.

Conclusions

In this chapter we have described our approach to the study of children's narratives. The reader will undoubtedly have detected a tension – for us it has been a creative tension – between a devotion to methodological standards that will allow us to make confident generalizations of our findings and a commitment to honoring the voices of the children who gave us their stories. On the 'scientific rigor' side of this tug of war, we have conscientiously implemented the highest standards of reliability assessment for transcriptions, coding, rating, and scoring, with virtually every variable assessed independently by at least two and often many members of the research team. We have paid attention to variability and to the shape of our distributions, and have used statistical procedures to uncover relationships between the narrative features we have assessed, as well as with empirically validated survey measures of academic and social-emotional adjustment. This we have done with modesty, recognizing that most of these procedures were designed for hypothesis testing, not for data exploration. On the 'interpretive rigor' side of the tug of war, we have intentionally developed and trained teams of undergraduate researchers who have studied stories while spending time each week working or playing with young authors in the same age group and while reading research and theory about human development. Hours spent over nearly twenty years in comparing stories and arguing about what they reveal about the author and the author's world have made us at once more confident and more humble. We have grown in confidence as we have experienced deepening insight and as we have seen our interpretations corroborated by other research and our continuing communication with our young authors and their teachers. The confidence has been regularly tempered by humility as we have continued to be surprised by the nuance in narrative productions of even our youngest children, and as we have grappled with interpretive differences between research team members. The tug of war we have enjoyed as we worked with these corpora, however muddied it has left us at times, has strengthened our devotion to an 'ever-which-way' program of research with a primary commitment to hear what children want to tell us and to communicate our clearest understanding of that to the grown-ups who have so much influence over the quality of their lives.

We have regularly presented our best take on this to teachers and counselors and administrators, mindful of our obligations both to honor our commitment to confidentiality and to credit the work of our young authors. Many times these audiences are receptive to our interpretive work, providing us with valuable on-the-ground insight and feedback that further informs this work; at times they are a little suspicious of the quantitative work, and are surprised that we consider these stories (which are such a common part of their daily experience) to be so very important. We have also presented findings to our colleagues at departmental and professional meetings. These audiences are more inclined to be interested in statistically documented differences between groups or relationships between variables, and they are often suspicious of the interpretive work, but they have been generous in helping us see how our work folds into ongoing research in other areas of child development.

In the chapters that follow, we reference the methods described in this chapter to present our assessment of what 1,600 elementary school children want grown-ups to know about what their conflicts are like.

References

Bahktin, M. (1981). *The dialogic imagination* (C. Emerson & M. Holquist Trans.). Austin, TX: University of Texas Press.

Baker-Ward, L., Bauer, P. J., Fivush, R., Haden, C. A., Ornstein, P. A., & Reese, E. (2007, July). Coding coherence in autobiographical narratives. Symposium conducted at the biennial meeting of the Society for Applied Research in Memory and Cognition, Lewiston, ME.

Briggs, J. L. (1992). Mazes of meaning: How a child and a culture create each other. In W. A. Corsaro & P. J. Miller (Eds.), *Interpretive approaches to children's socialization: New directions for child and adolescent development* (Issue No. 58, pp. 25–49). San Francisco, CA: Jossey-Bass.

Bruner, J. S. (1990). *Acts of meaning.* Cambridge, MA: Harvard University Press.

Edwards, D., & Potter, J. (1992). *Discursive psychology.* London: Sage.

Fiese, B. H., & Sameroff, A. J. (1999). I. The family narrative consortium: A multidimensional approach to narratives. *Monographs of the Society for Research in Child Development, 64,* 1–36.

Fivush, R., & Haden, C. A. (Eds.). (2003). *Autobiographical memory and the construction of a narrative self: Developmental and cultural perspectives.* Mahwah, NJ: Erlbaum.

Humphrey, R. (2013). The author's toolkit: Cultural voice as a springboard for other literacy skills. *Tennessee Reading Teacher, 40*(1), 4–9.

Labov, W., & Waletzky, J. (1997). Narrative analysis: Oral versions of personal experience. *Journal of Narrative & Life History, 7*(1–4), 3–38.

McAdams, D. P. (2006). The problem of narrative coherence. *Journal of Constructivist Psychology, 19,* 109–25.

McCabe, A., & Peterson, C. (1991). Getting the story: A longitudinal study of parental styles of eliciting narratives and developing narrative skill. In A. McCabe & C. Peterson (Eds.), *Developing narrative structure* (pp. 217–53). Hillsdale, NJ: Lawrence Erlbaum.

Miller, P. J., Koven, M., & Lin, S. (2011). Language socialization and narrative. In A. Duranti, E. Ochs, & B. B. Schieffelin (Eds.), *The handbook of language socialization* (pp. 190–208). Oxford: Wiley-Blackwell.

Stein, N., & Albro, E. (1997). Building complexity and coherence: Children's use of goal-structured knowledge in telling stories. In. M. Bamberg (Ed.), *Narrative development: Six approaches* (pp. 5–44). Mahwah, NJ: Lawrence Erlbaum.

Way, N. (2001). Using feminist research methods to explore boys' relationships. In D. L. Tolman & M. Brydon-Miller (Eds.), *From subjects to subjectivities: A handbook of interpretive and participatory methods* (pp. 111–29). New York, NY: New York University Press.

PART II

How Children Describe Their Own Conflicts

3

"FIGHTING ABOUT FRIEND SHIP"

Figuring Out What It Means to Be a Friend

So then me and her was best friends, and we never believed anything else that
someone said that wasn't true again.

Jalisa, fifth-grade girl, Community Wellness, Memphis

Children shared stories about conflicts with classmates and siblings, teachers and
parents, and a variety of other people; an especially interesting subset of stories
was about conflict with people designated as friends. Over 20% of stories reported
a conflict with a friend, a best friend, a bff (best friend forever), or as a former
best friend, ex-best friend, so-called friend, or frenemie. These stories provide a
glimpse into children's thinking about what friendship is and their struggles to
learn what it means to be a friend and to have friends. Consider Example 3.1:

EXAMPLE 3.1 NAOMI, FOURTH-GRADE GIRL, COLLEGE ELEMENTARY, MEMPHIS

One day I had a fight with my friend. I have to amet it was a silly fight. it happened on a thursday. We were fighting about friend ship. My freind thought I
was not playing with her a lot but I wasn't. I wanted to play with other people
besides my friend so I started to play with her more but she was really buging
me so I stoped playing whith her. but soon I realzide that with out my best
friend I feel really empty. So we made up and huged. I appolzide to her and
she did the same. but I relizide you are not complete with out your best freind
to help you or support you. but really I just was not thinking of others and their
feelings. I was thinking of me and only me. But from now on I will think of my
freind more often. The End! you are not alone with your freind. try not to fight
with your friend

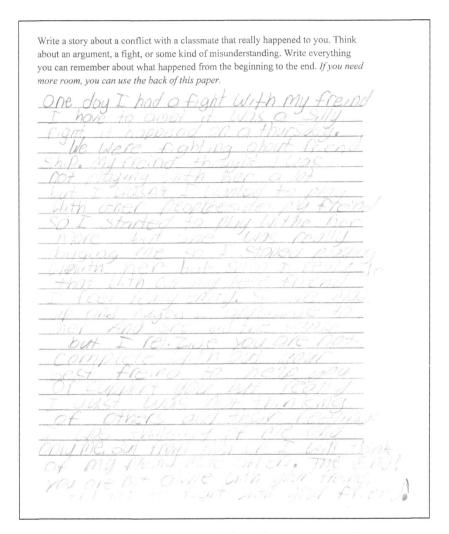

Write a story about a conflict with a classmate that really happened to you. Think about an argument, a fight, or some kind of misunderstanding. Write everything you can remember about what happened from the beginning to the end. *If you need more room, you can use the back of this paper.*

EXAMPLE 3.1 Naomi, fourth-grade girl, College Elementary, Memphis

Naomi not only tells us about a conflict with a friend, she tells us about a conflict that is *about* friendship. Her story touches on three themes that have dominated research on friendship and peer relationships in middle childhood: the struggle to understand the meaning and the obligations of friendship (e.g., "to help you and support you"), the varieties of friendship trouble that complicate the world of middle childhood (e.g., "I wanted to play with other people besides my friend"), and the importance of friendship in the development of a sense of self and in a sense of well-being ("you are not complete without your best friend"). This chapter is organized around these three broad issues that Naomi raised for us. As we consider what our authors had to say on each of these three areas, we will consider how it relates to the findings of previous researchers who have studied developing friendships in middle childhood.

"We were fighting about friend ship": The Meaning and Obligations of Friendship

In Naomi's story we recognize five features of friendship, and the conflict she describes is as much an internal conflict pertaining to her own understanding of her friendship obligations as it is a conflict between friends. Her friend complains that Naomi "is not playing with her a lot," and Naomi admits to this, in recognition that playing together is an expected feature of friendship. The fact that the friend "was really bugging me" was Naomi's justification for not playing with her, suggesting that friends should not annoy one another, or that they should enjoy their time together. The loss of the friendship was a threat to Naomi, for the reasons discussed above, but also because friends can be counted on "to help you or support you." Naomi is able to critique her own behavior in this relationship in a way that suggests an expectation that friendship requires a consideration for the feelings of others: "I just was not thinking of others and their feelings. I was thinking of me and only me." Finally, Naomi exhorts her reader to "try not to fight with your friend," suggesting that one of her expectations for friendship is the avoidance of conflict. In one 168-word story about a conflict, Naomi has suggested five features of friendship that were salient to her. Other children wrote stories suggesting many others. No wonder the achievement of satisfying reciprocal relationships is such a developmental feat in middle childhood. Just figuring out what friendship *means* is an impressive accomplishment.

Philosopher Gareth Matthews (1980, 1984) noted that the puzzlement and wonder and curiosity expressed by young children is the soil from which all great philosophical questions have grown. Indeed, two dominant questions raised by our young authors concerned what it means to be a friend and what obligations friends should have toward one another – the same questions posed by Socrates to Lysis in Plato's Dialogues and posed by philosophers from Immanuel Kant to Michel Foucault (Caluori, 2012). When researchers have looked at friendships in middle childhood, they too have struggled to find a definition that would encompass all the relationships we want to include in this category, without selecting a range of other relationships that share some features (e.g., siblings, acquaintances, parents). Hartup and Stevens (1997) defined friend ship as a dyadic relationship characterized by mutuality and symmetrical reciprocity. Bukowski, Motzoi, and Meyer (2009) elaborated on this notion by emphasizing the egalitarian interactions between two individuals who like each other and whose affect and behavior tend to be coordinated, responsive, and similar. Researchers tend to agree that friendships are recognized by both persons and are voluntary and that they tend to be stable over time (Rubin, Bukowski, & Bowker, 2015). Niobe Way (2011), in an important study of friendships among teenaged boys, encouraged us to recognize friendship as a cultural practice. When we take this approach, we see how the category 'friend' is locally defined as people interact with one another and negotiate the meanings of these interactions. Philosophers have worked to specify the defining features of friendship, and researchers have worked to operationalize these so that they can be studied empirically; but what children have to do as they come into middle childhood is negotiate with one another about what it means to be a friend.

While recognizing this negotiation is a part of the task of middle childhood, we were surprised to observe that adults' speech was exquisitely non-helpful. In several of the classrooms and in one of the community settings in which we collected data, the adults routinely used the word 'friends' to describe all the children present. At least one of the teachers in a classroom we observed was very explicit in telling her students that all members of the class are friends, and should therefore treat each other with kindness and that no child should be excluded from play. It was not at all uncommon for a teacher to announce our arrival to a classroom with something like, "We have some new friends visiting our class today," thus including in the category of 'friends' adults whom the children had not yet met. This kind of obligatory acceptance and positive regard may be an important expectation for peer relationships in many cultural communities, but it is not what philosophers or researchers have meant by 'friendship,' and it does not appear to be what most of our children meant when they used the word in their stories about conflict. Children's presentation of friendship in their narratives reflects their agency in their own social development; they are creating for themselves a new kind of relationship, different from the ones they have learned in their families and also different from what is presented to them by important authority figures.

When we looked at the stories children gave us about people they called 'friends,' it was clear that they were *not* using the word in the inclusive way their teachers often used it – they specifically did not consider all of their classmates or all of the children in the community center to be friends. Children used the word to refer to a more exclusive and, in many ways, more complicated relationship. Given the propensity of the adults to mean something quite different by the word, it is not surprising that our young authors focused a good bit of attention on trying to establish what friendship entails. What we have concluded from our work with children's stories is that this task includes not only developing friendships with prosocial peers but figuring out what it means to have a friend and to be a friend. Naomi was not alone in our sample in "fighting about friend ship." As we studied what children had to say about the roles their friends played in their conflicts, we were struck by how right Matthews was; below we examine how often these children raised the same questions that continue to puzzle philosophers and researchers, and we admire the astuteness of their analysis. We grouped the dozens of qualities of friendship children described in their conflict stories into five clusters, each related in interesting ways to previous research on children's friendships: (1) Friends should like each other and have fun together; (2) Friends should respect each other as equals; (3) Friends should support one another; (4) Friendships should persist over time; and (5) Friends should share their stories. These friendship features emerged in stories about interactions with friends and engagement in a cultural practice in which children negotiated the meaning and obligation of friendship.

Friends Should Like Each Other and Have Fun Together

Mutual liking may be the most important defining feature of friendship from the point of view of the adults who study children's friendship (Berndt & McCandless, 2009; Bukowski, Newcomb, & Hartup, 1996; Rubin et al., 2015). Most of the research on friendship in middle childhood identifies friends by asking children to list or circle the names of their classroom friends. When these selections are mutual, the children are considered to be friends (Gest, Graham-Bermann, & Hartup, 2001; Parker & Asher, 1993). Other procedures identify friends by nominations of 'liked' peers or ratings of 'liking.'

Our authors talked about liking as a feature of friendship in only 3.9% of the stories that described a conflict with a friend, but they did show evidence of seeing this as a defining feature of the relationship. One young author noted, "I don't like her, but she's still my friend," indicating, by the use of the counterfactual 'but,' that she considers it problematic that her friendship is lacking this feature. A fourth-grader used scare quotes to indicate that mutual liking is a defining feature of friendship ("Now her other 'friends' don't like her"). It is interesting to consider when and how children might come to recognize liking as a requirement of friendship. In their other relationships – with parents, siblings, teachers, caregivers – mutual affection might be a happy bonus, but it is neither a necessary nor sufficient condition for any of those relationships. Children's earliest experience with age-mates outside of the family are probably based on propinquity and opportunity to play (Ross & Lollis, 1989), and as we have noted above, adults are likely to call these playmates 'friends' whether or not the children show evidence of preferential liking. Research has shown, however, that children as young as two show preferences for playing with some peers rather than others (LaFreniere, Strayer, & Gauthier, 1984), and older preschoolers especially will initiate more interactions with their preferred playmates than with others (Martin & Fabes, 2001; Strayer & Santos, 2006). So we know that affection and enjoyment of time together has been a feature of elective relationships well before middle childhood.

Recognizing that mutual liking is expected between friends, children spent some time puzzling about the basis for this liking. It's a puzzle that has occupied philosophers since Aristotle and psychologists since William James, thinkers who would recognize the germs of their ideas in the stories of our elementary school children. For example, Aristotle considered the basis for liking to be the recognition of virtue in the friend (Rowe & Broadie, 2002), and in 7.8% of stories about friends, authors cited admirable qualities of the friend as a basis for liking. Fifth-grader Keila, whose story we examine in Example 3.9, said of her friend, "She tell the truth. I like to have a friend like that." The most common virtue cited was 'nice,' and most occasions of the attribute 'nice' were 'nice to me,' which we coded with "friends support you" rather than with "friends are virtuous or admirable." So we will not suggest that children regularly grounded their choice of friends in a search for virtue, but neither will we say that Aristotle was altogether wrong!

The notion that similarity might be the basis for interpersonal attraction was explored and elaborated by Berscheid and Walster (1969) in an important work that founded decades of research in relationship science (Reis, Aron, Clark, & Finkel, 2013). Similarly, Byrne and Griffitt's (1973) interpersonal attraction theory claimed that individuals are attracted to others with similar attributes to themselves. In middle childhood, many studies have found evidence for friendship attraction as a result of similarity. For example, previous research has shown that elementary school children select friends who are similar to themselves in multiple cognitive and behavioral domains (Logis, Rodkin, Gest, & Ahn, 2013). We found explicit mention of similarities between friends in just 2.9% of our stories, and it was usually presented as an appreciated feature of the relationship. But Example 3.2 illustrates how similarity between friends is both a source of delight and a potential source of trouble.

EXAMPLE 3.2 JACKIE, FIFTH-GRADE GIRL, IRONWOOD ELEMENTARY, MEMPHIS

One day a new girl from another school came to Ironwood. The girl's name was Jade Carver. We were almost identical. My other friends and I thought she was trying to act like me. We thought that because she came to school on the next day wearing the very same hairstyle. I had the day before. So, one day, when we were out one the playground, someone told her what we thought about her. I don't know who told her, but I was really mad. After that person told her, she came over to me and said, "I thought you were my friend!" I said, "I am your friend!" She said, "Well somebody told me that you and your other friends did not like me." After she said that she started crying. When all that happened we had a talk. We talked about what we like about each other. All of a sudden we had alot in common. When we had that talk, I start feeling alot better about myself. It gave me a chance to know her better. Since we had that talk she had become one of my bestfriends. We found out we were the only Taurus in our entire classroom. Out teacher even got our names mixed up.

Jackie's story makes it clear that liking is a necessary condition for friendship. Jade's challenge, "I thought you were my friend," was backed up by "Well somebody told me that you and your other friends did not like me." But the aspect of friendship that Jackie explores in her story is the basis for liking or disliking. Initially, the similarity between Jade and Jackie is problematized; it seemed to Jackie that Jade was trying to imitate her, and this failure of authenticity provoked derision. However, once the two "talked about what we liked about each other" they found that they "had a lot in common" and the similarities between them appear to be a source of delight. They are the only two children in the class born under the astrological sign of Taurus, and their teacher "even got our names mixed up." Similarity of preferences and interests appeared to be the basis for the enjoyment of shared activities, which may be a primary source of liking in middle childhood friendships. This "climate of agreement" between friends is presumed to underlie the potential for friends to influence each other's attitudes and behavior, thereby contributing to their developmental outcomes (Hartup, 1996).

In addition to the stories in which children explicitly talked about liking as important to their friendships, 4.5% of stories about conflicts with friends included reports about having fun together as the defining feature, or as evidence that the friendship was restored after conflict. One sixth-grader ended her story thusly: "We kept saying 'beast' and joking around. People looked at us like we were crazy. But we really didn't care because we were having fun!! [exclamation points made into a smiley face] My friends are the very, very, very, very BEST!!"

Friends Should Respect Each Other as Equal, Autonomous Actors

A critical feature distinguishing friendship from other close relationships is that friendships are voluntary associations among equals (Rubin, Bukowski, & Bowker, 2015). Only one child, among the nearly 1,600 children who gave us stories, used the word 'friend' to refer to an adult – a beloved teacher. This is a little surprising in light of the fact that many of the teachers addressed the children as friends or referred to the children as "my friends," or introduced adult researchers to the children as "new friends." Jean Piaget (1932/65) proposed that the emergence of relationships between age-mates in middle childhood promotes the development of a new and more mature kind of moral judgment. The moral thinking of younger children is grounded in a respect for authority; but as children come to spend more time with peers, they find themselves resolving conflicts by negotiating among equals about what is right and good. This results in a morality based on personal autonomy. Larry Nucci (1996) elaborated and extended these ideas, noting the importance of children's increasing experience of their own agency – their freedom to make choices about their own behavior (see also Nucci & Gingo, 2010). Nucci and many colleagues have studied a domain of behaviors thought to be the personal prerogative of individuals, not appropriately regulated by social convention or moral imperatives (e.g., Hasebe, Nucci, & Nucci, 2004; Lins-Dyer & Nucci, 2007). Among the personal prerogatives shown by these studies to be claimed by youth in Brazil, China, Hong Kong, Columbia, Japan, and the United States is the right to select one's friends or playmates.

As children share stories of their experiences of conflict, they claim agency and establish themselves as moral actors with the freedom to make choices. This freedom may be especially important in the relationships they designate as friendships. Several of our authors called attention to the idea that friendship requires respect for equality and agency. "She didn't treat me with respect and didn't treat me as her equal," complained one of our sixth-graders. "Bossing," "trying to tell me what to do," or failing to respect the friend's right to her opinions and preferences was problematized in 5.7% of the friend stories with children explicitly reporting that they did not like it when friends engaged in this behavior. Friendship, as we see in Example 3.3, requires a respect for the autonomous choices of the other.

> When you think about showing and getting respect from classmates, what does the idea respect mean to you? Give some examples.
>
> i have multiple friends and one of my friends likes pokemon and i do to, another friend hates pokemon i have to respect his feelings all i respect his opinion, so i dont tell him he sucks just because he hates pokemon by doing this we are very close buddies and we all get along

EXAMPLE 3.3 Evan, fourth-grade boy, College Elementary, Memphis

EXAMPLE 3.3 EVAN, FOURTH-GRADE BOY, COLLEGE ELEMENTARY, MEMPHIS

I have multiple frinds, and one of my frinds likes pokemon and I do to, another frind hates pokemon, I have to respect his feelings and respect his opinion, so I don't tell him he sucks just because he hates pokemon by doing this, we are very close buddies and we all get along

Friends Should Support One Another

Children perceive their close friendships as supportive relationships that can aid them during stressful circumstances and transitions (Berndt, 1989; Malecki & Demaray, 2003). Early in middle childhood, children acknowledge that friends provide instrumental support (e.g., helping with homework), but the appreciation and expectation for loyalty and dedication becomes an increasingly important feature of high-quality friendships among older children (Bukowski, Buhrmester, & Underwood, 2011). Whereas instrumental support can be provided by acquaintances or non-friends (e.g., "so I let him have my pencil"), social support in the form of showing up for a peer in a time of social need (e.g., "you better not talk about her that way!") may be unique to the friendship relationship. In 5.9% of the stories about friends, children expressed an expectation that friends should help each other in physical or material ways. Notice how important this was to Samuel in Example 3.4.

Write a true story about something that happened on the playground at ████ School. Tell everything that you can remember about what happened from the beginning to the end. *If you need more room, you can use the back of this paper.*

I was playing freeze tag one day. With abt of my friends we were having a tone of fun until. My best friend ████ fell + cut his hand we all quickly went over to help him. He was bleeding so i rushed inside to go ound get him a bandade he said thanks and we continued to play a game it was awesome I felt like a really awesome friend, And now we are really good friends. And by just that one thing we became really good friends

EXAMPLE 3.4 Samuel, fifth-grade boy, College Elementary, Memphis

EXAMPLE 3.4 SAMUEL, FIFTH-GRADE BOY, COLLEGE ELEMENTARY, MEMPHIS

I was playing frezze tag one day. With a lot of my friends we were having a tone of fun until. My best friend ralph fell & cut his hand we all quickly went over to help him. He was bleeding so i rushed inside to go and get him a bandade he said thanks and we continued to play a game it was awesome I felt like a really awesome friend. And now we are really good friends. And by just that one thing we became really good friends.

Samuel attributes the establishment of a "really good" friendship to "just that one" act of helping. He takes a great deal of pleasure in this: "It was awesome" to feel "like a really awesome friend."

An especially important way that children expected their friends to support them was to "watch my back" in conflict situations. Children cared a lot about a grouping of friendship features we can roughly call 'loyalty,' although our authors rarely used that word. Children conveyed the social protection that friends can (and should) provide for one another in 5.5% of the friend stories. Consider the following story written by a fifth-grade boy, Drew:

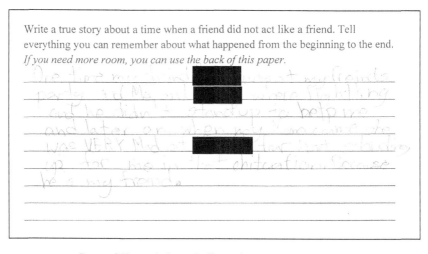

EXAMPLE 3.5   Drew, fifth-grade boy, College Elementary, Memphis

EXAMPLE 3.5   DREW, FIFTH-GRADE BOY, COLLEGE ELEMENTARY, MEMPHIS

One time my friend Dale was at my friends party and Me and Roy where fighting and he didn't stand up to help me and later on when my Mom came she was VERY mad at Dale for not standing up for me in that chituation. Because he is my friend.

Although he was asked to tell about a conflict, Drew did not choose to report what he was fighting about or about how the fight was resolved. What mattered to Drew was the fact that his friend did not stand up for him. His evaluation of this breach of friendship is given the authority of maternal anger: "when my Mom came she was VERY mad at Dale for not standing up for me." Children wrote about the disappointment of friends not 'having their back,' and they also wrote about the power of friends' protection, as in Amy's story in Example 3.6, describing an incident that happened in kindergarten that is still important to Amy three years later.

EXAMPLE 3.6 Amy, third-grade girl, College Elementary, Memphis

AMY, THIRD-GRADE GIRL, COLLEGE ELEMENTARY, MEMPHIS

A boy nammed Amal and he pulled the fire alarm in kindergarten. Geuss what? He blammed me. I did not get in trouble because my best friend Sapphire and my friend Lizzy backed me up by telling the princible and he had to admit that he pulled the alarm so every thing turned out ok.

"Guess what," Amy exclaims to her reader! We are invited to imagine the terrible consequences that might have ensued from this false accusation, if Amy had not had loyal friends who backed her up. It's the same protection that made Naomi reconsider her commitment to her friend in Example 3.1. Even though the friend was "bugging" her, Naomi decided that "you need your best friend to help you or support you." The power of friends' protection that children discussed in their stories is in line with some evidence suggesting that supportive friendships can buffer against the effects of negative relationships with others (Bagwell & Schmidt, 2013).

Friendships Should Persist Over Time

Research on friendship continuity during the elementary school years indicates that these relationships are moderately stable. For example, in one study, approximately 38% of mutually reciprocated best friendships that existed in the fall continued to exist in the spring of fifth grade (Bowker, Rubin, Burgess, Booth-LaForce, & Rose-Krasnor, 2006). Friendship stability has been linked to friendship quality, such that friendships high in quality are more likely to persist over time (Berndt, 1999). Friendship stability also is linked to children's adjustment, including higher prosocial behavior and lower aggression and victimization (Bowker et al., 2006). The stability of friendships increases across the elementary school years as well, indicating an increasing need or expectation for enduring relationships in middle childhood (Berndt & Hoyle, 1985).

In 16.3% of the stories about friends, children talked about their expectations that friendships should last over time, reported how long their friendship had lasted, or explicitly noted that even though they fight, their friendship remains intact. This corroborates research findings that even though friends have more conflicts with each other than do non-friends, they are more likely than non-friends to resolve the conflicts (Laursen, Finkelstein, & Betts, 2001). Consider Example 3.7 by third-grader, Olivia.

EXAMPLE 3.7 OLIVIA, THIRD-GRADE GIRL, COLLEGE ELEMENTARY, MEMPHIS

I started like this We talked about a game that we were going to play. And one of my friends got a part that I wanted in the game so my friend got mad and walked away. After that I got mad and walked away. I thought me and my friend were never going to be friend again. But a couple of days Later we were friends again. That has happened to me a lot but if we begin friends we stay friends. My friend stay to gether with me all the way through. If I meet a new friend we never make a change of not friends. That is how well I can make friends. We all talk a lot but if we have friendship we keep friendship I don't know about you but that is how my friendship goes! My teachers are the same way with friendship Keep it or lose it. My family is the same way too if you don't like your family that's wrong Keep friendship with your family like you do with friends.

Olivia is proud of her ability to make friendships last over time, "If I meet a new friend we never make a change of not friends. That is how well I can make

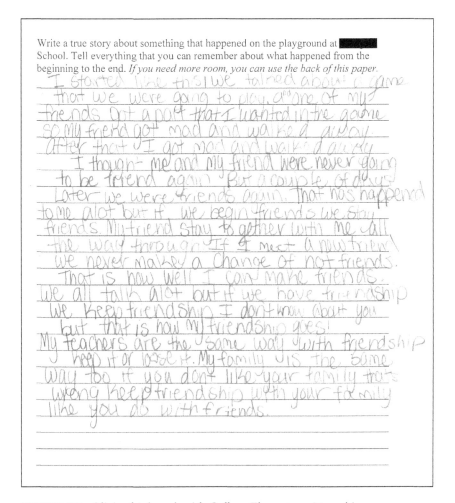

Write a true story about something that happened on the playground at ▮▮▮▮▮ School. Tell everything that you can remember about what happened from the beginning to the end. *If you need more room, you can use the back of this paper.*

I started like this I we talned about a game that we were going to play. and one of my friends got a part that I wanted in the game so my friend got mad and walked away. After that I got mad and walked away. I thought me and my friend were never going to be friend again. But a couple of days Later we were friends again. That has happened to me alot but if we begin friends we stay friends. My friend stay together with me all the way through If I meet a now friend we never make a change of not friends. That is how well I can make friends. We all talk alot but if we have friendship we keep friendship I don't know about you but that is how my friendship goes! My teachers are the same way with friendship keep it or loose it. My family is the same way too if you don't like your family that's wrong keep friendship with your family like you do with friends.

EXAMPLE 3.7 Olivia, third-grade girl, College Elementary, Memphis

friends." She asserts this as a value shared by the adults in her life, her teachers and her family, but her story gives us some understanding of how difficult this is: "I thought me and my friend were never going to be friend again. But a couple of days Later we were friends again." This seems a bit mysterious to Olivia, but she notes that, "This has happened to me a lot." Olivia considers the similarities between friendship and family relationships, noting that you ought to like your family, and she ends with a curious exhortation to us to "keep friendship with your family like you do with friends." Olivia seems to be trying to understand the roles of liking and of persistence in these two kinds of relationships. You ought to like your family (but those relationships will persist whether you like them or not), and you ought to "stay together all the way through" with your friends, even though those relationships are dependent on liking. Our authors did not talk explicitly about the requirement that friendship (unlike family relationships) be voluntary, and this story indicates that this distinction may be puzzling to them. Indeed, the requirement that friendships persist over time will almost certainly come to clash with the requirement that they be voluntary, and some of our children note that maintaining friendships requires them to play with children they no longer like. Fourth-grader Abby tells us, "Me and Carla have been friends longer, but I like Shar better." She explains her dilemma and ends her story with, "Carla is getting rely oning [really annoying]! What should I do!!!"

Gilligan, Lyons, and Hanmer (1990) found girls in middle school experienced considerable anguish over a need to be loyal to friends they no longer enjoyed or liked, at the expense of being honest. The elementary-aged children in our samples have not yet understood the complexities of this dilemma. They tended to assert continuity and persistence of friendship as an uncomplicated virtue (e.g., "My friend stay to gether with me all the way through"), and, as we discuss below, they asserted honesty in relationships as an uncomplicated virtue (e.g., "What kind of a friend would lie to you?"). But friendship conflicts like Olivia's and Abby's may be setting the stage for personal and moral dilemmas that will arise in adolescence – dilemmas in which honesty about which people they prefer is likely to hurt people's feelings and sever relationships. This will come into focus when we discuss sources of friendship trouble below, and in the next chapter on social aggression.

Friends Should Share Their Stories With Each Other

In the late 1970s, about twenty years before our earliest stories were collected, Bigelow and LaGaipa (1980) interviewed youth about their conceptions of friendship. They found a shift away from defining friendship by shared activities and mutual support in childhood toward a definition of friendship that included loyalty, commitment, and intimacy in adolescence. Friendship intimacy is characterized by self-disclosure and the exchange of personal information. This shift toward intimacy is consistent with Harry Stack Sullivan's (1953) suggestion that friends become important sources of social support during preadolescence and research by Furman and Buhrmester (1985), which found that fifth- and sixth-graders' ratings of intimacy with friends were higher than all other sources of social support with the exception of mothers, with whom they were similar. More recent research by Rose et al. (2012) found self-disclosure to be an important feature of friendship in middle childhood and especially in adolescence. We have already seen in Example 3.2 how important it was to fifth-grader, Jackie, that she and her friend "had a talk," in which she and the new girl found that they "had a lot in common." Jackie tells us that having this talk "gave me a chance to know her better." In 23.3% of our stories our authors reported "talking" as an activity they did with a friend. They referred to this as "having a talk" or "talking it out" or "just talking," and occasionally they reported that they "talked and talked." (Children also mentioned "talking about" or "talking behind [someone's] back" to refer to gossip, and we discuss these occasions below when we consider friendship trouble.) We found it interesting to examine the occasions in which children gave a label to a discourse practice. This meta-discursive talk showed us that children were noting certain communication practices as distinct activities, important enough to be named.

'Talking it out' was a term children used in 15.9% of stories about conflicts with friends to describe the kind of talk that resolved their conflicts. Three of our eight data collection sites were schools that had in place a formal peer mediation program. Children were selected by the classroom teacher to receive special training in facilitating conflict resolution. When conflicts erupted, the antagonists could elect to go to peer mediation or could be sent there by the teacher. In peer mediation sessions, each party to the conflict was given a chance to "tell your side of the story," and each was encouraged to demonstrate understanding of the others' 'take' on the situation. In all but one of the stories in which children talked about going to peer mediation, they reported that at the end of the process their antagonist was a friend. In the schools that did not have a formal peer mediation program, children still reported "talking it out" in their stories of conflict with friends, and the discourse practice described by this label always entailed a successful resolution. This is consistent with previous research showing that friends are more invested in the resolution of their conflicts than are other playmates (Newcomb & Bagwell, 1995). Our data led us to believe there are two things going on here, creating a virtuous cycle: (1) The activity of 'telling your side of the story' is a friendship-building discursive practice. When children tell stories about their own experience, they are doing the kind of self-disclosure that builds intimacy. In this sense, when conflicts provoke a cultural practice of 'talking it out,' they are actually serving as training for friendship; (2) At the same time, friendship between children is a powerful motivator of conflict resolution, especially in light of the imperative we saw Olivia articulate: "if we have friendship, we keep friendship." Friends are highly motivated to resolve their conflicts without ending their relationship, and the story-sharing that helps them resolve their conflicts has the potential to strengthen the friendship.

Whereas 'talking it out' referred to important, goal-directed talking, the expression 'just talking' was a curious discourse label that seemed to distinguish talking from other forms of play. "We don't to nothing on the playground just talking," reported third-grader, Glory. The activity of 'just talking' was attributed only to girls by our authors. Some previous research has suggested that in contrast to girl friendships, boy friendships are characterized by engagement in shared activities, whereas girl friendships are characterized by social conversation and self-disclosure, a practice that strengthens as children move from middle childhood to adolescence (Rose & Rudolph, 2006; Youniss & Smollar, 1985; cf. Way, 2013). Our data do not bear out this interpretation. Both girls and boys in our samples talked about engaging in play activities with friends, and both girls and boys used 'talking' as a discourse label. As we will see when we discuss sources of friendship trouble below, both girls and boys struggled with the discourse practice of sharing secrets. It does appear, however, that only girls participated in a cultural practice of sharing stories with each other, which was referred to with the modifier, 'just.' There are two ways to read this usage. 'Just' in this phrase may be a minimizer, and it therefore appears that 'just talking' is devalued in comparison to 'doing' something. (Glory saw it as "doing nothing"). On the other hand, the fact that the girls had a label they could use to refer to their time spent in conversation elevates the practice and underlines the exclusive significance (if only for girls) of sharing experiences and thoughts with one another. The expression "talked and talked" was another discourse label, used in ways similar to "just talking" to describe an activity at a sleepover or on the telephone that seemed to convey a highly valued friendship behavior. These story-sharing practices in middle childhood may be a good training ground for the intimacy expected and appreciated in adolescent friendships.

Write a true story about a time when a friend did not act like a friend. Tell everything you can remember about what happened from the beginning to the end. *If you need more room, you can use the back of this paper.*

Most time, my friend talk to their friend also my friend, so I can't really talk to them, so most time I feel boring so I in just think, my chinese friend is good, we can have fun, most time in the school, they are talking, I can't talking to them, they are more funny, so I feel boring.

EXAMPLE 3.8 MaeAnn, sixth-grade girl, College Elementary, Memphis

If we need further convincing that "talking" is at the heart of friendship, consider the heartbreaking story in Example 3.8 by a recent immigrant who is not yet confident about her English language proficiency.

EXAMPLE 3.8 MAEANN, SIXTH-GRADE GIRL, COLLEGE ELEMENTARY, MEMPHIS

Mosttime, my friend talk to their friend also my friend, so I can't really talk to them, so mosttime I feel boring so I'm just think, My Chinese friend is good, we can have fun. Mosttime in the school, they are talking, I can't talking to them, they are make funny, so I feel boring.

EXAMPLE 3.9 Keila, fifth-grade girl, Winterton Elementary, Memphis

We will close this section on how children understand friendship with a story by a fifth-grader, Keila, whose story illustrates the features of friendship we have identified and discussed above.

EXAMPLE 3.9   KEILA, FIFTH-GRADE GIRL, WINTERTON ELEMEMTARY, MEMPHIS

"My Best friend"

When I used to go to Winterton in the 1st grade I meet my best friend. Her name is Tamara Cooper. She is in the 5th grade. We will play together, share food, talk on the telephone. She come over my house. I come over to her house. She tell the truth. I like to have a friend like that. She take up for me. her birthday is in January 27, 85. The same year of my. I buy her a birthday gift and a xmas gift too. She will do the same for me. Her mother is die. I felt sorry for her. But we have a great times. She is like a sister to me. I love her like a sister too and she is kind, nice too. Her grandmom put[1] her.

The End

Keila doesn't tell us about a conflict; what she wants our research team to understand about 'what it is like to be a fifth-grader these days' is that middle childhood is enriched by important relationships, called "best friend." She wants to tell us what this relationship is like. She is explicit about liking, even loving her friend like a sister, and she explores several of the qualities that are the basis for this liking. Her attraction is partly based on admiration for Tamara's virtue – she tells the truth, she is kind and "nice too." Like Jackie in Example 3.2, Keila notes similarity between herself and her friend: they were born in the same year. She elaborates a good bit on the activities they share: they play together at each other's homes, share food, and she reports that they "have great times." Keila does not explicitly mention equality, but she lets us know that the two are born in the same year and that there is reciprocity in their exchanges of gifts. The friendship has persisted since the two girls met in the first grade. Keila reports that her friend takes up for her. Among the things they do together is 'talking on the telephone,' and this talk seems to have led Keila to know some significant parts of Tamara's life story. Tamara has lost her mother, and Keila expresses her compassionate concern for her friend, so the friendship entails mutual support. This single story covers all of the defining features of friendship we discussed above.

"I wanted to play with other people besides my friend": Sources of Friendship Trouble

As children used their narrative accounts to work through their puzzlement about what friendship means and about what it entails, they recounted their disappointments and struggles with these relationships. Two themes emerged as especially salient and frequent sources of trouble in their friendships. The first theme we call the 'honesty/trust complex,' in which children shared (and sometimes betrayed) secrets, or failed to deal honestly with one another. The second we call the 'exclusiveness/jealousy' complex. Here, we heard children struggle with an understanding of the extent to which their friendships ought to be exclusive and special. We will consider each of these themes below.

The Honesty/Trust Complex

Our authors were explicit about the expectation that friends should be honest with one another. One fifth-grader proclaimed, "friends should not lie." Not only should they be honest, they should trust one another to be honest. "I told her that she has to put more trust in her best friends," another fifth-grader wrote. These explicit reports about the honesty or trustworthiness of friends occurred in 8.2% of the friend stories. The development of trust between friends in middle childhood seems to be related in important ways to the 'he-said-she-said' of middle childhood gossip, and to the cultural practice of sharing secrets. Consider Example 3.10.

EXAMPLE 3.10   KENNETH, SIXTH-GRADE BOY, IRONWOOD ELEMENTARY, MEMPHIS

The Misunderstanding

One day I got into it with my best friend Mark, over what some other boy said. It was a mean argument we had, but once we set down and went over it we realized that Phillip was just trying to break up our friend ship. So we told him to butt out, and we promised we'd never argue or fight agan over what other people say.

The End

Kenneth doesn't tell us what Phillip said that was "trying to break up" his friendship with Mark, nor does he speculate about why Phillip was motivated to cause this break-up. The "mean argument" between the friends was easy enough to resolve, however. The boys only needed to "sit down" and "go over it." We see a similar situation in Uma's story in Example 3.11.

EXAMPLE 3.11 UMA, SIXTH-GRADE GIRL, CONNORS ELEMENTARY, MEMPHIS

an argument

One day In 6th grade My best friend [drawing here of heart broken in half] and I got into an argument. Cause someone told her that I said something about her. She believed it like a fool. She supposed to been my; best friend. A person told her that I said, "she was dum." So she come all up in my face. Then I came back in her face. It was almost on the school campest. Then we stared to talk things out. So now we are bestest friends again. From that day on I leaned not to talk about friends or people. Cause some times it mite hurt their feelings. I will never argue with my friend or friends. But now we are over that and moved on.

Uma expects to be trusted by her friend, and when the friend believes a classmate's report that Uma called her dumb, Uma considers the believing to be a violation of the friendship: "She supposed to been my; best friend." Interestingly, Uma never quite denies having made the insult. In fact, she reports that she learned, "from that day on," not to "talk about friends or people," inviting the inference that before this incident Uma was inclined to participate in such 'talk.' Maybe Uma *will* stop talking about people, based on this lesson she has learned, and maybe Kenneth and Mark will have learned not to be affected by "what other people say." The research evidence on what children talk about, however, leads us to doubt that either author will follow through on this. Susan Engel and her students have conducted observational studies that have looked at the content of the stories children spontaneously tell and of the questions they spontaneously ask (Engel, 1995; Engel & Li, 2004; Engel, 2015; and see also Dunn, 1988). This research shows that children's conversation is dominated by talk about their peers. Uma's negative assessment of 'talking about friends' as a hurtful activity is grounded in the experience she recounts and is probably consistent with the exhortations of the grown-ups around her. Gossip gets a bad rap. The word has negative connotations, and we tend to denigrate participation in gossip as either an idle waste of time or as destructive and harmful to relationships, or both. But despite this popular opinion, most scholars who have undertaken a study of the practice have found it to serve important functions. We have convincing evidence that the cultural practice of sharing information, speculating about, and evaluating other people can be credited with increasing social cohesion, with enforcing cultural norms, and with creating a local moral order for adults and children, and this evidence has been gathered by anthropologists (Besnier, 2009; Goodwin, 1980; Heath, 1983), by psychologists (Bamberg, 2004; Baumeister, Zhang, & Vohs, 2004; Parker & Gottman, 1989), and by sociologists (Corsaro & Eder, 1990; Fine, 1977). Engel (2015) argued that gossip is motivated by and encourages a healthy curiosity about other people's lives – a curiosity that can promote the development of empathy and that will produce the next generation of behavioral scientists. To this list of meritorious consequences of gossip, we would like to add the possibility that gossip in middle childhood helps children explore the role of honesty and trust in the development of relationships. We see this most clearly in the practice of secret-sharing, secret-keeping, and secret betrayals.

However much children were troubled by situations in which their friends did not trust or believe them, the pain of this was eclipsed by the heartfelt anguish or rage in the stories children told about a friend betraying a secret. Consider Examples 3.12 and 3.13.

Write a story about a conflict with another kid that really happened to you. Think about a fight, an argument or some kind of misunderstanding. Write everything that happened from the beginning to the end.

> There was a boy named ██████ and he alway spreaed rumurs about me. I Trusted ██████. We alway were such good friend. I came over to his house on Sunday. We played games. Then we went to his room. I told him I trusted him. He promised tell anybody. So I told him I liked someone. The next day at resess everybody was laughing at me. I said why are you guy laughing

EXAMPLE 3.12 *(continued)*

(continued)

> at me. Then they told me
> ███████ told me the news. I ran
> out to the feild and I hide
> behinde atree. I was so
> enbearrist. They could not stop
> laughing. The next day later
> he spreaded another rumur.
> So I went home and told my
> mom the sitchoration. I went
> to school the next day. I stood
> up for my self and he never
> spreaded any rumurs again.

EXAMPLE 3.12 Robert, third-grade boy, Magnolia Springs Elementary, Orlando

EXAMPLE 3.12 ROBERT, THIRD-GRADE BOY, MAGNOLIA SPRINGS ELEMENTARY, ORLANDO

There was a boy named Mike and he always spreaded rumurs about me. I trusted Mike. We always were such good friends. I came over to his house on Sunday. We played games. Then we went to his room. I told him I trusted him. He promised tell anybody. So I told him I liked someone. The next day at resess everybody was laughing at me. I said why are you guy laughing at me. Then they told me Mike told me the news. I ran out to the feild and I hide behinde a tree. I was so enbearrist. They could not stop laughing. The next day later he spreaded another rumur. So I went home and told my mom and sitchoration. I went to school the next day. I stood up for my self and he never spreaded any rumurs again.

> Write a true story about a time when a friend did not act like a friend. Tell everything you can remember about what happened from the beginning to the end. *If you need more room, you can use the back of this paper.*

One day a couple weeks ago I told my
friend a secret. I didn't swear her to secrty
because I thought I could trust her.
Turns out I probably should have 'cause
next thing ya' know she has told the
whole class. I felt like choking her
dancing on her grave. I was mad at her
for a few minutes, but I have trouble
staying mad at people. Besides, now I
know to make her swear to secrcy.

EXAMPLE 3.13 Francesca, sixth-grade girl, College Elementary, Memphis

EXAMPLE 3.13 FRANCESCA, SIXTH-GRADE GIRL, COLLEGE ELEMENTARY, MEMPHIS

One day a couple weeks ago I told my friend a secret. I didn't swear her to secrcy because I thought I could trust her. Turns out I probably should have 'cause next thing ya know she has told the whole class! I felt like choking her dancing on her grave. I was mad at her for a few minutes, but I have trouble staying mad at people. Besides, now I know to make her swear to secrcy.

The late elementary school classroom appears to be a training ground for the very difficult task of learning to trust. Research has described how difficult it is for adults to manage reciprocal self-disclosures as they negotiate gradually increasing vulnerability on the way to intimate relationships (Altman & Taylor, 1987; Collins & Miller, 1994). The process is plenty challenging for twenty-somethings. Yet we saw nine- and ten-year-olds taking it on with about equal parts trepidation and bravery. The betrayal of a secret can be a painful blow to friendship quality, but the discourse practice of sharing secrets also seemed to be tailor-made to let children practice the critical relationship skill of trust-building. In a cultural community fueled by the drama of secret-sharing, secret-keeping, and secret betrayals, children have the opportunity to learn which friends they can trust, as well as to be a trustworthy keeper of the secrets of others.

We have some evidence that children have been creating and passing down practices pertinent to the development of honesty and trustworthiness in many cultural contexts spanning many historical periods. In their fascinating collection of rites and rituals, songs and games of childhood depicted on Greek urns, and in ancient songs and tales, folklorists Iona and Peter Opie (2001) devoted an entire chapter to rituals they called "codes of oral legislation." Many of these 'codes' were gestures (e.g., crossed fingers) or words (e.g., "if I lie, stick a needle in my eye") or exchanges of objects (e.g., trust bracelets) that children, even in ancient times, used to test truthfulness or trustworthiness, or to secure their secrets. Francesca couldn't be too angry about her friend's betrayal because the ritual "swear to secrecy" had not been performed.

Children like Kenneth and Uma recognized the dangers of participating in the kind of relational gossip that occupies so much of peer interaction ("Cause some times it mite hurt their feelings," Uma comes to realize). And indeed, some children, like Robert, found themselves "so embarrassed" that they just wanted to hide. But Robert came out from hiding, and in general we believe that however painful and difficult these situations might be, they provide exactly the experience children need to participate fully in the kind of relationship that we (and they) know as friendship.

The Exclusivity/Jealousy Complex

The features of friendship discussed above could be exhibited in many relationships, but what makes friendship different (and often problematic) is that these features of friendship should be exhibited exclusively or at least primarily with the friend. You may like and enjoy the company of many people, but a friend is someone you like *more* than you like others. You may be supportive of many people, but it is especially egregious if you should fail to support your friend. You will share many stories with many people, but your special secrets are to be shared only with a trusted friend. This expectation that the friendship relationships should be special was the source of three related kinds of friendship trouble in many of our stories: a difficulty in negotiating how much time friends should spend together, a difficulty in managing the necessary exclusion of other children that this time together will require, and the feelings of jealousy and possessiveness that complicate both of these problems. This is at the heart of the problem that Naomi described in Example 3.1: her friend expects Naomi to play with her "a lot," and Naomi understands this to be a reasonable obligation of friendship, even if her friend is "bugging" her. The establishment

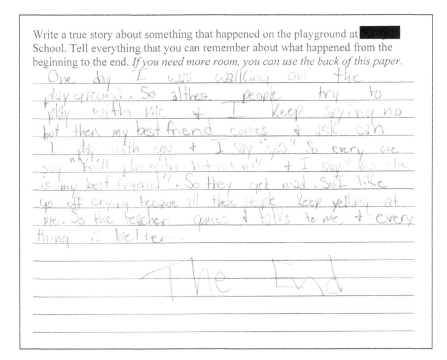

Write a true story about something that happened on the playground at ███ School. Tell everything that you can remember about what happened from the beginning to the end. *If you need more room, you can use the back of this paper.*

EXAMPLE 3.14   Isabel, third-grade girl, College Elementary, Memphis

of these special relationships in the context of a classroom is especially fraught. The same behaviors that establish one classmate as a preferred companion, especially liked, will necessarily be designating other classmates as less preferred. In an elementary school classroom, the work of establishing friendships entails acts of social rejection. Isabel describes the flip side of Naomi's dilemma in Example 3.14.

EXAMPLE 3.14   ISABEL, THIRD-GRADE GIRL, COLLEGE ELEMENTARY, MEMPHIS

One day I was walking on the play ground. So althese people try to play with me & I keep saying no but then my best friend comes & ask can I play with you & I say "yes" So every one say "You'll play with but not me" & I say "Yes she is my best friend". So they get mad. So I like go off crying because all these people keep yelling at me. So the teacher comes & talks to me, & every thing is better.

The End

Whereas Naomi wants to play with other children and experienced pressure from her friend to be more respectful of the exclusiveness of the friendship, Isabel wants to play exclusively with her best friend and is distraught at the consequences of rejecting the play invitations of others. What busy adult cannot relate to this? We have limited amounts of time and want to spend our precious free time with those to whom we are particularly close, whose company we enjoy. And, luckily for us, no one stands in the role of a well-meaning classroom teacher, telling us that everyone in the class is our friend and that no person should be excluded from having our attention. Isabel wants to meet her needs for intimacy and for time with her special friend without being the target of scorn from the classmates whose bids for her time she rejects. It is easy to see how this balancing act might lead to problems of possessiveness and jealousy in newly developing friendships.

The developmental tasks of middle childhood include establishing meaningful friendships *and* finding a place in a community of peers. Elementary-aged children develop several kinds of new relationships with peers as they engage together in academic tasks, in lunchroom conversations, and in playground and after-school activities. While previous research has focused on the development of friendships in middle childhood, a sizable amount of the peer relations literature is devoted to group-level variables such as group affiliation, peer acceptance, preference, liking, and popularity (e.g., Berger & Rodkin, 2012; Bowker, Rubin, Buskirk-Cohen, Rose-Krasnor, & Booth-LaForce, 2010). It might not be so difficult to develop special friendships if children did not also need to be attuned to their place in a complicated classroom social order, and finding their place and achieving status within the peer network might be easier if they were not also trying to develop special relationships with only a few people in the classroom. It is in this context, where the development of friendship requires selecting some classmates as preferred over others, that we see jealousy becoming a problematic emotion.

Jeff Parker and colleagues' work on friendship jealousy among young adolescents has revealed interesting findings about jealous notions of friendship that are linked to peer difficulties (including rejection) and social adjustment (Parker, Kruse, & Aikins, 2010; Parker, Low, Walker, & Gamm, 2005). This work defined friendship jealousy as "a negative reaction triggered by a close friend's actual or anticipated interest in or relationship with another peer and based upon the target's perception that the partner's relationship with someone else threatens their own, existing relationship with him or her" (Parker et al., 2010, p. 520). Our young authors spoke explicitly about the problems of jealousy in their relationships in 13.3% of friendship stories, and several described situations in which they managed to overcome these troubling feelings. Zia's story in Example 3.15 is a case of this.

Write a story about a conflict with a classmate that really happened to you. Think about an argument, a fight, or some kind of misunderstanding. Write everything you can remember about what happened from the beginning to the end. *If you need more room, you can use the back of this paper.*

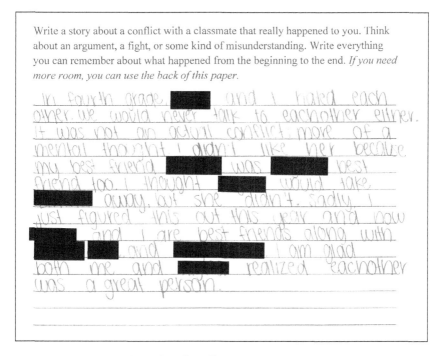

EXAMPLE 3.15 Zia, sixth-grade girl, College Elementary, Memphis

EXAMPLE 3.15   ZIA, SIXTH-GRADE GIRL, COLLEGE ELEMENTARY, MEMPHIS

In fourth grade, bridget and I hated each other. We would never talk to eachother either. It was not an actual conflict; more of a mental thought. I didn't like her because my best friend Selma was bridget's best friend too. I thought bridget would take Selma away, but she didn't. Sadly I just figured this out this year and now bridget and I are best friends along with Selma, Jordi, and Mary Joy. I am glad both me and bridget realized eachother was a great person.

Zia decided not to tell us about "an actual conflict." She wanted to tell us about an internal struggle, "mental thought," that caused her unnecessary problems last year. This year, in the fifth grade, Zia "figured out" that Bridget's friendship with Selma did not threaten Zia's relationship with Selma. "Sadly," this fear caused Zia and Bridget to hate each other in the fourth grade, even though Zia now knows that they were each "a great person." This insight, that a friend's attention to another person does not have to threaten the friendship, is hard won, and many children wrote about it. Third-grader Denise complained, "I tried to tell Alfreda that even if I am playing with Mari I'm still her friend, but she didn't understand." Zia came to understand this lesson in the fifth grade. Elyssa was in the sixth grade when she wrote about her best friend playing with others on the playground: "At first I was mad, then jealous. Then I realized she would always have friends other than me. So I moved on and went to play with my other friends." The relationship that children are coming to understand as 'friendship' requires special attention that will necessitate the exclusion of some classmates from some play and from some special talk (Wainryb, Komolova, & Brehl, 2014). But friends must also play with others, and expectations for exclusiveness provoke feelings of jealousy and conflict. What a delicate balancing act is required of elementary school children!

As we summarize this section, we note that the struggles with the honesty/trust complex and the exclusivity/jealousy complex that children discussed in their stories about friendship appeared to undermine the quality of those friendships. Thomas Berndt (2002) described friendship quality as being characterized by high levels of positive features, such as intimacy, and low levels of negative features, such as conflicts and rivalry. Berndt's and others' research on friendship quality has illuminated its association with other aspects of children's social adjustment (Bagwell & Schmidt, 2013). The children in our samples seemed to recognize that the stress that a lack of trustworthiness and jealousy brought to their friendships affected multiple aspects of their social-emotional well-being. Nevertheless, they seemed to find the benefits of friendship to be worth the risk. Indeed, we have come to believe that the same troubles that lower friendship quality (e.g. 'talking about' and secret betrayals) provide the experiences children need to enhance that quality.

"You are not complete without your best friend": The Importance of Friendship to the Development of a Sense of Self and to Well-Being

An impressive body of research has made it clear that the development of satisfying relationships with peers in middle childhood is crucial to multiple domains of well-being, including social-emotional and academic adjustment (Furman & Buhrmester, 1985; Bukowski et al., 2011). The benefits of having a high-quality friendship have been documented as well (Bagwell & Schmidt, 2013). When we examined what children chose to note about the importance of having friends, we found support for these beneficial claims. In stories about interpersonal conflict, children recognized the importance of friends and friendship to their well-being. It was relatively rare for children, in their descriptions of conflicts, to tell us what they considered to be the benefits of friendship, but those few stories in which they did so are instructive. Most of the benefits they mentioned fell into three categories: Friends provide (1) a sense of personal well-being and completeness,

(2) companionship, and (3) comfort. We review these below, as they relate to previous research on the importance of friendship to children in middle childhood.

"When we had that talk, I started feeling alot better about myself": Friendship Promotes a Healthy Self-Concept

Naomi, in Example 3.1, introduces a notion that friendship is critical to the development of selfhood so that a loss of a friend made her feel "really empty," and she advises the reader that friendship is required for completeness. These are surprising metaphors of personal development from the pencil of a fourth-grader. Her insights are nicely aligned with the theorizing of Sullivan (1953), who deemed friendship intimacy as the most crucial social accomplishment during preadolescence, as well as with the decades of empirical research since Sullivan's writing demonstrating the importance of intimate friendships for children's well-being in late childhood and beyond (Bagwell & Schmidt, 2013). Sullivan claimed that such close friendships allow the preadolescent to develop a more realistic sense of self through the eyes of a chum, as well as bring about prosocial behavior, including sensitivity to what matters to another person. For Sullivan, social relatedness was not just about what a child receives from someone else, but also what a child is able to give in the relationship. Naomi comes to the same conclusion in her story: "but really I just was not thinking of others and their feelings. I was thinking of me and only me. But from now on I will think of my freind more often."

Our stories provide many examples of how children delighted in their friendships; the stories (even though they recounted conflicts) often emphasized fun and play. Even though most of our stories were given to us in writing, we can hear joyfulness in the voice of the fourth-grade author who wrote, "We held our hands and said loudly, 'Best friends forever!'" In addition to the pleasure they took in their declarations of friendship, we also hear pride in the stories of children whose success at friendship boosts their estimation of their own efficacy. Recall Samuel, in Example 3.4, who felt "awesome" about being a "really awesome friend." Jackie, in Example 3.2, reported that the talk she had that established her friendship with Jade made her feel a lot better about herself. We clearly heard the pride in Olivia's account in Example 3.7 of her ability to make her friendships last. Children in our study recognized that their sense of self and self-assessments were enhanced by friendship.

"You are not alone with your friend": Friendship Provides Companionship

Previous scholars have theorized about the importance of companionship and a need for intimacy with peers during middle childhood (Sullivan, 1953; Hartup, 1996). After reviewing a vast body of social and personality psychology literature,

Baumeister and Leary (1995) concluded that individuals need frequent, positive interactions with the same individuals within the context of long-term, caring relationships: people need to belong. Empirical work on the need for companionship with peers has supported these claims for children. For example, the fifth- and sixth-graders in Furman and Buhrmester's (1985) study reported that best friends were the greatest source of companionship (e.g., children frequently played and spent fun time with their best friends). Having someone to play with, someone to sit beside at lunch or on the bus, and someone to talk to was of significant importance for the children who wrote stories for us. In multiple stories children shared comments such as, "Luckly I always have a friend at my table and she's always by my side," reflecting the shared view that enjoyment and fun were defining features of friendship. Lacking a companion was a serious concern to children and being "all alone" on the playground appeared to be an especially onerous fate. For example, fifth-grader Bonnie shared the following story:

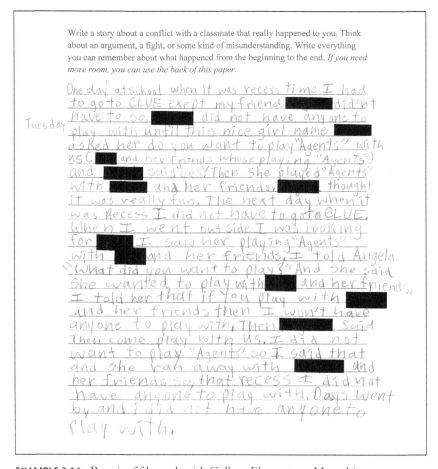

EXAMPLE 3.16   Bonnie, fifth-grade girl, College Elementary, Memphis

EXAMPLE 3.16   BONNIE, FIFTH-GRADE GIRL, COLLEGE ELEMENTARY, MEMPHIS

One day at school when it was recess time I had to go to CLUE exept my friend Candace did'nt have to so, Candace did not have anyone to play with until this nice girl name Andrina asked her do you want to play "Agents" with us (Andrina and her friends whose playing "Agents") and Candace said "yes"! Then she played "Agents" with Andrina and her friends. Candace thought it was really fun. The next day when it was Recess I did not have to go to CLUE. When I went outside I was looking for Candace. I saw her playing "Agents" with Andrina and her friends. I told Candace "what did you want to play?" And she said she wanted to play with Andrina and her friends. I told her that if you play with Andrina and her friends then I won't have anyone to play with. Then Candace said Then come play with us. I did not want to play "Agents" so I said that and she ran away with Andrina and her friends so, that recess I did not have anyone to play with. Days went by and i did not have anyone to play with.

Bonnie's story clearly shows that not having anyone to play with at recess is a troubling situation. Our stories reveal many experiences of children rejected by their peers and we elaborate on this in Chapter 4. In Bonnie's and others' tales of lacking a friend to play with or have fun with, children recognized the value of companionship that friendships provided.

"Friends share your joy and comfort your sadness": Friendship Promotes Emotional Competence

Most of the time when children talked about supporting one another, they were talking about either physical or material support (e.g., "doing things together like helping with all kinds of work") or social support (e.g., "So my best friend helped me fight them back and we were a good team working together"). There was, however, an interesting set of stories in which children talked about getting, giving, or expecting emotional support from friends, and typically this involved responses to negative emotions and experiences. Previous work has included emotional support under the umbrella of social support (Bokhorst, Sumter, & Westenberg, 2010), but we found that emotions and emotion regulation was a distinct topic of conversation for the elementary school children who wrote stories for us. Larry, a third-grade boy, tells us about the content of his conversation with his "new friend," Landon: "We were taking a bout makes us more comftorbole. And by that I mean less angry or sad." Children inquired about and wondered about their friends' emotional states in 4.9% of the friends' stories. "One day My friend ray asked me what was wrong with me. Because I had been crying because my Friend or I dont know if he's my friend now hit me," reported Benjamin, a fifth-grader. He goes on to describe how his friend, Ray, sought the help of a teacher. When their friends were angry or sad, children wanted to understand why. When they recognized negative emotions in their friends, children reported efforts to help each other manage them. In 3.9% of the 490 stories in which children designated an actor as a friend, the author describes a friend making deliberate efforts to calm or cheer or otherwise improve the emotional state of another. Fifth-grader Serena tells us in Example 3.17 how her friend helped her overcome her fear.

Number _ _

Write a story about something that happened to you.

Once last year we went on a field trip to East-End Skating ring. I was in fifth Grade with my teacher ████ ████████ She was a nice lady and caring to. She taught us Every Subject we know. One day we were going on a field trip to the skating ring I was scared because I did and I didn't know how to skate. I was also excited because it was my first time going to a skating ring so big and tall, but I got over my fear because my friend ████████ gave me courage. We started talking and playing. So we went and skated. I also had the best time

EXAMPLE 3.17   Serena, fifth-grade girl, Winterton Elementary, Memphis

EXAMPLE 3.17   SERENA, FIFTH-GRADE GIRL, WINTERTON ELEMENTARY, MEMPHIS

Once last year we went on a field trip to East-End Skating ring. I was in 4th grade with my teacher Mrs. Morris. She was a nice lady and caring to. She taught us every subject we know. One day we were going on a field trip to the skating ring. I was scared because I did and I didn't know how to skate. I was also excited because it was my first time going to a skateing ring so big and tall, but I got over my fear because my friend Maya gave me courage. We started talking and playing. So we went and skated. I also had the best time.

Serena sets us up to expect that it will be her teacher (who taught her every subject she knows!) who would help her resolve the conflict she reports in this story. She makes sure we know there was a "nice and caring lady" available, but when it came down to conquering her fear of skating in the rink "so big and tall" it was not the teacher, but her friend who gave her courage. It seems that Maya did this by "talking and playing."

In addition to helping them get over their fears, children told us about their friends helping them manage hurt feelings, control their anger, get over disappointments, and manage embarrassment. Third-grader Rashanna tells us that her friend Tiarra "always tries to cheer me up Because she doesn't like me getting my feelings hurt." When her friend "got really angry," fourth-grader Veronica reported, "I told her to calm-down and lets see if we can resolve this problem." Fourth-grader Wanda tells us how she and her friend Kathryn "both were a little inberesed about swimming in front of our classmates. So we started talking about it together." The result of their talking, Wanda tells us, is that "we went through swimming together not half as inberresed as we planned on being."

Researchers have found links between the ability to regulate emotional expressiveness and peer success in the elementary school years (Murphey et al., 2004; Sokol & Muller, 2007; Conduct Problems Prevention Research Group, 1999). It is not difficult to understand how the children who have developed strategies to regulate their own negative emotions will be better at managing peer relationships than those whose emotions are extreme. Conflicts between age-mates are likely to provoke anger, and the ability to down-regulate anger will open up the possibility of non-violent conflict resolution. The possibility of social rejection is likely to provoke fear and anxiety. The experience of such rejection will undoubtedly provoke sadness and disappointment. The whole enterprise of finding a place among peers is likely to be fraught with difficult emotions – emotions that can sabotage relationships if they are not managed successfully. Children who can recognize these negative experiences in themselves and in their peers, and who have strategies for de-escalating, will clearly have more success (Halberstadt, Denham, & Dunsmore, 2001; Zeman et al., 2006).

The question of how children develop these emotion regulation skills has most often focused on infants and young children (Calkins, 1994), and has often focused on the physiological and neurological substrates of emotional experience (Calkins & Keane, 2004). Much research has noted the role of early attachment and the emotion socialization by parents and caregivers (Morris et al., 2007; Thompson & Meyer, 2007). Relatively few researchers have considered the possibility that friends in middle childhood help each other with the management of emotions (cf. Howes, 2009). Amy Halberstadt and colleagues (2001) proposed an elegant model of affective social competence that includes management of one's own emotional experience and management of the sending and receiving of emotion messages with social partners. We discuss this model further in Chapter 11 and show how the sharing of stories facilitates emotional competence. The stories we have studied show us that friends are curious about each other's emotional experience; they talk about how they feel and they make explicit efforts to calm each other down and to cheer each other up. When they feel bad, they "talk it out" with a friend, and sixth-grader Connie tells us "that's what friends are for." Fifth-grader Harrison, in Example 3.18, shows us how communication about emotional experience helps to moderate negative emotions and maintain friendship.

Everybody gets angry sometimes. Sometimes you get angry at school and your friends know that you are angry. Tell us about a time a friend knew you were angry at school and tell us what your friend did. Tell us everything that happened from beginning to end.

> last week, or atleast last week from when i write this, i was mad. see, most of my friends are in the other class and we don't do outside recess much because of the harsh conditions outside so i pretty much never get to see them so i had to go over to their class to deliver something but when i went i saw the class having a lot more summer recess than ours and it made me kinda disapointed but one of my only friends in this class, ███ was mad too so i sat down and he told me his problem and i made him feel better then i told him my problem and he made me feel better. i like having friends but it s painful to watch them slowly drift away due to lack of communication :C

EXAMPLE 3.18 Harrison, fifth-grade boy, College Elementary, Memphis

EXAMPLE 3.18 HARRISON, FIFTH-GRADE BOY, COLLEGE ELEMENTARY, MEMPHIS

last week, or at least last week from when i write this, i was mad. see, most of my friends are in the other class and we dont do outside recess much because of the harsh conditions outside so i pretty much, never get to see them so i hed to go over to their class to deliver somthing but when i went i saw the class having a lot more funner recess than ours and it made me kinda dissapointed but one of my only friends in this class, noah was mad too so i sat down and he told me his problem and i made him feel better then i told him my problem and he made me feel better. i like having friends but it is painful to watch them slowly drift away due to lack of communication :(

Harrison doesn't really describe how he made Noah feel better or how Noah made him feel better; he only tells us that they sat down and took turns telling their problems to one another. It may be that the "communication" that Harrison recognizes as critical to friendships, the communication that might be painfully drifting away for Harrison and his friends, is as important to emotion regulation as it is to maintaining friendships (Harris & Walton, 2009; Pasupathi, Wainryb, Mansfield, & Bourne, 2016). We don't doubt the neural bases of emotion regulation, or that it is a skill developed in infant–caregiver interactions, scaffolded by preschool teachers, and refined as children learn to use language to label the emotional expressions of others and to use emotion words to report their own experience (Gross, 2013). By the time they get to be fourth and fifth-graders, however, their interactions with people they call friends may be the critical site for the development of emotion regulation skills. Emotion regulation both promotes friendship and is promoted by friendships (Bell & Calkins, 2000).

Conclusions

Previous work on children's friendships has shed light on the significance of these relationships for social, emotional, and moral development during middle childhood. The stories we have studied have corroborated the findings of previous researchers in many ways. The five features of friendship that were regularly highlighted by child authors (liking/enjoyment, equality/autonomy, mutual support, continuity, and self-disclosure) are all features that have emerged as important in previous research. The problems our authors identified most frequently in their friendship relationships (the honesty/trust complex and the exclusiveness/jealousy complex) have been recognized and studied by researchers using survey methodologies. Our elementary school writers spontaneously remarked about the benefits of friendship (personal growth, companionship, and emotion regulation) that have been described by theorists and researchers. For the most part, our work affirms and underlines an impressive body of previous research in this field, but three important insights emerged in our work that have not often been emphasized in the work on friendships in middle childhood. These include (1) a clearer picture of friendship as a cultural practice that is established and maintained by negotiation between children, (2) a recognition of friendship development as uniquely child-guided, and (3) an appreciation and deep respect for the struggles required to accomplish friendship in middle childhood, and for the courage and creativity of the children who undertake the struggle.

Children Creating Culture: Friendship as a Cultural Practice

Much of the previous work on children's friendship has emerged from a cognitive-constructivist or cognitive-behaviorist theoretical approach. This means that researchers have been interested not only in how children behave with their friends, but also in how they think about these relationships (Crick & Dodge, 1994). We have also been interested in children's ideas about friendship, and we have been eager to learn how they express these ideas in their own words. However, as we listened and did close readings of children's descriptions, we moved closer and closer to a socio-cultural approach, in which the most interesting developments are happening in the meanings children create together as they enact a set of very local cultural practices. Friendship emerges as one of these cultural practices, defined by a set of interactional rituals, ways of talking, and ways of legitimizing certain behaviors. When we think about friendship this way, our attention is drawn to how ideas 'work' in everyday interactions. The children who wrote stories for us seemed to be less engaged in the social cognitive task of defining friendship and more in the social interactive task of enacting the obligations of friendship – and in the critical work of negotiating about what those obligations are.

Children Creating Friendship: The Invention of Friendship in Middle Childhood

Friendships may be unusual among human relationships in the extent to which they emerge without the scaffolding of adults. Barbara Rogoff (2003) described how most complex cultural practices and relationships get passed along from generation to generation by a process she called guided participation. More competent members of a community interact with new members in ways that gradually bring the new member into fuller and fuller participation. Children come to take on duties in their families, and to take on roles as students, because more experienced people structure the children's experience, giving them just as much responsibility as they can handle, and gradually increasing what is expected. To the extent that friendship is constituted by interactions between equals, the course of its development differs a bit from this pattern.

In elementary school, it is not surprising that children flounder a little as they figure out how to establish and maintain this distinctive type of relationship. They will certainly use some of the skills they have learned from their early attachment relationships, but those relationships have not been grounded in mutual responsibilities or respect for equality. Children have to negotiate about the obligations of friendship in ways they never had to negotiate their primary attachments – and the partner in those friendship negotiations is likely to be similarly inexperienced. We suspect the grown-ups (at least the teachers) may actually increase the difficulty of the task, because of their commitment to maintaining a congenial classroom environment in which no child is rejected. We are not surprised that we see children struggling with the establishment of friendships, but we find their struggles to be truly remarkable. They do not take up the simple obligation of friendship that their teachers frequently use ("Be nice to everyone"). Instead, they puzzle about the costs and benefits of friendship, they endure the disappointments of rejection and betrayal, they deliberate about the morality of privileging some relationships over others, and they keep negotiating, because all of these matters are in constant flux. As they and their friends increase in maturity, the cultural practice they call "being friends" will be continually re-created.

The Courage of Elementary School Children: Friendship as a High-Risk Endeavor

As several generations of college students sat through weekly meetings on our research teams, reading and re-reading children's stories, we regularly found ourselves overwhelmed with a powerful empathy and respect. We had forgotten how *difficult* it is to be a child! The stories we read made us remember the pain of having our secrets betrayed, or of being cruelly misquoted in one of those 'he-said-she-said' encounters. It made us wonder how so many children could find so much courage to risk continued participation in the practices that might lead to the joyful pleasures of friendship, but also might lead to devastating rejection. As we moved back and forth between these empathy-driven readings and our more 'objective' coding practices, we came to treasure three insights especially.

First, we came to understand that the cultural practices of gossiping and secret-sharing (and even of secret betrayals) were not just unpleasant aggressive behaviors. At times, these practices were serving critical functions that brought the cultural practice of friendship into being. By participating in "talking about," and in secret-sharing, however much they risked a sense of well-being, children were inventing a new kind of relationship. They were making honesty, trust, and self-disclosure defining features, or defining practices, of the relationships they were calling friendship.

Second, we came to appreciate how seriously the classroom, as a setting for the establishment of friendships, is fraught with moral ambiguity. In a cultural community of around twenty-five children, each child needs to find a few with whom they will spend more time, have more fun, share more about themselves, provide more attentive support – a few good friends. At the same time, they are learning to manage multiple group memberships, including what it means to be a member of a particular gender category, and to achieve status in multiple realms of a complex social world in which they must earn the affection and respect of the other twenty or so classmates. They have the nearly impossible task of establishing relationships that are by definition exclusive, without committing acts of social exclusion that we have tended to call social aggression. At one point, in one of our research team meetings, a college student exclaimed, "How can they do this? They are only ten years old!"

Finally, our admiration for the young authors who told us about their conflicts grew out of an increasing recognition of how much they attended to each other's emotional experience and tried to help each other manage the disappointments, frustrations, fears, anger, and sadness that were provoked by the work they were doing together. We read their reports that described their friends' emotions (as well as their own), their reports about inquiries or puzzlement as they tried to understand how their friends were feeling, their reports about deliberate attempts to calm each other down or cheer each other up, and their willingness to credit their friends with giving them courage, or helping them 'get over' their negative emotions. Before reading these stories, we had not understood how critical a friendship practice is to emotion regulation in middle childhood.

We began this chapter with a story by fourth-grader Naomi, whose fight "about friend ship" organized our investigation and helped us get a better view of the world of middle childhood. As much as we respect Naomi, at the end of this journey, we have to object to her report that "it was a silly fight." Her struggles and those of her age-mates are anything but silly. They are the strivings of a new generation to invent for themselves an essential type of human relationship. They are creating friendship.

Note

1 We are not certain about what Keila meant to say here. It is possible that she planned to continue the story, but ran out of time. However, the fact that she wrote "The End" calls this interpretation into question. It may be that Keila meant to write "got her," as a way of telling us that the grandmother got custody of Tamara after her mother died.

References

Altman, I., & Taylor, D. (1987). Communication in interpersonal relationships: Social penetration theory. In M. E. Roloff & G. R. Miller (Eds.), *Interpersonal processes: New directions in communication research* (pp. 257–77). Newbury Park, CA: Sage.

Aristotle. (2002). In C. J. Rowe & S. Broadie (Eds.), *Nicomachean ethics*. Oxford: Oxford University Press.

Bagwell, C. L., & Schmidt, M. E. (2013). *Friendships in childhood and adolescence*. New York, NY: Guilford Press.

Bamberg, M. (2004). Talk, small stories, and adolescent identities. *Human Development*, 47, 366–9.

Baumeister, R. F., & Leary, M. R. (1995). The need to belong: Desire for interpersonal attachments as a fundamental human motivation. *Psychological Bulletin, 117*(3), 497–529. doi:10.1037/0033-2909.117.3.497.

Baumeister, R. F., Zhang, L., & Vohs, K. D. (2004). Gossip as cultural learning. *Review of General Psychology, 8*(2), 111.

Bell, K. L., & Calkins, S. D. (2000). Relationships as inputs and outputs of emotion regulation. *Psychological Inquiry, 11*, 160–209.

Berger, C., & Rodkin, P. C. (2012). Group influences on individual aggression and prosociality: Early adolescents who change peer affiliations. *Social Development, 21*, 396–413.

Berndt, T. J. (1989). Obtaining support from friends during childhood and adolescence. In D. Bell (Ed.), *Children's social networks and social supports* (pp. 308–31). New York, NY: John Wiley & Sons.

Berndt, T. J. (1999). Friends' influence on students' adjustment to school. *Educational Psychologist, 34*(1), 15–28.

Berndt, T. J. (2002). Friendship quality and social development. *Current Directions in Psychological Science, 11*, 7–10.

Berndt, T. J., & Hoyle, S. G. (1985). Stability and change in childhood and adolescent friendships. *Developmental Psychology, 21*(6), 1007.

Berndt, T. J., & McCandless, M. A. (2009). Methods for investigating children's relationships with friends. In K. H. Rubin, W. M. Bukowski, & B. Laursen (Eds.), *Handbook of peer interactions, relationships, and groups* (pp. 63–81). New York, NY: Guilford Press.

Berscheid, E., & Walster, E. H. (1969). *Interpersonal attraction.* Reading, MA: Addison-Wesley.

Besnier, N. (2009). *Gossip and the everyday production of politics.* Honolulu, HI: University of Hawaii Press.

Bigelow, B. J., & LaGaipa, J. J. (1980). The development of friendship values and choice. In H. C. Foot, A. J. Chapman, & J. R. Smith (Eds.), *Friendship and social relations in children* (pp. 15–44). New Brunswick, NJ: Transaction Publishers.

Bokhorst, C. L., Sumter, S. R., & Westenberg, P. M. (2010). Social support from parents, friends, classmates, and teachers in children and adolescents aged 9 to 18 years: Who is perceived as most supportive? *Social Development, 19*, 417–26. doi:10.1111/j.1467-9507.2009.00540.x.

Bowker, J. C. W., Rubin, K. H., Burgess, K. B., Booth-LaForce, C., & Rose-Krasnor, L. (2006). Behavioral characteristics associated with stable and fluid best friendship patterns in middle childhood. *Merrill-Palmer Quarterly, 52*(4), 671–93.

Bowker, J. C., Rubin, K. H., Buskirk-Cohen, A., Rose-Krasnor, L., & Booth-LaForce, C. (2010). Behavioral changes predicting temporal changes in perceived popular status. *Journal of Applied Developmental Psychology, 31*(2), 126–33.

Bukowski, W. M., Newcomb, A. F., & Hartup, W. W. (1996). *The company they keep: Friendships in childhood and adolescence.* Cambridge, MA: Cambridge University Press.

Bukowski, W. M., Motzoi, C., & Meyer, F. (2009). Friendship as process, function, and outcome. In K. H. Rubin, W. M. Bukowski, & B. Laursen (Eds.), *Handbook of peer interactions, relationships, and groups* (pp. 217–31). New York, NY: Guilford Press.

Bukowski, W. M., Buhrmester, D., & Underwood, M. K. (2011). Peer relations as a context for development. In M. K. Underwood & L. H. Rosen (Eds.), *Social development* (pp. 153–79). New York, NY: Guilford Press.

Byrne, D., & Griffitt, W. (1973). Interpersonal attraction. *Annual Review of Psychology, 24*, 317–36.

Calkins, S. D. (1994). Origins and outcomes of individual differences in emotion regulation. *Monographs of the Society for Research in Child Development, 59*, 53–72.

Calkins, S. D., & Keane, S. P. (2004). Cardiac vagal regulation across the preschool period: Stability, continuity, and implications for childhood adjustment. *Developmental Psychobiology, 45*, 101–12.

Caluori, D. (2012). *Thinking about friendship: Historical and contemporary philosophical perspectives.* New York, NY: Palgrave Macmillan.

Collins, N. L., & Miller, L. C. (1994). Self-disclosure and liking: A meta-analytic review. *Psychological Bulletin, 116*(3), 457–75.

Conduct Problems Prevention Research Group. (1999). Initial impact of the Fast Track prevention trial for conduct problems: II. Classroom effects. *Journal of Consulting and Clinical Psychology, 67*, 648–57.

Corsaro, W. A., & Eder, D. (1990). Children's peer cultures. *Annual Review of Sociology, 16*, 197–220.

Crick, N. R., & Dodge, K. A. (1994). A review and reformulation of social information-processing mechanisms in children's social adjustment. *Psychological Bulletin, 115*(1), 74.

Dunn, J. (1988). *The beginnings of social understanding.* Cambridge, MA: Harvard University Press.

Engel, S. (1995). *The stories children tell: Making sense of the narratives of childhood.* New York, NY: W. H. Freeman and Company.

Engel, S. (2015). *The hungry mind: The origins of curiosity in childhood.* Cambridge, MA: Harvard University Press.

Engel, S., & Li, A. (2004). Narratives, gossip, and shared experience: How and what young children know about the lives of others. In J. M. Lucariello, J. A. Hudson, R. Fivush, & P. J. Bauer (Eds.), *The development of the mediated mind: Sociocultural context and cognitive development* (pp. 151–74). Mahwah, NJ: Lawrence Erlbaum.

Fine, G. A. (1977). Social components of children's gossip. *Journal of Communication, 27*(1), 181–5.

Furman, W., & Buhrmester, D. (1985). Children's perceptions of the personal relationships in their social networks. *Developmental Psychology, 21*(6), 1016–24.

Gest, S. D., Graham-Bermann, S. A., & Hartup, W. W. (2001). Peer experience: Common and unique features of number of friendships, social network centrality, and sociometric status. *Social Development, 10*, 23–40.

Gilligan, C., Lyons, N., & Hanmer, T. J. (Eds.). (1990). *Making connections: The relational worlds of adolescent girls at Emma Willard School.* Cambridge, MA: Harvard University Press.

Goodwin, M. H. (1980). He-said-she-said: Formal cultural procedures for the construction of a gossip dispute activity. *American Ethnologist, 7*(4), 674–95.

Gross, J. J. (Ed.). (2013). *Handbook of emotion regulation.* New York, NY: Guilford Press.

Halberstadt, A. G., Denham, S. A., & Dunsmore, J. (2001). Affective social competence. *Social Development, 10*, 79–119.

Harris, A. R., & Walton, M. D. (2009). "Thank you for making me write this." Narrative skills and the management of conflict in urban schools. *The Urban Review, 41*, 287–311.

Hartup, W. W. (1996). The company they keep: Friendships and their developmental significance. *Child Development, 67*(1), 1–13.

Hartup, W. W., & Stevens, N. (1997). Friendships and adaptation in the life course. *Psychological Bulletin, 121*(3), 355.

Hasebe, Y., Nucci, L., & Nucci, M. (2004). Parental control of the personal domain and adolescent symptoms of psychopathology: A cross-national study in the U.S. and Japan. *Child Development, 75*(3), 815–28.

Heath, S. B. (1983). *Ways with words: Language, life and work in communities and classrooms.* Cambridge, MA: Cambridge University Press.

Howes, D. (2009). Friendship in early childhood. In K. H. Rubin, W. M. Bukowski, & B. Laursen (Eds.), *Handbook of peer interactions, relationships, and groups* (pp. 180–94). New York, NY: Guilford Press.

LaFreniere, P., Strayer, F. F., & Gauthier, R. (1984). The emergence of same-sex affiliative preferences among preschool peers: A developmental/ethological perspective. *Child Development, 55*(5), 1958–65.

Laursen, B., Finkelstein, B. D., & Betts, N. T. (2001). A developmental meta-analysis of peer conflict resolution. *Developmental Review, 21*, 423–49.

Lins-Dyer, T., & Nucci, L. (2007). The impact of social class and social cognitive domain on northeastern Brazilian mothers' and daughters' conceptions of parental control. *International Journal of Behavioral Development, 31*(2), 105–14.

Logis, H., Rodkin, P. C., Gest, S. D., & Ahn, H-J. (2013). Popularity as an organizing factor of preadolescent friendship networks: Beyond pro-social and aggressive behavior. *Journal of Research on Adolescence, 23*, 413–23.

Malecki, C. K., & Demaray, M. K. (2003). What type of support do they need? Investigating student adjustment as related to emotional, informational, appraisal, and instrumental support. *School Psychology Quarterly, 18*(3), 231–52.

Martin, C. L., & Fabes, R. A. (2001). The stability and consequences of young children's same-sex peer interactions. *Developmental Psychology, 37*(3), 431–46.

Matthews, G. B. (1980). *Philosophy and the young child.* Cambridge, MA: Harvard University Press.

Matthews, G. B. (1984). *Dialogues with children.* Cambridge, MA: Harvard University Press.

Morris, A. S., Silk, J. S., Steinberg, L., Myers, S. S., & Robinson, L. R. (2007). The role of the family context in the development of emotion regulation. *Social Development, 16*, 361–88.

Murphey, B. C., Shepard, S. A., Eisenberg, N., & Fabes, R. A. (2004). Concurrent and across time prediction of young adolescents' social functioning: The role of emotionality and regulation. *Social Development, 13*, 56–86.

Newcomb, A. F., & Bagwell, C. L. (1995). Children's friendship relations: A meta-analytic review. *Psychological Bulletin, 117*(2), 306–47.

Nucci, L. (1996). Morality and the personal sphere of actions. In E. S. Reed, E. Turiel, & T. Brown (Eds.), *Values and knowledge* (pp. 41–60). Hillsdale, NJ: Erlbaum.

Nucci, L., & Gingo, M. (2010). Moral reasoning. In U. Goswami (Ed.), *Blackwell handbook of childhood cognitive development* (2nd ed.) (pp. 420–45). Oxford: Blackwell.

Opie, I., & Opie, P. (2001). *The lore and language of schoolchildren.* Oxford: Oxford University Press.

Parker, J. G., & Gottman, J. M. (1989). Social and emotional development in a relational context: Friendship interaction from early childhood to adolescence. In T. J. Berndt & G. W. Ladd (Eds.), *Peer relations in child development* (pp. 95–131). New York, NY: Wiley.

Parker, J. G., & Asher, S. R. (1993). Friendship and friendship quality in middle childhood: Links with peer group acceptance and feelings of loneliness and social dissatisfaction. *Developmental Psychology, 29*, 611–21.

Parker, J. G., Low, C. M., Walker, A. R., & Gamm, B. K. (2005). Friendship jealousy in young adolescents: Individual differences and links to sex, self-esteem, aggression, and social adjustment. *Developmental Psychology, 41*(1), 235–50.

Parker, J. G., Kruse, S. A., & Aikins, J. W. (2010). When friends have other friends. In S. L. Hart & M. Legerstee (Eds.), *Handbook of jealousy: Theory, research, and multidisciplinary approaches* (pp. 516–46). Malden, MA: Wiley-Blackwell.

Pasupathi, M., Wainryb, C., Mansfield, C. D., & Bourne, S. (2016). The feeling of the story: Narrating to regulate anger and sadness. *Cognition and Emotion, 10*(1), 1–18.

Piaget, J. (1932/65). *The moral judgment of the child.* London: Free Press.

Reis, H. T., Aron, A., Clark, M. S., & Finkel, E. J. (2013). Ellen Berscheid, Elaine Hatfield, and the emergence of relationship science. *Perspectives on Psychological Science, 8*(5), 558–72.

Rogoff, B. (2003). *The cultural nature of human development.* Oxford: Oxford University Press.

Rose, A. J., & Rudolph, K. D. (2006). A review of sex differences in peer relationship processes: Potential trade-offs for the emotional and behavioral development of girls and boys. *Psychological Bulletin, 132*(1), 98.

Rose, A. J., Schwartz-Mette, R. A., Smith, R. L., Asher, S. R., Swenson, L. P., Carlson, W., & Waller, E. M. (2012). How girls and boys expect disclosure about problems will make them feel: Implications for friendships. *Child Development, 83*(3), 844–63.

Ross, H., & Lollis, S. (1989). A social relations analysis of toddler peer relationships. *Child Development, 60,* 1082–91.

Rubin, K. H., Bukowski, W. M., & Bowker, J. C. (2015). Children in peer groups. *Handbook of child psychology and developmental science, 4*(5), 1–48.

Sokol, B. W., & Muller, U. (2007). The development of self-regulation: Toward the integration of cognition and emotion. *Cognitive Development, 22,* 401–5.

Strayer, F. F., & Santos, A. J. (2006). Affiliative structures in preschool peer groups. *Social Development, 5*(2), 117–30.

Sullivan, H. S. (1953). *The interpersonal theory of psychiatry.* New York, NY: Norton.

Thompson, R. A., & Meyer, S. (2007). Socialization of emotion regulation in the family. In J. J. Gross (Ed.), *Handbook of emotion regulation* (pp. 249–68). New York, NY: Guilford Press.

Wainryb, C., Komolova, M., & Brehl, B. (2014). Children's narrative accounts and judgments of their own peer-exclusion experiences. *Merrill-Palmer Quarterly, 60*(4), 461–90.

Way, N. (2013). Boys' friendships during adolescence: Intimacy, desire, and loss. *Journal of Research on Adolescence, 23*(2), 201–13.

Way, N. (2011). *Deep secrets: Boys' friendships and the crisis of connection.* Cambridge, MA: Harvard University Press.

Youniss, J., & Smollar, J. (1985). *Adolescent relations with mothers, fathers and friends.* Chicago, IL: University of Chicago Press.

Zeman, J., Cassano, M., Perry-Parrish, C., & Stegall, S. (2006). Emotion regulation in children and adolescents. *Developmental and Behavioral Pediatrics, 27,* 155–68.

4

"SHE WOULD KERCE ME OUT PRACTEDLY EVERY DAY"

Social Aggression in Elementary School

> he talks about my mother very very wrong.
>
> *Megan, fifth-grade girl, Magnolia Springs Elementary, Orlando*

In a preschool classroom, if Collin were to sit down next to three-year-old Abby at story time, and she moved to the opposite side of the circle and said, "I don't want to sit next to him!" the scenario would be familiar, and not too concerning to his teacher. Preschool teachers are accustomed to observing and working to socialize the aggressive urges of young children. However, when eight-year-old Josh Francis tells Shakenya, a participant in our study, "YOUR NOT MY FRIND ANYMORE," Josh's teacher is much more likely to feel concern, perhaps reprimanding him and spending time discussing the importance of accepting and not excluding others. By the time they are eight or ten, children are expected to find ways to satisfy their own wishes without trampling on the well-being of others.

In elementary school classrooms, this is not an easy feat. The tasks of gaining the acceptance of peers, and of satisfying the human need for a sense of belonging, must be accomplished in a group of twenty to thirty other children, all of them just beginning to establish a sense of their own identity, to demand autonomy over new domains, and to claim agency in a new moral universe. Clashes are inevitable. The distinction between social acceptance and social dominance may be a little subtle for nine-year-olds, and finding strategies that defend one's own interests without threatening the social position of another child is no small challenge. Accordingly, researchers have given no small amount of attention to understanding aggression in middle childhood. The 2015 edition of the *Handbook of Child Psychology and Developmental Science* included a chapter on aggression that references over 300 studies (Eisner & Malti, 2015). Definitions and classifications of types of aggression vary from one article to the next in the research literature and can leave the reader of these studies bewildered and frustrated. Lamb and Harré (1983) suggested that these definitions share two features: (1) perpetrators intend to harm and (2) victims must feel hurt. Among our 2,811 conflict stories, 91% described acts of child aggression by this definition. Our analysis of these 2,530 stories was done in constant conversation with the important research and theory that preceded our work.

The authors in our studies accused one another of threatening or causing harm in three core developmental domains of the self: physical, psychological, and social. They described physical aggression that harmed the body (and we examine this in Chapter 5); they inflicted psychological harm by threatening a developing sense of identity or self-concept, and they attempted to damage relationships or social standing. Approximately 2,431 (96.1%) of the stories that reported child aggression described at least one of these, and many stories included more than one. The ninety-nine (3.9%) child conflict stories that did not fall into these categories were either disputes about property rights or descriptions of disagreements in which no child was positioned as an aggressor. There were many behaviors described by the authors in our studies as harmful to the developing self-concept and to social relationships and status, and the most common of these fell into three categories: (1) name-calling and face-to-face insults, (2) spreading rumors and insulting people behind their back, and (3) rejecting or excluding individuals from play or other activities. These behaviors are typically grouped together in a more general category of relational or social aggression in other research (Underwood, 2003). In our work, we've distinguished name-calling and face-to-face insults (as a type of psychological aggression that threatens the developing self) from behind-the-back aggression and explicit exclusion (as types of social aggression that threaten social status and relationships) (Walton, Harris, & Davidson, 2009). Although we recognize that these categories overlap – harm to social relationships inevitably harms the self and harm to the self threatens social relationships – the conceptual distinction is useful in organizing our analysis and it has led to a more nuanced and culturally relevant understanding of when and how children talk about non-physical aggression. Our work to address these distinct forms of aggression focused our attention on the social and moral universe of middle childhood, and we came to see a powerful role for narrative accounts in early identity development and social development.

"She called me a loser made me cry and hurt me": Name-Calling and Face-to-Face Insults

In 878 stories (approximately 34.7% of those stories that included any child aggression), authors described name-calling or direct insults, a type of psychological aggression that threatened the developing sense of self. Children wrote about name-calling in all of our samples, and in all samples they described this practice as hurtful. Third-grader Marvin gave us a sense of how expected this behavior is: he described his first day at a new school with: "I thought that I would be laughed at and be call things by other children but later on that day I made new friends." It was noteworthy for Marvin that he did *not* get ridiculed by other children, and he may have been right to expect it. The practice of name-calling appears to be customary in all the settings in which it has been studied (Crozier & Dimmock, 1999; Goodwin, 2002). Opie and Opie's (2001) description of the folklore of childhood included chapters on nicknames, name-calling, taunts, and jeers that children have used to insult one another, collected from communities across the British Isles and beyond, going back to Shakespeare's time, and continuing to modern schoolyards.

Most of the time, children did not tell us the specific name they were called (e.g., "he . . . call me dum-dum"), instead referring to the event by one of several discursive labels. They used the expression 'calling names' or 'called me a name' or 'cursed me out,' without reporting the exact insult. Children in predominantly African American schools in Memphis used three expressions to talk about varieties of name-calling or insults: "called me out my name," "your momma," and "checking." The expression "called me out my name" referred to name-calling that involved 'bad words,' generally words that the children were reluctant to repeat or to write down. The expression "your momma" functioned as short-hand for a class of insults that insulted the mother, usually among boys. Rarely in our sample did children report the full content of this kind of insult. Most commonly, African American Memphian children referred to an exchange of insults, often including insults of the family, as 'checking.' A sixth-grade boy, Deon, from Connors Elementary, explains, "Sometimes people in the class want to check and when they do the other person starts and the checking just goes back and forth until someone's feelings get hurt." Sociolinguist William Labov (1972, 1997) described discourse practices similar to the insult exchanges that were called 'checking' in Memphis among African American children and teens where they are referred to as 'playing the dozens,' 'signifying,' or 'sounding.' In ethnographic studies of African American children, Shirley Brice Heath (1983) and Marjorie Goodwin (1990) described similar practices in ways that highlighted the verbal fluency and creativity that was an integral part of neighborhood play for these children. Many of the sociolinguists who study these insult games describe them as banter that hones verbal skills and promotes the sophisticated use of language that has given rise to jazz and rap and spoken word poetry – part of a cultural aesthetic to be valued (e.g., Kochman, 1983). The children who wrote about checking in our samples presented the activity as hurtful or mean, but there was at least occasional recognition that the practice required a valued skill. Fourth-grader Kayla reported, "It started out as, well, just Her checking me and me checking her back. When I did a really good one, she got really mad." When skillfully performed, checking made use of humor. Fifth-grader

Jessica complained about a classmate who "messed with me almost every day," explaining that "Lacey said that she could check my grandma so bad that her hole family would laugh at what she says." The suggestion of sociolinguists that insult play serves a positive cultural function raises an interesting question about the function of teasing and name-calling for all children in the elementary school years. A close examination of children's stories about the insults they endure from one another provides some insight into the social developmental function of this common discourse practice.

When U.S. children wrote about name-calling and did tell us the specific name they were called, we found that they fell roughly into four overlapping categories: gender insults, body insults, character assassinations, and racial or ethnic slurs. The 9% of these that concerned gender are discussed in Chapter 7. The largest category, making up 40.4% (and many of these were gendered), insulted an aspect of the appearance or function of the body. Children were taunted for being fat or skinny, tall or short, for having big ears, lips, or teeth, for having the wrong hair-style or hair color, for ill-fitting clothes, for stinking, for being dirty or ugly. They were sometimes called by body parts ("Hey, butt-head") or by body excrements ("poo-poo" or "doo-doo"). Another 24.0% of the insults ridiculed or demeaned some feature of the character or psyche. There were taunts that called into question the intelligence or sanity of the victim ("stupid," "idiot," "crazy"), taunts about maturity ("baby" or "crybaby") and taunts about moral failings ("mean," "traitor," "liar"). A small number of taunts (5.7%) were clearly about race or ethnicity ("white," "mixed," "nigger," "vietnesees rat"), and sometimes these were directed at members of the same racial or ethnic group and other times they were reported in cross-racial interactions; some of the body/appearance taunts also seemed to have racial meanings (e.g., those about facial features or hair). Many of the taunts had to be classified in multiple categories, impugning both physical and psychological or moral character. Children were called by the names of cartoon characters (e.g., Pinocchio, Oscar), and by the names of a variety of animals (dog, monkey, donkey, chicken), and these probably had meanings that impugned the child's character. What all of this name-calling seems to require of children is that they defend core features of their identity. In Example 4.1, sixth-grader Faye describes how difficult this is.

EXAMPLE 4.1 FAYE, SIXTH-GRADE GIRL, COLLEGE ELEMENTARY, MEMPHIS

This isn't really a fight it's more of a misunderstanding. Today we were discussing the Houston trip that we just got back from. We were talking about the Holocaust and people involved I made a comment about the people. Dying of starvation and they were just skin and bone's. So some of the boys only some started to laugh. They started checking me under their breath, but loud enough so I could her. I am nothing like those people. They think so. If this isn't a mis understanding you tell me. I'm urging to leave this class but I want to stay. Boys just can't grow-up. They must start to grow up in the real world it's to close to kid around.

Faye was a tall, thin sixth-grader whose class was studying the Holocaust. She tells us that she was moved to express her distress at the pictures she has seen of starving people ("just skin and bone's"), but the boys in her class ("only some" – Faye is careful not to overgeneralize) found this an opportunity for 'checking.' Their insults were ostensibly made "under their breath," but they found the insults amusing, and they made sure Faye could hear them. Faye doesn't repeat the content of the checking, but she defends herself against them by asserting that she is "nothing like" those Holocaust survivors, even though "they think so." Faye wants to take these matters seriously, and the failure of her classmates to "grow up in the real world" makes her debate with herself about whether she even wants to remain a part of this class. This child, on the cusp of adolescence, is trying to defend a sense of herself as a serious and mature person. We noted that children's reports of name-calling and insults were often accompanied by similar attempts to claim a developing self and identity.

The kinds of name-calling children reported about differed little from sample to sample in the United States, but children in Shenzhen reported about defending themselves from quite different kinds of insults. In U.S. stories, gendered insults (9% of all insults) and body insults (40.4%) were common, but both were much less common in Shenzhen (5.9% and 11.1%, respectively). A full 64.5% of the Shenzhen children's insults (as compared to 24.0% in the US) included at least one report of a character insult. Some of these insults were familiar – we could easily have been reading stories by American children when they called each other idiot, stupid, psycho, or annoying. Like U.S. children, they reported about calling one another various animals (dog, wolf, pig, sheep). All of this was familiar. What distinguished the Shenzhen stories from all of our U.S. samples was the frequency with which they wrote about defending themselves against threats to their moral character. Among our U.S. samples, insults based on moral character traits were relatively rare, and were predominated by the attribution, "mean." In Shenzhen, however, the most frequent category of name-calling children wrote about ascribed a moral character flaw, and there was a rich variety of moral failings alleged. Shenzhen children used words that we translated as heartless, inhumane, boorish, shameless, uneducated, selfish, stingy, violent, bad-tempered, spoiled, ungrateful, show-off, bad-mannered, uncompassionate, and 'useless in society.'

What is clear to us is that early identity development happens and is shaped within cultural communities. In the United States, elementary school children began the work of claiming a gender identity, of establishing the acceptability of their body presentations, and of positioning themselves as intelligent and mature.

The insults they endured challenged those identities, suggesting that gender, age, and body characteristics were features of the self that are especially important to early identity development in the US. In Shenzhen, children of the same age were working to secure a reputation as a humane person, aligned with Confucian principles of 'ren' (仁) and 'li' (禮). The concept of ren includes ideals of gentleness, genuineness, and an ability to look at one's own failures as opportunities for self-cultivation. 'Li' concerns propriety and attention to social harmony and good relationships. These were features of character that were important to the emerging identities of children in ChunTian Primary School and so these were the fodder for the name-calling and insults with which they taunted one another.

Most research on identity development focuses on adolescence and recently on early adulthood (Schwartz, Donnellan, Ravert, Luyckx, & Zamboanga, 2012). It is clear, however, that the foundations that support the building of an identity are laid much earlier, when children come to compare themselves to their peers and to find significance in differences in size, appearance, and skills; when they come to assume moral agency and to find themselves blame- and praise-worthy, and when they identify themselves and their peers as members of social categories that are differentially valued by the larger society they enter. This early identity work is threatened by name-calling and by the insult practices of middle childhood. When we give children opportunities to author narratives about their own experience, we give them the authority to assert a valued identity for themselves. Faye, in Example 4.1, may not have been able to persuade her classmates (only some of them) to take her seriously, but when we invited her to 'tell a story about a fight, an argument, or some kind of misunderstanding that really happened to you,' she was able to create a coherent narrative, in which she positioned herself as the kind of person she wants to be. Maybe those boys in her class were not convinced, but she's won *us* over!

Children create challenges for themselves in the domains of important developmental accomplishments. We saw in Chapter 3 how much courage children exhibited as they shared secrets and risked rejection in learning to have and to be friends. Here again, we see the cultural practices of middle childhood challenging the critical developments of the period. This take on middle childhood name-calling may make some sense of the meta-linguistic attention that African American communities give to insult-exchanging practices. African American children were similar to the white, Hispanic, and Asian children we observed in our samples in their frequency of reporting name-calling and in the anguish they described when they suffered personal insults. What we did see from them was a greater attention to the naming and the ritualizing of the practice. When children are part of a marginalized community, so that their identity is likely to come under various forms of attack, their cultural communities may need to be more attentive to the defenses they develop against those attacks. The development of a healthy sense of self among African American youth may be particularly challenging when their societal status is devalued; counteracting racial victimization may require, on the one hand, resisting negative stereotypes or insults and, on the other hand, owning those insults and modifying their function to achieve self-liberation and valuation (Stevens, 1997). To the extent that insult exchanges are ritualized (Goodwin, 1990; Labov, 1997), and especially if, as Kochman (1983) argued, these rituals highlight valued features of the cultural community (such as verbal fluency and facility with improvisation), then we may see African American children better prepared to defend their identity as African Americans than they would be without this experience. When Lacey bragged that she can make her whole family laugh with her insults, she was claiming a proficiency with improvisation, humor, and oratory that is highly valued in her community.

The interpretation above should not be understood as a justification or apology for a kind of aggression that can indeed produce genuine suffering and can leave lasting scars for many children (Crozier & Skilopidou, 2002). Just because name-calling plays a role in acculturation doesn't mean it is good for children. When we ask our college students what they remember about teasing or name-calling in elementary school, many of them recount poignant memories of being taunted for the same things our children reported in their stories. Some confessed that they continue to be self-conscious about their bushy eyebrows or their freckles or for being too loud or too quiet – whatever feature of the self made them the brunt of middle childhood taunts. Name-calling is a special kind of mean behavior, and the young authors who reported about these events recognized it as such. Children's conflict narratives revealed that they were reflecting on the wrongness of psychologically aggressive acts and on the perspectives, the inner worlds, of themselves and others during these experiences. Children who wrote about name-calling and face-to-face insults included significantly more explicit moral evaluations in their stories than children who wrote about other aggressive acts (Walton, Harris, & Davidson, 2009). Acts that threaten or insult children's sense of self, just at a time when they are laying a foundation for identity development, present a serious problem for many elementary school children.

Threats to Social Status and Relationships

In addition to reporting about threats to the developing self, children wrote about aggressive acts that threatened their social status, their friendships, and their relationships with other classmates. Two specific types of this social aggression that children reported in their stories included spreading rumors and insulting people behind their back, and rejecting or excluding individuals from play or other activities.

"Keep my name out of your mouth!": Behind-the-Back Aggression

Some previous researchers have distinguished direct and indirect aggression (Card, Sawalani, Stucky, & Little, 2008) and the children who wrote stories for us clearly made a distinction between "in my face" and "behind my back" aggression. Children reported considerable distress about what other people said about them to others. As reflected in Mike's and Francesca's stories shared in Chapter 3, we found numerous instances of the pain and anguish children described when their peers gossiped about them and, especially, when friends betrayed secrets and spread rumors behind their backs. Although children in all of our samples wrote about this kind of aggression, and reported it as harmful, we found cultural differences in the ways children talked about it. In our well-resourced schools, children described gossip and rumor-spreading as disloyal when done by friends and as mean when done by others. In our less affluent schools, however, we saw children orienting to a norm that valued direct conflict and that denigrated behind-the-back aggression as cowardly or dishonorable. We can hear Nadia's disdain in Example 4.2.

EXAMPLE 4.2   NADIA, SIXTH-GRADE GIRL, CONNORS ELEMENTARY, MEMPHIS

Today in class my friend Tianna told me that someone put my name an a argument and it was something I didn't do. But if I did say it she didn't have no busy putting my name and it. I hope that she keep my name out of her mouth, because if she was some kind of friend she could told me and my face. I don't mean no harm but, Rebecca could just stay out of my wonderful face.

"Some kind of a friend," Nadia asserts, would have told her to her "wonderful face." Nadia denies having said whatever it was that Rebecca accused her of saying, but she asserts that even if she had done it, Rebecca had no business "putting my name in it." The word 'confront' or 'confrontation' was used frequently by children in these communities and never by children in the university-affiliated school. "Everyone who was talking about me, I confrontd them," sixth-grader Helen reports with pride. Brian, another sixth-grader, writes that, "Later that day we confronted the person that was speading the rumors. Now me and Hope are friends."

This difference between cultural groups has been observed in girls by Gilligan, Lyons, and Hanmer (1990), who studied girls in an elite boarding school. Those authors expressed concerns about the ways that most of the white girls in their study "went underground" as they entered adolescence, choosing indirect communication and avoiding the expression of open disagreement. The African American girls they interviewed, by contrast, were much more inclined to speak their minds, even when this risked conflict. In in-depth interviews of ethnically diverse high school students from poor and working-class families who attended an urban, under-resourced school, Niobe Way (1998) found girls affirming the importance of speaking one's mind, even when it threatened direct conflict, believing this to be critical to relationships. Our university-affiliated school was not so elite as the Emma Willard School studied by Gilligan and her colleagues, and our authors were four to six years younger than Way's participants. Nevertheless, our findings are consistent with their observations. We found both boys and girls from the less affluent communities expressing respect for direct conflict and a disdain for behind-the-back aggression.

Too often, behind-the-back social aggression has been construed naively as girls' aggression. This stereotype is propped up by the 'bitchy' Mean Girls and Gossip Girls portrayed in the media. We will see, in Chapter 7, that children know and sometimes affirm this stereotype, referring to behind-the-back aggression as "little girl games." Some research has supported the notion that when girls aggress, they tend to engage in relatively more social aggression than physical aggression (Goodwin, 2002; Underwood, 2003), but findings are mixed in regard to whether girls engage in this type of aggression more than boys (Card et al., 2008). Indeed, some studies have found that boys engage in more social aggression compared to girls (Henington, Hughes, Cavell, & Thompson, 2008; Salmivalli & Kaukiainen, 2004). We found that girls wrote about relatively more social aggression and less physical aggression compared to boys, but only when girls wrote about girl antagonists and boys about boy antagonists. Girls and boys did not differ in their reports of psychological aggression (Walton et al., 2009). Further, 19.1% of boys wrote stories about social aggression, and similar to the girls in our studies, boys were distressed by this type of aggression that attempted to harm their social standing and relationships. We saw Kenneth, in Example 3.10, describe how Phillip used behind-the-back aggression in an attempt to break up Kenneth's friendship with Mark. Robert in Example 3.12 described his anguish concerning his friend Mike, who "always spreaded rumors about me." A fifth-grader, Draymond, (Example 4.3) described the behind-the-back aggression of one of his classmates as a troubling experience.

EXAMPLE 4.3 DRAYMOND, FIFTH-GRADE BOY, MAGNOLIA SPRINGS ELEMENTARY, ORLANDO

There was a boy who thought I sed that I want to fight him. So ever day he would say something to me and I would turn around and say what. And he would be scard to say something else to me. One day when we went to lunch I had to sit with him. It was the first school they give us asyne seats so I had to sit with him then I sed why you want to fight me. He sed Tyrell sed that I want to fight him then I looked at Tyrell and sed why did you tell me a story. after that me and him was cool with eachother. [smiley face]

> Write a story about a conflict with another
> kid that really happened to you. Think
> about a fight, an argument or some kind of
> misunderstanding. Write everything that
> happened from the beginning to the end.
>
> There was a boy who thought I sed that I
> want to fight him. So ever day he would say
> Something to me and I would turn around and
> say what. And he would be scard to say something
> else to me. One day when we went to lunch
> I had to sit with him. It was the first school
> they give us asyine seats so I had to sit
> with him then I sed why you want to fight me.
> He sed ▬▬▬▬▬ sed that I want to
> fight him then I looked at ▬▬▬▬▬ and
> sed why did you tell a story. After that me
> and him was cool with each other. ☺

EXAMPLE 4.3 Draymond, fifth-grade boy, Magnolia Springs Elementary, Orlando

Draymond shares a 'he-said-he-said' story, describing how his classmate, Tyrell, shared false information ("a story") with another "boy" when he asserted that Draymond "sed that I want to fight him." After days in which the boy muttered something to Draymond from behind him in class, the assigned seating arrangement at lunch gave Draymond the perfect opportunity to confront the boy, "why you want to fight me." After learning that Tyrell was responsible for the misunderstanding with his behind-the-back remarks, Draymond and the other boy "were cool with eachother." Notice how Draymond provides us with a good deal of information about the internal worlds of the characters in his story (e.g., "a boy who *thought* I sed that I *want* to fight him"; "he would be *scard* to say something else"). Although boys wrote about this type of aggression less frequently than girls did, when they wrote about behind-the-back aggression, they sounded very similar to the girls and boys Niobe Way described in *Deep Secrets*, her 2011 study of boys' relationships. Like Harrison in Example 3.18 who wrote "I like having friends but it is painful to watch them slowly drift away due to lack of communication," boys expressed the same expectations for human relationships that we found in girls stories. They were similarly hurt when these relationships were threatened by social aggression. Overall, we found the similarities more striking than the differences.

"Days went by and I did not have anyone to play with": Acts of Exclusion or Explicit Rejection

In addition to covert behind-the-back aggression, when describing aggressive acts that threatened their social status and relationships, children occasionally wrote about exclusion or unequivocal rejection. In our samples, reports of social rejection and exclusion took several forms, primarily explicit statements that "you can't play" or "you're not my friend" and non-verbal actions such as eye-rolling, walking away, and ignoring (e.g., not responding to a question or "not talking to me"). Belongingness is a very fundamental need and social rejection is an affront to this most basic human necessity. Often, experiences with rejection are part of an extended pattern of social interactions with a 'friend' or group of peers and not simply a single incident of being left out. Peer relations researchers have studied the group phenomenon of rejection for decades, observing that children who are rejected by their classmates tend to experience a host of negative psychological, social, and academic outcomes concurrently and longitudinally (Rubin, Bukowski, & Bowker, 2015). To assess peer rejection, researchers often use sociometric procedures where elementary-age students are presented with a list of classmates and asked to circle the names of students whom they liked least. A 'rejection' or 'disliking' score is created for each child by dividing the number of nominations for 'liked least' received by the nominators in the classroom or by standardizing the number of nominations received by class to account for varying numbers of nominators across classes (Davidson, Walton, Kansal, & Cohen, 2016; Serdiouk, Rodkin, Madill, Logis, & Gest, 2015).

In two of our samples, Magnolia Springs and College Elementary, we were able to examine peer nomination data from each classroom, and to identify the children in each room who were least liked by the other children (Davidson, Walton, & Cohen, 2013; Davidson et al., 2016). We were surprised to find that, with two exceptions, the children who were very high in liked least nominations (with scores more than 1 standard deviation above the mean number of nominations in their class) simply did not write about rejection and exclusion. They wrote about a variety of other forms of aggression, and their stories overall included less psychological mindedness and less moral analysis. In fact, the children who did write about rejection and exclusion, on average, tended to be well below the mean liked least nomination score (i.e., they were not disliked by peers). In our Florida sample, we also had academic information about the participants in our study, and we found that those children who described social rejection or exclusion had higher peer academic reputations (i.e., the average of four items for which peers nominated who was good/not good at reading and who always/never knows the right answer in class) and higher teacher ratings of academic skills compared to children who did not write about rejection. The children who were writing about rejection did not appear to be the children who were most frequently experiencing rejection at school: as a group, they were better adjusted academically and socially than the children who wrote about other forms of aggression. Our efforts to explore this finding led us to look closely at who wrote stories about rejection and at what those stories were like.

Here again, we found a striking difference between the children in our U.S. samples and the children from Shenzhen. In the US, children's stories described rejection or exclusion only 12.8% of the time. By contrast, children in Shenzhen included rejection in 34% of their stories. Our U.S. children may have found it difficult to write about this type of peer aggression in great part because it requires writing about something that *didn't* happen (e.g., "they didn't play with me"), as opposed to writing about something that occurred (e.g., "she called me fat and ugly"). Jack's story in Example 4.4 reveals how difficult this is.

Write a true story about something that happened on the playground at ▮▮▮ School. Tell everything that you can remember about what happened from the beginning to the end. *If you need more room, you can use the back of this paper.*

Once my class got a erleay recess. I was going out side and noticed the fith graders were still out. That morhing I had been wanting to play soccer, but when I got to the soccer field the fith graders would not let me play. sometimes people exclude you but someone in my class got to play. It just did not make sense

EXAMPLE 4.4 Jack, third-grade boy, College Elementary, Memphis

EXAMPLE 4.4   JACK, THIRD-GRADE BOY, COLLEGE ELEMENTARY, MEMPHIS

Once my class got a erlealy recess. I was going out side and noticed the fith graders were still out. That morning I had been wanting to play soccer, but when I got to the soccer field the fith graders would not let me play. sometimes people exclude you but someone in my class got to play. It just did not make sense.

Jack wrote briefly about being excluded from a game of soccer at recess. He seems to have accepted as a part of social life that "sometimes people exclude you." Then, his use of the counterfactual 'but' signals that this situation is different because one of his classmates was allowed to play. Jack concludes that it "just did not make sense." Why would the fifth-graders allow another classmate, but not him, to play? He shares few details about the aggressive act, perhaps because there were few details to share. Jack was not pushed or kicked, insulted or taunted, nor was he the target of gossip. He simply was left out of an activity he "had been wanting to play." We noted other examples of these aggressive non-events across our samples, such as fifth-grader Kendall, who wrote, "Once when I said hi to my friend Nicole, she wouldn't answer me. I asked her what was wrong and she said nothing."; fifth-grader Destinee who wrote about a peer who "didn't talk to me the whole way there. We went into the movie room to whatch a movie and she went across the room so she wouldn't sit next to me."; and third-grader Luis who shared that "my friend conpletly ignored me. I came a cross him once in a [while] but he still ignored me."

TABLE 4.1 Psychological mindedness in stories about conflict

Variable	Example
Reports of own emotions	"I was sad because my mom took me over to my auntie's house."
Reports of others' emotions	"she was mad because I was sitting by my other friend"
Reports of collective emotions	"We were glad she let us go."
Reports of own mental states	"But I knew she made a mistake"
Reports of others' mental states	"so Kito thought that we were trying to avoid her and ignore her."
Reports of collective mental states	"We knew we were in for it."
Reports of own motives	"I was just trying to do my work."
Reports of others' motives	"And she said she wanted to play with Andrina and her friends."
Reports of collective motives	"We wanted to play outside but she said not to go out."

In Chapters 1 and 2, we discussed how Bruner's landscape of consciousness is critical to fleshing out a good story, and we described our efforts to account for children's considerable awareness of psychological selves in their stories. (Appendix C describes our coding of psychological mindedness.) Pairs of undergraduate researchers independently coded each story, making counts of children's use of emotional state words (e.g., afraid, happy, mad), emotional behavior descriptors (e.g., crying, screaming, frowning), mental state descriptors (e.g., thought, believed, wondered), and volitional or motivation words (e.g., wanted, wished, was trying to). Separate counts were made for own and other internal states, with strong inter-rater reliabilities (assessed using a Pearson's r correlation) ranging from $r = .80$ to .96, where perfect agreement between coders would yield an r of 1.0 and random scores would yield $r = 0$. (See examples in Table 4.1.)

Although U.S. children infrequently wrote about social rejection and exclusion, interestingly, when they did write about this type of aggression, they were more psychologically minded and attentive to their own and others' motives than when they did not. Notice how much thought Brandi gives to thoughts, feelings, and motivations in Example 4.5.

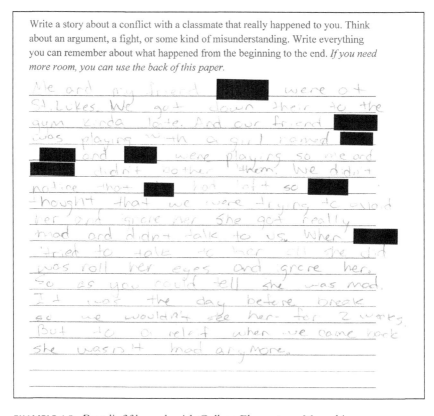

EXAMPLE 4.5 Brandi, fifth-grade girl, College Elementary, Memphis

EXAMPLE 4.5 BRANDI, FIFTH-GRADE GIRL, COLLEGE ELEMENTARY, MEMPHIS

Me and my friend cameron were at St. Lukes. We got down their to the gym kinda late. And our friend Kito was playing with a girl named Sheena. Kito and Sheena were playing so me and Cameron didn't bother them. We didn't notice that Sheena had left so Kito thought that we were trying to avoid her and ignore her. She got really mad and didn't talk to us. When cameron tried to talk to her all she did was roll her eyes and ignore her. It was the day before break so we wouldn't see her for 2 weeks. But to a relief when we came back she wasn't mad anymore.

Brandi's story illustrates how problematic exclusion or 'ignoring' is in this fifth-grader's social world. Recognizing that her own (non-)behavior could be interpreted as exclusion, she frames it as "not bothering" Kito and Sheena. She further explains her failure to play with Kito as her own failure to "notice that Sheena had left." Notice the impressive complexity here: Brandi is recognizing how her own non-behavior is interpreted, and she attempts to influence the reader's interpretation of this by her labeling of the behavior and also by reporting about what she did not know. This is an author thinking about what the reader knows about what the characters in the story know about the other characters in the story at a particular time in the story. Without explicitly stating that she and Cameron were not purposefully excluding Kito, Brandi convinces us that she was not engaged in a socially aggressive act. She lets us know that Kito thought otherwise about the author's motives, "so Kito thought that we were trying to avoid her and ignore her." The result of this anger, Brandi suggests, is intentionally exclusionary behavior this time by Kito, who wouldn't talk to her friends. Brandi describes an effort by Cameron to repair the situation, but the efforts were rebuffed, "all she did was roll her eyes and ignore her." There was special urgency to this problem because of an upcoming two-week break, during which Brandi and Cameron would not see Kito. Brandi reports her own emotional relief when, at the end of the break, Kito's anger had dissipated. This story clearly illustrated how much psychological and social-cognitive sophistication is required to explain incidents of social exclusion. According to the psychological states coding scheme reported in Table 4.1, Brandi reported three instances of other emotions or mental states ("She got really *mad*," "she wasn't *mad* anymore," "Kito *thought* we were trying to avoid her"), two instances of collective (her own and Cameron's) emotions or mental states ("We didn't *notice*," "to a [our] relief"), one instance of other motives ("Cameron *tried* to talk to her"), and two instances of collective motives ("we were *trying*," "Kito and Sheena were playing *so* me and Cameron didn't bother them").

We saw similar perspective-taking and psychological work in the stories written in Shenzhen about rejection and exclusion, and we puzzled about why these conflicts were so much more frequently described in that sample. Example 4.6 suggests a possible explanation.

平日，每个人都可能会与别人发生矛盾。请回忆自己亲身经历的一次矛盾冲突。和同学、兄弟姐妹，朋友，或邻居的小朋友等都可以（和大人的冲突除外），无论发生在学校、家里，社区或别的地方都行。这个冲突可以是意见不和，争吵，误会，或相互动手等等。请如实写下事情的经过，包括你能记起的所有细节（如何开始，中间都发生什么事情，结果怎样，你的感受如何等等）。

> 一天，我和 ▇▇▇ 正在讨论问题，但到了问题解决的第二步，我和他开始争论起来，一下子便开始了一场目利辩论会。结果我们俩都没成功，而且还闹起了矛盾，从此再也没有打过交道。
>
> 有一天，老师在班上开展了"手拉手"活动，让我们写一封信。于是我借这个活动给 ▇▇▇ 写了一封信：
>
> ▇▇▇：
>
> 您好。
> 您之前和我争少的事情，我希望它能永远沉入我们广阔的心胸。我也想能跟你再次打交道，成为一对好朋友，行吗？
>
> 你的同学
> ▇▇▇
> ~~2010~~ 2009.9.16
>
> 后来，我也收到了 ▇▇▇ 的回信，说他也这么想。于是，我和他又成为了一对好朋友。

EXAMPLE 4.6 Jiang Ji-Long, sixth-grade boy, ChunTian Primary, Shenzhen

EXAMPLE 4.6   JIANG JI-LONG, SIXTH-GRADE BOY, CHUNTIAN PRIMARY, SHENZHEN

One day, I was discussing a question with Li Zi-Hui, but on the second step, we started to argue. Suddenly it turned into a debate. In the end we couldn't convince each other, And we had conflict. Since then we had no contact with each other. One day, teacher held a "hand in hand" activity in class, asked us to write a letter. So I wrote a letter to Li Zi-Hui in this activity. Li Zi-Hui: hello! About the thing we had argument before, I wish it could sink to the bottom of our heart. I also want to talk with you, be friend with you, can I? Your classmate Jiang Ji-Long 09/16/2009 Later on, I got Li Zi-Hui's reply, said that he wanted too. So, he and I are good friends again.

Jiang Ji-Long's story is similar to many of the rejection stories from Shenzhen: friends argue and, subsequently, they stop playing together, or begin to ignore one another, or stop walking home together, or "Since then we had no contact with each other." In the U.S. samples it was rare for children to write about a teacher or classmate intervening in these situations, but such interventions were frequently reported in Shenzhen. Fifth-grader Deng Yan wrote a long story describing her friendship with Chen Tian Tian since preschool. When a series of conflicts resulted in "a cold war" between them, Deng Yan reported, "One day, our teacher gave us a lesson, the book told a story about how two friends make up after conflicts, So I went to talk with Chen Tian Tian to clear things up." Shenzhen authors also wrote about intervening when classmates were ignoring one another. Fifth-grader Li Fan reported that one of his classmates asked: "why good brothers ignored each other?" The classmate "wanted to help us make up, so he treated us with food during weekend. Gradually, we felt it, so we made up." These efforts didn't always work. Sixth-grader, Ying Ke, wrote about her despair when her efforts to get two of her friends to reconcile had failed, "I looked at the sky, why the sky is so blue, clouds are so white, the birds are so cheerful, people are so complex, could it be?"

People are indeed complex, and instances of exclusion and rejection may well be the most complex of the peer conflicts children experience. Primary education in China includes explicit lessons in classes the children wrote about as 'moral class' (Li, 2012). These include curriculum activities designed to help children learn to achieve 'right relationships.' Shenzhen children wrote stories that quoted lessons about filial piety (孝 xiao) governing parent–child relationships, fraternal piety (悌 ti) governing sibling relationships, and mutual piety (信任 xin ren) governing friendship relationships. Our hunch is that elementary school children in China and in the United States struggle similarly with experiences of rejection and exclusion. When is withdrawal the best response in the face of a conflict? When is 'ignoring' an act of aggression? How should we interact with people we do not like? How should we respond when we are ignored or excluded? We doubt that children in China experience more or less of these dilemmas than children in the United States. We think that they write about this more often because their educators are more intentional about giving them the language they need for making sense of such experience. In Chapters 9 and 10 of Part III, we make recommendations for incorporating a narrative practice into elementary school classrooms.

In the US, it was the children with stronger narrative skills who ventured to write stories about rejection or exclusion. Like the children in Shenzhen, they were able to report about their own and their antagonists' thoughts, emotions, and motives. They were able to take on a difficult subject and to process a personal experience that challenged their feelings of belongingness. Their ability to consider their own and others' perspectives in stories about these events may have assisted them in making meaning out of experiences with peers that were both distressing and mystifying, and may be related to their ability to resolve, prevent, or avoid negative peer interactions. The children who most frequently experienced these negative peer interactions were much less likely to write about it. Our findings suggest that those who are socially, emotionally, and psychologically healthier, and have stronger narrative skills, are able to write about experiences with rejection. It is possible that the ability to write about this difficult topic promotes healthier relationships, and our recent longitudinal work indicates that narrative skills facilitate peer adjustment across school years (Davidson et al., 2016). We elaborate on this in Chapter 10.

Conclusions

In this chapter, we examined children's stories about aggression that threatened a developing sense of identity or self-concept, and social status or relationships. Children's descriptions of psychological and social aggression fell into three main categories: name-calling and face-to-face insults, behind-the-back aggression, and rejection and exclusion. When we looked closely at these behaviors designated by children as the cause of conflicts, we came to see how the children were aligning themselves with selected cultural norms. We saw them adopting and defending or resisting culturally ascribed identities and we became convinced that the identity work of middle childhood is shaped within specific cultural communities. Among our U.S. samples, insults and identity threats based on moral character traits were relatively rare; in Shenzhen, however, the most frequent category of name-calling children wrote about ascribed a moral character flaw. African American children were similar to the white, Hispanic, and Asian children we observed in our samples in their frequency of reporting name-calling and in the genuine suffering they experienced from personal insults. They, however, were more attentive to the naming and the ritualizing of the name-calling practice, perhaps because, as a member of a marginalized community, their identity was more likely to come under various forms of attack. As the author of their own story, they had the authority and perhaps the responsibility to name and defend this identity.

We also got a glimpse of the moral thinking and moral negotiations that govern elementary schools. We saw that behind-the-back aggression was viewed as cowardly and described with relatively more contempt among children from the less affluent schools compared to children from well-resourced schools. As authors, children get to report about their own motives and thoughts and emotions, and, if they choose, they have the authority to ascribe motives, thoughts, and emotions to the other characters. If they recognize a role for intentionality in establishing culpability, then they may ascribe intentional states to the characters they deem blameworthy. However, when topics and experiences are so difficult to understand and explain, children may struggle with how to make sense of the actions and cognitions of the characters involved. We found that experiences of explicit rejection and exclusion were more complex and difficult to describe when compared to other types of aggression. This type of social aggression is so difficult to write about because often it requires children to explain and make sense of non-events, such as being left out or ignored. Yet our research shows that the children who wrote about this difficult subject did so with more attentiveness to the internal worlds of themselves and others compared to the children who wrote about other types of aggression. We were impressed by children's ability to negotiate what it means to be a friend in Chapter 3, and we are no less fascinated by the ability of eight- to eleven-year-olds to cope with and make sense of experiences with psychological and social aggression as they embark on a complex identity quest.

References

Card, N. A., Sawalani, G. M., Stucky, B. D., & Little, T. D. (2008). Direct and indirect aggression during childhood and adolescence: A meta-analytic review of gender differences, intercorrelations, and relations to maladjustment. *Child Development, 79*(5), 1185–229.

Crozier, W. R., & Dimmock, P. S. (1999). Name-calling and nicknames in a sample of primary school children. *British Journal of Educational Psychology, 69*, 505–16.

Crozier, W. R., & Skilopidou, E. (2002). Adult recollections of name-calling at school. *Educational Psychology, 22*, 113–23.

Davidson, A. J., Walton, M. D., & Cohen, R. (2013). Patterns of conflict experience that emerge in peer reports and personal narratives during middle childhood. *Journal of Applied Developmental Science, 17*(3), 109–22.

Davidson, A. J., Walton, M. D., Kansal, B., & Cohen, R. (2016). Narrative skills predict peer adjustment across elementary school years. *Social Development*.

Eisner, M. P., & Malti, T. (2015). Aggressive and violent behavior. *Handbook of Child Psychology and Developmental Science, 3*(19), 1–48.

Gilligan, C., Lyons, N., & Hanmer, T. J. (1990). *Making connections: The relational worlds of adolescent girls at Emma Willard School*. Cambridge, MA: Harvard University Press.

Goodwin, M. H. (1990). *He-said-she-said: Talk as social organization among black children*. (Vol. 618). Bloomington, IN: Indiana University Press.

Goodwin, M. H. (2002). Exclusion in girls' peer groups: Ethnographic analysis of language practices on the playground. *Human Development, 45*(6), 392–415.

Heath, S. B. (1983). *Ways with words: Language, life, and work in communities and classrooms*. Cambridge, MA: Cambridge University Press.

Henington, C., Hughes, J. N., Cavell, T. A., & Thompson, B. (2008). The role of relational aggression in identifying boys and girls. *Journal of School Psychology, 36*(4), 457–77.

Kochman, T. (1983). The boundary between play and nonplus in black verbal dueling. *Language in Society, 12*(3), 329–37.

Labov, W. (1972). *Language in the inner city: Studies in the black English vernacular*. Philadelphia, PA: University of Pennsylvania Press.

Labov, W. (1997). Rules for ritual insults. In N. Coupland & A. Jawoski (Eds.), *Sociolinguistics: A reader* (pp. 472–86). London: Palgrave Macmillan.

Lamb, R., & Harré, R. (1983). *The encyclopedic dictionary of psychology*. 1st MIT Press ed. Cambridge, MA: MIT Press.

Li, J. (2012). *Cultural foundations of learning: East and west.* New York, NY: Cambridge University Press.

Opie, I. A., & Opie, P. (2001). *The lore and language of schoolchildren.* New York, NY: New York Review Books.

Rubin, K. H., Bukowski, W. M., & Bowker, J. C. (2015). Children in peer groups. *Handbook of Child Psychology and Developmental Science, 4*(5), 1–48.

Salmivalli, C., & Kaukiainen, A. (2004). "Female aggression" revisited: Variable- and person-centered approaches to studying gender differences in different types of aggression. *Aggressive Behavior, 30*(2), 158–63.

Serdiouk, M., Rodkin, P., Madill, R., Logis, H., & Gest, S. (2015). Rejection and victimization among elementary school children: The buffering role of classroom-level predictors. *Journal of Abnormal Child Psychology, 43*(1), 5–17. doi:10.1007/s10802-013-9826-9.

Schwartz, S. J., Donnellan, M. B., Ravert, R. D., Luyckx, K., & Zamboanga, B. L. (2012). Identity development, personality, and well-being in adolescence and emerging adulthood: Theory, research, and recent advances. In I. B. Weiner (Series Ed.) & R. M. Lerner, A. Easterbrooks, & J. Mistry (Vol. Eds.), *Handbook of psychology,* Vol. 6: *Developmental psychology* (pp. 339–64). New York, NY: John Wiley and Sons.

Stevens, J. W. (1997). African American female adolescent identity development: A three-dimensional perspective. *Child Welfare, 76*(1), 145–72.

Underwood, M. K. (2003). *Social aggression among girls.* New York, NY: Guilford Press.

Walton, M. D., Harris, A. R., & Davidson, A. J. (2009). "It makes me a man from the beating I took": Gender and aggression in children's narratives about conflict. *Sex Roles, 61,* 383–98.

Way, N. (1998). *Everyday courage: The lives and stories of urban teenagers.* New York, NY: NYU Press.

Way, N. (2011). *Deep secrets.* Cambridge, MA: Harvard University Press.

5

"BECAUSE THE BUYER HAD A GANG IN THE DARK CORNERS OF ALL AROUND"

Making Sense of a Violent World

We are all human beings. Why he has such a bad temper, and has such an aggressive character? Maybe he is spoiled at home. In society, a person like him is doomed to be useless.

Feng Jin-Yun, fifth-grade boy, Chun Tian Primary School, Shenzhen

We began our work with children's stories nearly twenty years ago as part of a violence prevention program in two inner-city schools. Although we wanted to learn how children understood violence and how they described the violence they experienced and observed in the world around them, we did not ask them to tell us about violence. We asked them to tell us about conflicts. A minority of the conflicts they wrote about described horrific physical violence, and we consider those at the end of this chapter, but most of their stories described ordinary, child-sized conflicts – the kinds of disputes we expect to be a part of childhood.

The stories we described in Chapters 3 and 4 gave us a view of children guiding one another into participation in a relatively civil society, where people can develop satisfying relationships. We saw that stories about betrayals and insults, rumors and rejections gave painful evidence of how difficult it is to accomplish civility and fulfilling relationships. The stories that are the focus of this chapter, by contrast, describe aggressive behavior that is, in many ways, simpler. Physical aggression tends to be easily identified (acts that harm the body, as compared to rumors or exclusion, for example). Acts of physical aggression are often morally clear violations of an imperative to avoid harming others. We are reminded every day that vicious rumors, direct and indirect insults, and acts of exclusion and rejection continue to be a part of our social worlds, well into adulthood. They continue to provide material for ordinary personal narratives and for dramatic fiction.

Physical aggression is different. We write during a presidential election season in the United States, and we see debating presidential candidates using some of the same insults used by the young authors in our study (e.g., 'loser,' 'liar'). Sometimes, the result of their name-calling appears to be a rise in voter approval. By contrast, if one of them were to physically attack an opponent, we are quite sure they would be deemed unqualified to run for office, and they would likely be prosecuted.

The conflicts our research participants wrote about included at least one act of physical aggression between 35.9% and 58.0% of the time, depending on the sample. For stories that were told in an oral story-sharing circle, reports of physical aggression were made in between 12% and 34.8% of the stories. We examine written stories about physical aggression in this chapter. Our examination of the stories children wrote about this type of aggression began with a consideration of what they included in their descriptions. In the first section we ask how children explained and evaluated physical aggression. We describe the attention they gave to the interior experience of the characters in their stories of physical aggression (reports of thoughts, emotions, motives, etc.), and the moral/evaluative work they did to assign responsibility for the consequences of the aggression they described. In the second section, we compare the stories in which children were surprisingly astute in these areas to those stories in which they neglected these critical features of narrative form. Throughout, we consider the role of narrative in helping children make sense of the physical aggression and violence they describe.

"I know it was wrong. But I don't think it was wrong": Moral and Psychological Complexity in Children's Stories of Physical Aggression

In Chapter 4 we described some of the ways we assessed the psychological mindedness in children's stories. A fairly straightforward counting of uses of mental state and emotion vocabulary gave us a good index of children's attentiveness to the landscape of consciousness. Our assessment of the moral evaluative work we have called moral voice was more complex. Consider Example 5.1.

EXAMPLE 5.1   GRACE, FOURTH-GRADE GIRL, IRONWOOD ELEMENTARY, MEMPHIS

The misunderstanding I had was with my sister. At first we were arguing. Then she got louder and louder. After that she started to push me. Then she pulled my hair like she was crazy. Later, she yelled more and more. Something was wrong with her. I tried to get her to stop. I walked away. She was very mad. My sister thought she was bad. My sister was very angry. I do not know why she was angry. She made me angry. I was not angry at all. I do not like when she makes me mad. Then she gets me in trouble. I did not start the fight she did. She is always starting something. I never start a fight with her.

Grace describes a "misunderstanding" that escalates to yelling, pushing, and hair-pulling by her sister. The central tension of the story concerns Grace's effort to explain her sister's extreme behavior. "Something was wrong with her," and Grace seems genuinely puzzled about how to interpret this "crazy" behavior. She posits an emotional state ("She was very mad" and "My sister was very angry") but these explanations are unsatisfactory, because Grace cannot discern a reason for the anger. Grace suggests, "My sister thought she was bad." Note that Grace is thinking here about what her sister thinks about herself, a kind of perspective-taking described by Selman (1980) as emerging in middle childhood. This statement reflects a fairly sophisticated understanding that a person's self-assessment might explain behavior. In addition to the attention Grace gives to her sister's thoughts and feelings, Grace tells us a bit about the impact of all of this on her own interior life. She reports about her uncertainty about her sister's experience ("I do not know why she was angry"). She describes the impact of her sister on her own emotional state ("She made me angry. I was not angry at all"), and she reports that she does not like it when her emotions are manipulated this way by her sister ("I do not like it when she makes me mad").

Grace works to position herself in her story as blameless and her sister as culpable. She reports her motive to de-escalate ("I tried to get her to stop. I walked away"). She blames her sister for getting her in trouble, noting that it is her sister who is "always starting something." It is important to Grace that she "did not start the fight." She is calling on a cultural norm that evaluates the first attacker as more blameworthy than the person who retaliates. Grace assures us that she would "never start a fight with her." Grace's story is full of psychological mindedness, and this was not difficult to score. Quantifying the moral evaluation in this story was much more difficult. When Grace calls her sister "crazy" and asserts that "something was wrong with her," are those moral evaluative assessments as well as assessments of her sister's mental state? When Grace says that her sister "thought she was bad," is the word 'bad' a negative moral assessment, or is this a colloquial use that might mean something like, "thought she was a big shot"? Is "always starting something" a moral evaluation?

After much training, we were able to achieve acceptable reliability between independent coders who counted the number of moral concerns expressed in children's stories (see Appendix B). We found, however, that our overall impressions of the moral stance authors took could be reliably rated on a three-point scale, where a score of 0 indicated no moral evaluation at all and a score of 2 indicated a clear and explicit evaluation. Table 5.1 provides examples of explicit positive and negative moral assessments of self and other.

TABLE 5.1 Moral assessments of self and other

Moral explicitness variable	Example rated as explicitness = 2
Moral justification of self	I decided to be the better man and apologize for checking his family.
Moral critique of self	I thought I was guilty.
Moral justification of other	I admit, she did not do anything wrong.
Moral critique of other	He not supposed to hit girls.

Each story was given four moral explicitness scores. Grace's story was scored 2s for her explicit justification of herself and her explicit critique of her sister. She made an implicit critique of herself (scored 1) when she said "She gets me in trouble," but she makes no attempt to make a moral justification of her sister (scored 0).

When children described physical aggression in their stories, they usually accompanied their descriptions with some moral/evaluative work, and this was as we expected. We began our investigation of children's conflict narratives with the expectation that the moral evaluation of physical aggression would be fairly simple and straightforward. Parents begin at an early age to socialize toddlers not to hit, not to throw things, and not to do harm (Drummond, Paul, Waugh, Hammond, & Brownell, 2014). By elementary school, we expect children to have bought into this moral imperative to avoid physical aggression and violence. What we found, however, as we read their accounts, was that the moral evaluation of physical aggression often presented children with significant challenges to their moral thinking. Consider the analysis done by the sixth-grader in Example 5.2.

EXAMPLE 5.2 HELEN, SIXTH-GRADE GIRL, IRONWOOD ELEMENTARY, MEMPHIS

What I've been in is a lot about aurguing, fighting, and misundersanding. My aurguing was about people talking about me every one who was talking about me. I confronted them and it lead into a light of misunderstanding but they were wrong not me. Next I've been in an fight because some wants to fight me and when they wan't to fight me I fight back. Because my mother always told me if someone hits me hit them back. my next aurgument was about me and my cousin but she's only nine and she put her hand in my face and I moved her hand and we start fighting. But even though I don't like her she's still my cousin but I know it was wrong. But I don't think it was wrong because she pushed me. But still I won. Because my grandmather gat mad and I said she make me sick and she told my mother and my mather said well. Because my mother said she shouldn't have put her hand in my face.

Helen begins with a quote of the prompt, which asked her to "Think about an argument, a fight, or some kind of misunderstanding." She goes on to identify two experiences she labels as arguments (one of which led to misunderstanding), and one that she labels as a fight. Although nothing in the assignment directed the children to establish who was right or wrong, it is clear that Helen understood this to be a part of what she must do in relating her experience. In the first "argument," she simply declares that "they were wrong not me." In the second episode, when she tells about her "fight," she cites a moral authority – "my mother always told me" – to justify her own behavior as retribution: "if someone hits me, hit them back" ("when they wants to fight me I fight back"). Helen lives in a community in which she can expect to be challenged to fight and her mother has prepared her to face those challenges head on.

The moral good is much more difficult for Helen to establish in the third episode she relates, and she gives us a clear sense of her struggle. She calls upon two norms that problematize a fight with this antagonist: "but she's only nine" (you should not fight with children younger than yourself) and "she's still my cousin" (you should not fight with members of your own family). Her first analysis of the situation here is that fighting is not justified: "But I know it was wrong." However, it is really not this simple, and she follows her admission of guilt directly with "But I don't think it was wrong, because she pushed me." She contrasts knowing and thinking here, indicating more uncertainty about her self-justification than about her critique. Helen, like all children, lives in a world that provides her with multiple interpretive repertoires that can lead to mutually contradictory evaluations of the same behavior. There is an imperative to fight back when threatened and to retaliate when mistreated, and there is an imperative to keep the peace within the family and to avoid fighting with younger children. Which should provide the interpretive frame for this conflict? Before she resolves this, Helen throws in just a hint of a third repertoire: a 'winning is everything' or 'might makes right' interpretation in which right and wrong matter less than who won the fight. As she prepares to close her story, Helen seems to imply that there is a difference of opinion between her grandmother and her mother. The grandmother was mad about the fighting, but the mother said "Well." Helen finally goes with maternal authority, ending her story with an indirect quote of her mother establishing that the cousin was blameworthy in this situation. For now, for Helen, the imperative to retaliate when attacked wins out over the imperative to keep the peace. How could we have imagined that the moral evaluation of physical aggression would be simple?

When Authors Failed to Claim a Moral Voice

The stories presented above illustrate clearly how impressive the psychological and moral analysis of elementary children can be. But not all of the children in all of their stories included this kind of interpretive work. We made many comparisons as we sought to understand the circumstances in which children did and did not exercise a narrative voice that claimed moral authority and that demonstrated the ability to "get into other people's heads" that Bruner posited to be the fundamental power of narrative. The physical aggression of boys, for example, tended to be presented with less evaluation than the physical aggression of girls – and this is discussed in Chapter 7, when we take a close look at gender. Any physical violence that the child presented as punishment (spankings, whoppings, whippings, etc.) is discussed in Chapter 6 when we talk about how children described adults. In the sections below, we present three types of stories that tended to be less attentive to the kind of moral analysis we saw in Grace's and Helen's stories.

Severity of Violence and the Moral Work in Children's Narrative Accounts

In both of the examples we considered above, children described physical aggression that did not result in significant injury or harm. Did children do similar moral analysis in stories about more severe violence? Pairs of undergraduate researchers independently read each story and made a rating of the severity of violence described in the story. Reliability for these ratings was strong ($r = .97$, where 1.0 would indicate perfect agreement between coders). Table 5.2 presents examples of the violence described at each level. We discuss differences between communities below, but it is worth noting here that in all of our samples a sizable majority of the stories included no violence or mild physical aggression. Across all of our samples, however, we found examples of violence producing injury, and we found a small but disturbing set of stories that described criminal or life-threatening violence.

When we grouped the stories according to the level of violence described, we found stronger moral analysis and greater attention to the interior lives of

TABLE 5.2 Severity of violence reported in children's stories

Violence level	Definition	Example
0	No physical aggression described	She bosses me around all the time.
1	Physical aggression or annoyance not causing pain or injury	He kept bumping me in line and poking me.
2	Violence producing pain, but not injury	She pulled my hair and I slapped her.
3	Violence resulting in injury requiring first aid	He got a bloody nose and I got a black eye.
4	Criminal or life-threatening violence	Jon got his dad's gun and went out after Chrimane.

actors when the level of violence described was mild or moderate than when it was severe or life-threatening. Specifically, we found more reports of characters' emotions, thoughts, and motives in stories coded as level 1 and level 2 violence than in those coded as level 3 and 4 violence (Walton, Harris, & Davidson, 2009). Emotion words, in particular, steadily declined from stories with no violence to stories with life-threatening violence. In addition to this psychological mindedness in reports of stories with milder aggression, we found that children were more likely to include moral justifications of the self and other in stories describing mild to moderate physical aggression than in stories describing more extreme violence. This is illustrated by comparing Example 5.3 to Examples 5.1 and 5.2.

EXAMPLE 5.3   PEARSON, SIXTH-GRADE BOY, IRONWOOD ELEMENTARY, MEMPHIS

On the 3rd day of school in the Fourth Grade When we went to the bathroom. When we were washing our hands I heard someone talking about me. So I told him stop checking me, Then he was still checking me So I hit him in the jaw. then he hit me back then I hit him again then blood came out of him then the teacher caught me then called our parents and My dad had a conference with Mr. Green. Then After that day the big brother tried to fight me. So it was another fight with both of us was bleeding and I got wrote up and sent to the office because the Safety Council saw the whole thing happen the other boy Got suspended and his big brother I was about to go to permediation but I didn't go to it.

Pearson reports acts of quite serious physical aggression ("both of us was bleeding") that resulted in suspensions for two students. He describes these without explanation or moral evaluations. The narrative does not consider possible motives for anyone's behaviors. There are no descriptions of or speculations about the emotions or thoughts of any actors. It is noteworthy that the mechanisms in place at this school to respond to and prevent violence were not effective for the children in this story. A teacher got involved only after a fight in the boy's bathroom had resulted in a child bleeding. A conference with parents did not prevent an escalation of the violence with the addition of an older brother. The fact that the second fight was observed by the Safety Council assured that punishment (suspension) would be meted out, but the peer mediation program didn't get an opportunity to operate, and there is no evidence of reconciliation, and no evidence that the author learned anything about how to avoid violence.

This author has clearly mastered some aspects of narrative form. The story starts by establishing a clear setting, scored as a 3, the maximum on the contextual subscale of the Narrative Coherence Coding Scheme (NaCC) discussed in Chapter 2 (Baker-Ward, Bauer, Fivush, Haden, Ornstein, & Reese, 2007). The sequence of events is clear; the author makes some explicit causal connections using the conjunctions "so" and "because," and the reader can easily make inferences about other causal links. This clear chronology was also given the maximum score of 3 on the chronological dimension of the NaCC. Unlike the narratives written by Grace and Helen, however, this story does not have the dual landscape that Bruner (1990) described as a critical feature of narrative form. There are no motives or intentions or goals and because of its minimal thematic coherence, this story was scored a 1 on the NaCC. We speculate that children who tell us stories of mild or moderate physical aggression have attentional and socio-cognitive resources to concern themselves with the meaning of the aggression. By contrast, when children wrote about violence that caused or threatened to cause serious injury, their attention may be so captivated by the salience of the violent acts, by blood and bruises and by threats of serious injury, that they are distracted from the narrative work of taking a moral stance. Especially when such violence is rare and traumatic, children may become overwhelmed and unable to marshal the emotional and cognitive capacities to process and explain violent events.

When Violence Comes Into the Family

If children lacked resources to explain and evaluate serious violence when it was perpetrated by other children, they were even less prepared to make narrative meaning when serious violence happened in their homes. By far, the most disturbing stories we read were those describing serious family violence. These stories were rare, but they were shared in every sample except Shenzhen, and they raised serious ethical issues for us as researchers. When we found one of these stories among those that children wrote for us, we made sure that the child was in the care of a school counselor who was attentive to the situation. Indeed, in all of these stories, when we alerted the school counselor or staff professional, we found that they were already aware of the special needs of that child, and the child was in care.

In the samples in which we collected stories orally, accounts of family violence offered an even more serious challenge. Many of our stories were shared in sessions we called KidsTalk. Groups of five to eight children sat in a circle and took turns sharing stories in response to a weekly prompt. These prompts often matched the educational themes of the facility that week (e.g., during first-aid week at a summer camp, we asked, "Tell a story about a time somebody got hurt"). Most of our KidsTalk sessions were not a part of our data collection, and many of these prompts did not elicit stories about conflicts, but sometimes they did. KidsTalk facilitators were trained to interrupt a child who began to tell a story that seemed to be about to reveal family violence or criminal behavior in their family. The facilitator would say, "This sounds like it is going to be a really important story that needs to be told to a trusted grown-up. Can you wait until after KidsTalk and then tell me or Ms. [name of staff member] the whole story?" Then the facilitator quickly told another story designed to divert the attention of the other children from the troubling story. In twenty years of running weekly KidsTalk sessions at a dozen different facilities, we have had only half a dozen of these occasions, and in all six instances, the child was willing to talk to a staff member about the incident. In each case the staff members followed up with intervention to assist the child and the family. For this reason, we have descriptions of dangerous or criminal behavior in children's families only in our written stories.

There was a second critical ethical question raised for us in working with these stories. We told the children that we were collecting their stories because we want to learn what it is like to be a child their age. Most children were very clearly telling us what they wanted us to know about their experience. Sometimes, however, as we read stories of significant trauma, it seemed clear that the child needed to get the story out – that the story made its way into the child's writing, whether the child intended it or not. Consider Example 5.4.

Write a story about something that happened to you.

→ One day me and my family went to the
Fair and to the ear doctor they put
a tube in my ear now they said
they are going to take it out out
But a long time ago ████████ kill my mom
He was guilty I was so glad. But my Mo
alway Be in my heart But I still
Know But my Mom is no longer alive
an she still loves me and she is
in my heart

EXAMPLE 5.4 Timothy, third-grade boy, Winterton Elementary, Memphis

EXAMPLE 5.4 TIMOTHY, THIRD-GRADE BOY, WINTERTON ELEMENTARY, MEMPHIS

One day me and my family weat to the fair and to the ear doctor they put a tube in my ear now they said they are going to tack it out But a long time ago Harry kill my mom He was guilty I was so glad. But my mom alway be in my heart But I still know But my mom is no longer alive an she still loves me and she is in my heart

Timothy started to tell a story about going to the fair, but then switched topics to tell about a trip to the ear doctor. But neither of those is the story that Timothy really needed to tell, and the more difficult and significant story seems to intrude. Timothy's mother was murdered "a long time ago." This child experienced not only the loss of his mother, but also the trauma of an investigation and court proceeding that resulted in a guilty verdict, which gave Timothy some comfort ("I was so glad"). The child has been in counseling, and he has family members who have assured him that his mother's love continues to be in his heart. Nevertheless, Timothy is not able to create a coherent narrative about what he has experienced. The story inserts itself, we believe, because this child needs to be able to make narrative sense of what he has been through.

Research inspired by Jamie Pennebaker's expressive writing intervention has produced decisive evidence that opportunities to write about troubling life events increase young adults' ability to resolve negative feelings and foster resilience (Frattaroli, 2006; Sexton & Pennebaker, 2009). This "writing cure" has been used successfully with children on the cusp of adolescence (Daiute & Buteau, 2002), although evidence for the effectiveness of this for child victims of trauma is much less clear than for adults. Several narrative researchers have urged caution based on evidence that children are unable to do the kind of narrative meaning-making that is the basis of therapeutic effects in adults (Fivush, Marin, Crawford, Reynolds, & Brewin, 2007; McLean, Breen, & Fournier, 2010). Despite this concern, a recent meta-analysis of twenty-one experimental studies of interventions in which youth aged 10–18 were asked to write about difficult or troubling situations found modest positive effects for the intervention, with the 10–13-year-olds not different from the older teens (Travagin, Margola, & Revenson, 2015). Writing about personal experiences has been shown to be effective in reducing aggression for children as young as twelve, and Sullivan (2011) found that seventh-graders in an experimental study who regularly wrote personal narratives were rated by their teachers as less aggressive two months later than were peers who did not have the writing practice. The benefit of the writing increased as the level of neighborhood violence went up.

We do not recommend that teachers, or others working with children in ordinary classroom or afterschool settings, encourage those children to write about traumatic experiences. This should only be done in settings where there is a professional prepared to guide the child and to exercise judgment about the child's readiness for this work. We do, however, believe that the creation of a narrative practice, in which all children are encouraged to write about their experiences, will facilitate the development of interpretive skills and meaning-making that will promote resilience for all children and will be especially important for those whose experience includes traumatic exposure to violence. Children who are given the opportunities to practice their narrative skills will be likely to create the stories they need to tell. For those children whose experience has included traumatic violence, their ability to cope and thrive will be enhanced if they get better and better at creating coherent narratives. The authority of authorship can give these children an opportunity to take a moral stance and to position the self in alignment with the good. The control they have as an author can allow them to report about their emotions or to leave the emotional content out until they are ready to explore it. We discuss further and provide specific examples of this kind of story-writing practice in Chapter 10. The experience of fifth-grader Ulysses, reported in Examples 5.5 and 5.6, is consistent with our argument.

EXAMPLE 5.5   ULYSSES, FIFTH-GRADE BOY, IRONWOOD ELEMENTARY, MEMPHIS

When me siter die it was bad she got shot in the head. Her in me bother was playing with a gun they did not no the gun was rallye [?]. the buttel whit strat thro her brown! not olly was it sad to me but to me mom I want tro [?] couser for thero yers. The prodley was I thou it was my flot.

If we attempt to correct spelling and punctuation for this story, it reads as follows:

> When my sister die, it was bad. She got shot in the head. Her and my brother was playing with a gun. They did not know the gun was really loaded. The bullet went straight through her brain! Not only was it sad to me but to my mom. I went to the counselor for three years. The problem was I thought it was my fault.

This story was written by Ulysses in November of his fifth-grade year, and he can barely make a readable report of this horrendous experience. He tells us that his sister and brother were playing with a loaded gun, and that the sister was shot. Surprisingly, this author seems to have a better grasp of the landscape of consciousness than of the landscape of action. Although he gives us only the barest details about the what, where, and when of his story, he does report his own emotion and his mother's. The central problem of the story, he tells us, concerns his own moral analysis – he has struggled with a sense that he himself was responsible for his sister's death. We were not able to learn more about the details of this child's story. The guidance counselor at his elementary school, with respect for the privacy of Ulysses' family, told us only that she knew the situation and that the child was getting appropriate services. We did not discuss his story with his teacher, Ms. Erwin, but she told us that she was especially concerned about Ulysses. She also told us that it was her practice to arrive at school each morning and spend several minutes in her car in the parking lot praying that she would be able to give Ulysses and each of her other students what they need.

When we came back to Ulysses' classroom in April of the same school year, he wrote the following story.

EXAMPLE 5.6 ULYSSES, FIFTH-GRADE BOY, IRONWOOD ELEMENTARY, MEMPHIS

Once I was in school when a boy walked up to me in push me then he call me a buck. In Talk about my mother. so I push him back. Then later That day when we went to soppert he kipe on picking at me trying to start a fight. but at last I got tried of him picking with me so I jump in start to hit him. I got a in school supcecht for thier days. I was the last one to eat, not going to support, not being and my class, room eating by my self, not learing, not playing with my firends, or talking to my firends. I said to myself I would never do it agine. in ses then I have never did It agin becaus I do not want lo go throw want I went throw last time.

Here, we correct spelling and punctuation in Ulysses' story:

Once I was in school when a boy walked up to me and push me. Then he call me a punk and talk about my mother. So, I push him back. Then, later that day when we went to support, he kept on picking at me, trying to start a fight. But at last I got tired of him picking with me, so I jump in, start to hit him. I got an in-school suspension for three days. I was the last one to eat, not going to support, not being in my classroom, eating by myself, not learning, not playing with my friends, or talking to my friends. I said to myself, I would never do it again. And since then, I have never did it again because I do not want to go through want I went through last time.

Four and a half months after our first visit to her class, Ms. Erwin was eager to tell us that Ulysses had made impressive progress in his writing skills. "He's just doing so much better," she told us. Ulysses' April story recounts a significant conflict in which he is punished with a three-day in-school suspension. But this is a story Ulysses has the power to tell. He provides a clear report about the sequence of events that led to his suspension. He explains his own behavior as retaliation ("I push him back") and as an emotional response ("at last I got tired"). He describes in some detail the consequences of his punishment, and among these is the loss of the opportunity to see the guidance counselor ("not going to support"). Ulysses concludes his story by telling us about his internal dialogue ("I said to myself I would never do it agine"), and with an update that assures the reader that "since then I have never did It agin." Ulysses' narrative coherence scores improved from fall to spring. Noting that the conflict occurred "in school," he scored a 1 on 'contextual coherence' (compared to a 0 in the fall). With more than 50% of the temporally relevant action statements in chronological order, he scored a 2 on 'chronological coherence' (compared to a 0 score in the fall). With several elaborations, Ulysses substantially develops the theme of his second narrative, scoring a 2 on 'thematic coherence' (compared to a 1 in the fall).

Although we have had research team meetings in which tears were shed over stories like Ulysses', we are not ultimately inclined to despair. Ulysses will have much work to do to recover from the trauma he has experienced, but we think he is on his way. Despite the fact that he attends a "failing school" (so designated because of low performance on high-stakes standardized tests), Ulysses has a devoted teacher who is eager to see him make progress. He values the "support" provided by his guidance counselor. And he is learning to tell his own story. We believe that these supports for resilience give this child, and many of the others who described traumatic violence, a fighting chance to be a part of the 'ordinary magic' that Ann Masten (2015) described as the most typical response to adversity.

In contrast to Ulysses, we are more concerned about Ilanna (see Example 5.7).

EXAMPLE 5.7   ILANNA, FOURTH-GRADE GIRL, WINTERTON ELEMENTARY, MEMPHIS

This is about a fight. It was new year night. My dad and his borther got into a fight. Went my next door. They had guns. they was going to killd him went the gun. They hite him in the month. Then my uncle girl fenrid call the police. The police had came put my dad in the car. Then they take him out went my gandmother came. Then we want home. The police left. My gandmother left. And the next door nader moving.

The End

Write a story about something that happened to you.

This is about a fight.
It was new year night. My dad and his
brother. Got into a fight. went gray next door.
They had guns. they was going to killd
him went the gun. They bite him in the mouth.
Then my uncle girl friend call the police.
The police had come put my dad in the
car. Then they toke him out went my
Gandmother came. Then we want home.
The police left. My gandmother left.
And the next door was ic moving.

I   End

EXAMPLE 5.7   Ilanna, fourth-grade girl, Winterton Elementary, Memphis

If we correct Ilanna's spelling and punctuation, the story reads:

> This is about a fight. It was New Year night. My dad and his brother got in a fight. I went next door. They had guns. They was going to kill him with the gun. They hit him in the mouth. Then my uncle's girlfriend called the police. The police had came, put my dad in the car. Then they take him out when my grandmother came. Then we went home. The police left. My grandmother left. And the next door neighbor is moving.
>
> The End.

Ilanna's story includes no attention to her own thoughts or emotions, or to the thoughts, emotions, or motives of any of the actors. She makes no evaluative claims or moral analysis. Without revealing any of her own emotion, this author powerfully provokes *our* emotion as she reports the sequential removal of all her supports. The police left. The grandmother left. The next door neighbor is moving away. Ilanna is left with no clear link to safety at "The End." This child, we believe, needs more opportunities to write about her experiences.

Finally, we recognize yet a third ethical dilemma that pertains to our decision to share stories of this type. Our commitment to the children who participated in our studies is to try to represent them as they want to be understood. It is important to us that these young authors will grow up to be adults who might read our take on the stories they wrote as children. If they do so, we do not want them to be sorry that they shared their story with us. When adults give permission for researchers to use their data (or their children's data), we are usually confident that they understand the implications of doing so. This is not so clear with children. They tell us their stories without knowing how they will be interpreted by adults. We have spent many hours trying to discern whether sharing these stories is the right thing to do. We believe that it is important for adults to see how children make sense of the trauma they experience. We hope we have gotten this right, and we hope that the children who wrote these stories have become young people who are glad that we decided to share their stories here.

When Violence Becomes Commonplace

EXAMPLE 5.8   TAN, THIRD-GRADE BOY, WINTERTON ELEMENTARY, MEMPHIS

A story about something happen to me

One day I was walk down the state I say a women. A car bast by he pull the women and to the car and dive of the men ho was dive said that i will be bake to geat you. That night i was skard i was taking that they were gone to get me i was skart. Of three weeks I call the poile and said a women was take they foun the women she was die the plice give me a gift at was some money that is my story about something that happed to me.

If we correct Tan's spelling and punctuation, the story reads:

A Story about Something Happen to me

One day I was walk down the street. I saw a woman. A car past by. He pull the woman into the car and drive off. The man who was drive said that, "I will be back to get you." That night I was scared. I was thinking that they were gone to get me. I was scared. Of three weeks, I call the police and said that a woman was take. They found the woman. She was die. The police give me a gift. It was some money. That is my story about something that happened to me.

Write a story about something that happened to you.

A story about something happen to me

Once Day I was walk down the state I say a women. A car past by he pull the women and to the car and dive of the men ho was dive and that i will be take to geat you. That night i was skaid i was taking that they were gone to get me i wes skaid. Of three weeks I call the poink and said a women was take they foun the women she was die the plice give me a gift at was some money that is my story about something that happed to me.

EXAMPLE 5.8 Tan, third-grade boy, Winterton Elementary, Memphis

Tan was a recent immigrant, and his literacy skills are way below grade level, but he was able to make a narrative account of a very frightening experience. One day he was walking down the street and he saw a woman. A car passed by and Tan observed the woman being pulled into the car. Before the car drove away, the driver told Tan, "I will be back to get you." Tan tells us twice about his own fear. Some time passed (three weeks, Tan tells us) before Tan reported to the police what he had observed. Many residents in this community were distrustful of police and were often reluctant to make reports when they observed crimes. The city had in place a program called "Crime Stoppers" that was designed to encourage members of the community to cooperate with investigations. They offered cash rewards for information that led to an arrest. Tan received one of these rewards for the information he gave. Despite the fact that this child struggled to write, he managed to get down the basic facts of his story in chronological order. He offers no explanations for what has happened – how could he? We read similar stories about children's encounters with gang members, with people they believed to be kidnappers, and with drive-by shooters.

The communities in which we collected stories differed in many ways, with one of the most striking differences being the prevalence of violent crime in the neighborhoods. One of our schools served children living in one of the most troubled zip codes in Memphis, a city that was then third in the United States in the prevalence of violent crime, according to the FBI Uniform Crime Report. A study commissioned by the mayor in the year we collected data found 70% of the adult residents of that neighborhood were afraid to walk on their streets. Three of the community centers where we collected stories also served families living in neighborhoods they perceived to be dangerous for their children. Faced with almost daily violence around them, these families had a variety of strategies for keeping their children safe. The principal of the school in our most challenged neighborhood knew every family and had visited most of the homes of the enrolled children. The neighborhood centers included regular instruction for the children on such matters as gun safety, "stranger danger," and strategies to resist gang recruiting. Most families had their children involved in churches that had programming designed to "keep our children off the streets." One of our data collection sites was an afterschool program in one of these churches, and we visited others. We were deeply touched by the intentional care with which they celebrated the accomplishments of their children. After the choir sang, for example, the minister invited the ten young teens in the choir to step forward so that the whole congregation could celebrate the fact that these children were using their talents and were not joining gangs. Those children who had made the honor roll in school were invited to stand and the congregation cheered. However distressed these neighborhoods were, we saw a fierce commitment to and love for the children by almost everyone we met. Still, we observed children playing 'funeral' in the playground, and were astounded by their familiarity with the texts and liturgies of their community's funeral practice (and we were more than a little impressed with their mastery of oratory). Most of the children knew someone who had died or had been wounded in violent encounters. How might this exposure to violence impact the kinds of stories children told?

First, we want to stay mindful of the fact that, even in our highest-crime neighborhood, 42% of the stories children told us about their conflicts included no physical aggression at all. Many of the stories told in our most high-crime and high-poverty neighborhood were about the ordinary problems of childhood – all of the struggles to figure out how to 'do' friendship that we saw in Chapter 3, and all the challenges presented by the social aggression we discussed in Chapter 4. We saw astute moral analysis in stories from every sample. Nevertheless, we saw differences between the stories from our high-stress neighborhoods and those from schools serving central-city children whose streets were not so dangerous. Children in the high-stress neighborhood told more stories that described criminal or life-threatening violence. This was not surprising given that such violence was commonplace in the streets where they lived. What disturbed us more was the difference we observed in the *way* that both criminal violence and less serious physical aggression was described – with little attention to the thoughts, intentions, and emotions of protagonists in their stories and with less moral evaluation and fewer explanations than we saw from children in less stressed neighborhoods (Walton, Harris, & Davidson, 2009). When children described criminal aggression and violence between adults, they rarely demonstrated the moral and psychological analysis that was more common in stories of child violence. Consider Example 5.9.

EXAMPLE 5.9   OCTAVIUS, SIXTH-GRADE BOY, IRONWOOD ELEMENTARY, MEMPHIS

> One Sunday I was over my daddy's house. Then a white man shot the door so my brother and I fell to the floor and got under something. My daddy came to see if we were all right, and he return fire. I don't know why this happened, but it end with the white man going to jail.

Octavius is aware of the expectation that violence such as this requires explanation – this is why he remarks on his inability to tell us "why this happened." We are given a report about the consequences of the violence ("the white man going to jail"), but the author does not speculate about the feelings or thoughts of any characters, does not report his own feelings, does not venture to make a moral judgment, and simply cannot propose an explanation.

Most of the time, when children wrote about physical aggression, they made some attempt to explain why the aggression happened. We classified these explanations into three categories. Coders reliably identified explanations for aggression as emotion explanations ("she got really mad"), character attributions ("She's always trying to start something"), or as retribution or retaliation ("someone hits me I hit them back"). Overall, children's stories included more explanations when they reported physical aggression than when they reported about the kinds of social aggression we described in Chapter 4. This was not true, however, when they described criminal aggression by an adult. Children rarely provided any of these three kinds of explanation when they reported violent behavior of adults.

A plausible explanation for children's disinclination to take a moral stance in stories about adult physical aggression is consistent with Piaget's (1926, 1977) emphasis on the importance of equal status and peer interactions for advancing moral development. According to Piaget, because of their unequal power relations and their asymmetric social interactions with adults, children are likely to abandon their own ideas in favor of ideas presented by adults, even without investigating, critiquing, or verifying those ideas. In this way, children's moral thinking is not promoted through compliance with adult authority, and because adults are seen as authorities, the appropriateness of their behavior is unquestioned. From this perspective, children are more likely to explain physical aggression when it is perpetrated by another child because such aggression is in a moral realm that is accessible to them and available for critique. When adults behave badly, and especially when their behavior includes serious violence, children may report about it, but they rarely do the narrative work that makes sense of their experience of such violence.

Conclusions

We began this chapter with a recognition of how much social-cognitive and moral work children do when they create narrative accounts of their experience with physical aggression. Children give impressive consideration to the thoughts and feelings of the actors in their stories. They report their own motives and speculate about the motives of their antagonists. They do the evaluative work that brings them into the moral discourse of their cultural community, positioning themselves as moral authorities, with an authorial responsibility to evaluate what has happened and to specify what should have happened instead.

We found important and often disturbing exceptions to this inclination to include sophisticated interpretive analyses in their narrative accounts, and we explored three categories of these exceptions. When children told stories about especially dangerous violence, causing or risking serious injury, they showed less psychological mindedness and less moral astuteness. They were much less likely to attend to the interior lives of their characters and less likely to make moral evaluations in stories with severe violence, as compared to stories with mild or moderate violence. For some children, severe violence may be rare, yet so salient and so disturbing that it overwhelms the child's ability to exercise a moral voice or to do a proper narrative interpretation. Stories of severe violence tended to be 'bare bones' stories that reported only the who-what-where-when of the story, without attending to the 'why' or the 'so what.'

A small but important subset of the stories we collected told about traumatic violence in the child's own family. We believe that children told us these stories because they needed to do so. The power of narrative to facilitate meaning-making renders 'telling the story' a critical component of recovery for individuals who survive trauma (Kiser, Baumgardner, & Dorado, 2010). We will elaborate in Part III of this book our belief that we should nurture classroom, neighborhood, and family environments in which children have multiple opportunities to write or tell their own "story about something that really happened to you." As they create stories about the ordinary peer and sibling conflicts that are an inevitable part of middle childhood, they practice interpreting social situations and participating in the moral discourse of their communities. This sets them up in important ways to make their own lives meaningful – even in situations where they may face significant challenges. We believe that the development of a strong narrative voice is especially critical in contexts that include violent conflict and exposure to criminal or traumatic violence.

Children were unlikely to do moral evaluative work when adults were the perpetrators of physical aggression in their stories. The aggression of adults was simply described. There are, of course, many reasons why we do not want children to witness adult physical aggression. We don't want such aggression modeled for them, and we don't want them to experience the fear and sense of insecurity that must accompany a recognition that the adults in their world are so out of control. Our data suggest that we should also worry about the exposure of children to adult physical aggression because of the way it silences their moral voice. Conflicts between children, even when they involve physical aggression, usually evoke narrative reports that include condemnation of violence. Not so for aggression that is perpetrated by those in positions of authority.

Although children from a variety of cultural communities were similar in their tendency to report social aggression, we saw more stories about physical violence written by children whose neighborhoods were troubled by high rates of violent crime. More disturbing than the fact that these children wrote about severe violence was the finding that they were more likely than children from less distressed neighborhoods to report violence without explanation. Narrative form encourages the story-maker to explain those behaviors and outcomes that are exceptional and to background those that are commonplace and expected by those who will hear the story. If violence is too common in the everyday lives of our children, we are concerned that they will not benefit from the narrative practices that encourage us to evaluate and critique such harmful behaviors. This explanation may seem contradictory to the first explanation we considered, the notion that a severely violent incident may overwhelm a child's capacity to interpret and explain it, but we believe that both are plausible. Violence may be backgrounded by some children living in high-stress communities when it is severe and common, but not so personally life-threatening that it overwhelms children's processing capacities. This 'everyday' violence is horrific, but quite different from the life-altering violence written about by Timothy, Ulysses, and Illana.

References

Baker-Ward, L., Bauer, P. J., Fivush, R., Haden, C. A., Ornstein, P. A., & Reese, E. (2007). Coding coherence in autobiographical narratives. Symposium conducted at the biennial meetings of the Society for Research in Memory and Cognition. Lewiston, ME.

Bruner, J. S. (1990). *Acts of meaning*. Cambridge, MA: Harvard University Press.

Daiute, C., & Buteau, E. (2002). Writing for their lives: Children's narratives as supports for physical and psychological well-being. In S. J. Lepore & J. M. Smyth (Eds.), *The writing cure: How expressive writing promotes health and emotional well-being* (pp. 53–73). Washington, DC: American Psychological Association.

Drummond, J., Paul, E. F., Waugh, W. E., Hammond, S. I., & Brownell, C. A. (2014). Here, there and everywhere: Emotion and mental state talk in different social contexts predicts empathic helping in toddlers. *Frontiers in Psychology, 5*, 361.

Fivush, R., Marin, K., Crawford, M., Reynolds, M., & Brewin, C. R. (2007). Children's narratives and well-being. *Cognition and Emotion, 21*(7), 1414–35.

Frattaroli, J. (2006). Experimental disclosure and its moderators: A meta-analysis. *Psychological Bulletin, 132*(6), 823–65.

Kiser, L. J., Baumgardner, B., & Dorado, J. (2010). Who are we, but for the stories we tell: Family stories and healing. *Psychological Trauma: Theory, Research, Practice and Policy, 2*(3), 243–49. http://doi.org/10.1037/a0019893.

Masten, A. S. (2015). *Ordinary magic: Resilience in development*. New York, NY: Guilford Press.

McLean, K. C., Breen, A. V., & Fournier, M. A. (2010). Adolescent identity development: Narrative meaning-making and memory telling. *Journal of Research on Adolescence, 20*(1), 166–87.

Piaget, J. (1926/77). *The language and thought of the child*. New York, NY: Harcourt Brace & Company.

Selman, R. L. (1980). *The growth of interpersonal understanding*. New York, NY: Academic Press.

Sexton, J, D., & Pennebaker, J. W. (2009). The healing powers of narrative. In S. B. Kaufman & J. C. Kaufman (Eds.), *The psychology of creative writing* (pp. 264–73). New York, NY: Cambridge University Press.

Sullivan, T. N. (2011). A school-based expressive writing intervention for at-risk urban adolescents' aggressive behavior and emotional lability. *Journal of Clinical Child and Adolescent Psychology, 40*(5), 693–705.

Travagin, G., Margola, D., & Revenson, T. A. (2015). How effective are expressive writing interventions for adolescents? A meta-analytic review. *Clinical Psychology Review, 36*, 42–55. doi:10.1016/j.cpr.2015.01.003.

Walton, M. D., Harris, A. R., & Davidson, A. J. (2009). "It makes me a man from the beating I took": Gender and aggression in children's narratives about conflict. *Sex Roles, 61*, 383–98.

6

"I TOLD MY MOM & SHE HELPED COMFORT ME"

The Roles Children Give to Adults in Their Stories

One day I had told the teacher they was messing with me, and then the teacher told the principal and the principal got them suspended for three days.

Casey, fourth-grade girl, Community Wellness, Memphis

Scholars in many disciplines have theorized about the variety of ways that adults attempt to bring children in line with accepted roles and practices in their cultural communities (Bornstein & Cheah, 2006). Rogoff (2003) described how parents in many parts of the world find ways to guide their children's participation in the practices that organize life in their culture. There are enormous differences across the globe and across historical time in the autonomy granted to children and the ages at which children are expected to manage a variety of ordinary tasks on their own, and there are wide-ranging differences in the ways adults become involved in bringing children toward more and more adult-like behavior. Even within a socio-historical context (such as twenty-first-century North America) researchers have described important and interesting differences in the ways parents go about socializing their children. Decades of research have considered the impact of these different strategies on children's behavior and on their well-being, but we know very little about how the children understand the efforts their grown-ups are making. Our studies did not ask children to tell us about adults. We asked them to tell us about their experience with conflicts, and in some studies we specifically asked them about conflicts with peers. Nevertheless, in our combined samples adults were mentioned in about half of children's conflict stories. In 11.9% of stories that included adults, the adult was incidental to the conflict; for example, "Then my dad came to pick me up so I went home." In 4.8% of the stories that included an adult, the adult was involved in the kind of community or family violence we described in Chapter 5 (criminal violence that the child did not describe as punishment). Excluding these, in this chapter we consider almost 1,300 stories in which the author described an adult's involvement in the author's own conflict. How these young authors positioned the adults, and how they evaluated the behavior of the adults, gives us a rare opportunity to understand what children make of the efforts of grown-ups to influence them.

We found that the children who put adults in their stories most often positioned the adults as enforcers of rules or standards for behavior. In 73.2% of the stories that included adults in the conflict, the grown-ups' role was to regulate the behavior of the children by some kind of coercion. They administered or threatened punishments ("so I got spended for three days"), and in 9.5% of the stories these punishments involved physical violence ("He knew Mr. Jerrell would paddle him"). In 31.2% of the 1,300 stories, adults were described as controlling children's behavior by issuing commands ("finally Miss Davis told him to stop"), or they intervened by controlling resources ("Then my mom gave the remote to my borther"). In 14.2% of third- and fourth-grader stories and in 29.5% of fifth- and sixth-grader stories adults were positioned as consultants in the story; their role was to make suggestions, offer advice, or to encourage the children to resolve their conflicts ("We went to the counser and she helped us solve our broblem").

This distinction between adults-as-enforcers and adults-as-consultants was cross-cut by an evaluative dimension. Sometimes, the children positioned the grown-up as on the side of right and good. From the point of view of the child author, the adult was effective in achieving a desired end. This occurred in 25.9% of stories in which adults were involved in the child's conflict. In Chapter 5, we saw Ulysses in Example 5.6 after describing his experience of being suspended for fighting, declare that "ses then I have never did It agin becaus I do not want to go throw want I went throw last time." Ulysses' story presents his punishment as achieving the desired effect. For fourth-grader York, however, suspension was not so effective: "and then both of us got on punishment which didn't work because we still get into it," and this was the case in 12.7% of conflict stories describing adult involvement. Sixty-one percent of the time, however, children described the role of the adult in their conflict without any evaluative comments, so that we do not know how the child assessed the adult's role. In Figure 6.1, we see that children's inclination to use the moral authority of authorship to assess the effectiveness of the adults in their stories differed, depending on the role those adults played. When they chose to tell us about conflicts in which they described adults as enforcers (and especially when adults enforced violently by administering any kind of corporal punishment), children were much more likely to remain silent on the matter of the effectiveness or the appropriateness of the adult behavior than when they positioned the adults in their conflicts as consultants who made suggestions or gave advice.

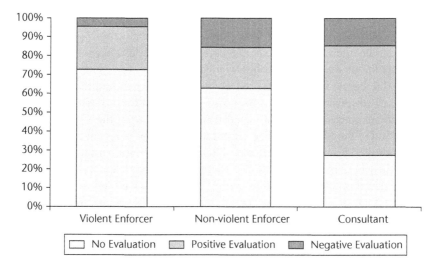

FIGURE 6.1   Children's evaluation of adults depending on the role of adults in the conflict

In the sections below, we examine first the three main ways that children described adults. Following this, we discuss previous research in this area, and we consider how cultural differences in parenting behaviors and differences in the educational philosophies that guide school disciplinary policies might have influenced the way our young authors described adults in their stories. We show how the role of adults in children's conflict narratives is related both to children's moral maturation and to the philosophies that direct adults' approaches to the socialization of children.

How Children Described Adults

Separate from their evaluation of adults as effective (positive) or ineffective (negative) authority figures, children who put adults in their story positioned them in three main ways: as enforcers and adversaries (where authors described resistance to the efforts of adults to control them), as enforcers and allies (where authors recognized the value of adult control), and as consultants (where authors sought advice, information, or suggestions from adults to solve problems).

"My mom came and washed my mouth with soap":
Adults as Enforcers and Adversaries

Children sometimes chafe under the expectations adults have for their behavior. In school, they are required to manage their biological, cognitive, emotional, and social needs in accordance with rules and standards established by others. They must 'sit still and pay attention' when this facilitates the classroom enterprise, not when it suits their own interests and energy levels. Adults have many ways to overrule the un-socialized impulses of children. Grown-ups control most of the material resources in most of the settings in which children find themselves, and this was a major source of coercive power in many of the stories children told. In 41.9% of conflict stories that included an adult character, the adult meted out some kind of punishment, and 32.5% of the time that punishment took the form of removal of privileges or the imposition of some unwanted but non-violent consequence. Children reported, for example, that they were required to miss recess, that they were given extra chores, or that they were restricted from use of the phone or video games. They told about official school suspensions – a word that was delightfully opaque for our young writers: they wrote about being spended, dispended, sensed, dispensed, and one special misbehaver was given a three-day pension. Most of the time, as can be seen in Figure 6.1, children did not venture an evaluation of adults in these situations, and when they did, they were about equally likely to consider the punishment appropriate as inappropriate (as we noted above with the comparison of Ulysses and York). Even when children made it clear in their stories that the adult was mistaken or that the punishment was undeserved, they rarely made explicit criticisms of the adult. This is illustrated in Example 6.1.

EXAMPLE 6.1 OPHELIA, FIFTH-GRADE GIRL, IRONWOOD ELEMENTARY, MEMPHIS

One day my mom called me into her room. "Your cousin just called and told me that you told her that their was no Santa Claus, is that true?" she asked. "No." I replied "Well I don't think that she would just call me and tell me a lie!" my mom said. "She is only six years old." "Well I didn't tell her that!" I shouted. Then my mom grounded me for the rest of the day for yelling. The next few days my mom got more calls form Quinn telling her that I said that their was no toothfairs and that their was a witch in her closet and things like that. Everyday she called was another day that I was grounded. The very next day, over my grandma's house I asked her why did she lie on me. and she said "I don't know!" After that I made her tell my mom everything from beginning to end. She never did anything like that again.

This author has to deal with an adult who is clearly getting it wrong. Poor Ophelia is grounded, first for saying something she did not say, and then for expressing her frustration at not being believed. She is in a terrible predicament, because every day her cousin calls and the punishment is extended. Ophelia criticizes her cousin's behavior and seeks to find a motive by asking, "why did you lie on me?" Ultimately, she is able to get the cousin to confess to the mother. Notice, however, that Ophelia does not in any way criticize her mother. The wrongdoer in the story is the cousin.

The realization that grown-ups can make mistakes may constitute an insight with considerable importance for moral development, as when the teacher in Robin's story in Example 1.3 called down the wrong child. Sometimes a child author seemed to be amused at catching an adult in a mistake, as when a teacher called down the wrong child for making a funny noise, to the delight of all the knowing classmates. In other stories, as we saw in Chapter 5, the shortcomings of the adult are not so amusing. We read stories about fathers who drink too much, stories about parental extramarital affairs, and stories about family fights that involved weapons and threaten serious violence. We have seen that a critical power given to children as we encourage them to author their own stories is the authority of a moral voice. The tentative first steps toward claiming this authority may be taken when a child creates a story about an occasion in which a parent or teacher is positioned as wrong. Here the authority of authorship is pitted against the authority of adulthood. It is not surprising that we see only halting steps toward claiming a moral voice in such stories. See how Owen describes his father's mistake in Example 6.2, a story he told in a KidsTalk session at a summer camp.

EXAMPLE 6.2   OWEN, FIFTH-GRADE BOY, FLASH CAMP, MEMPHIS

One time that wasn't fair was when – was when my family lost – lost one of the chargers and we were all looking for it and we can't – and we couldn't find it. And so the next day they said that I'm grounded, and I said, "You don't even know it's me!" Then my dad started yelling at me. And then, and then later that day after school, we said, "Maybe it's in one of our pockets." And then my dad went to his drawer and checked one of the pockets, and the charger was in there. Yeah, so he got the talk from my mom.

Owen is fully in control of his story, using direct and indirect quotation and dramatic voicing when presenting his own position ("you Don't even know it's me!" and "maybe it's in one of our pockets"). He underlines his own vindication with the assertion, "Yeah," and he articulates the words "the talk" with dramatic emphasis. More interesting than Owen's account of his father's mistake was the reaction of the other children in the KidsTalk circle. The report that Owen's dad got "the talk" from Owen's mom elicited giggles, followed by questions. "Did your dad say sorry?" "Were you still grounded?" A story in which a grown-up admits to a mistake and rescinds a punishment, and even gets reproached by the mom – this is a story that held the rapt attention of the other campers.

It was unusual for children to criticize adults in stories where the adult used non-violent coercions such as grounding, and it is even more rare for them to do so when they choose to tell us about occasions when adults used physical violence to punish. We found that 13.0% of the stories that positioned adults as enforcers (9.5% of all the stories that included adults) were reports about adult violence that was explained as punishment. Authors or their siblings or classmates got whoopings, whoppings, whippings, spankings, beatings, beat-downs, and paddlings. Corporal punishments were administered by parents, teachers, and principals. Physical violence, used by adults to punish children, was reported in each of our samples – in the Southeastern United States and in Southeastern China, in summer camps serving professional families and in community centers serving homeless children, in well-resourced university-affiliated schools, and in central-city schools designated by the state as "failing." In all of these settings, our young authors described this kind of physical violence by adults without questioning the legitimacy of these punishments. Although children used their narratives to criticize adults and to evaluate the behavior of adults in some circumstances, they rarely did this when they told about adults using physical violence as a punishment (only five times in 123 stories that included physical punishment). When children did venture a moral evaluation of punishment violence, their analysis did not exhibit insight about either their own or the adult's motives or culpability. Consider Example 6.3.

EXAMPLE 6.3   CLIFTON, SIXTH-GRADE BOY, IRONWOOD ELEMENTARY, MEMPHIS

When I was in second grade I came to school and we had a substitute. His name was Mr. Deangelo. After he introduced himself he told us to read a story from a story book. After I read the story I picked up a book of my choice and read it. Mr. Deangelo came over to me and asked me why I was reading a different book. I told that I was all read it, but he didn't listen. He picked up all of my books and threw them. Later in the day I axcidentally drop my pencil. I got out of my desk to get it. When I bent down Br. Deangelo hit me in the back with ruler. Luckily I got to leave early that day because of a doctor appointment.

Clifton creates a coherent story, telling us clearly what happened. He tells us that Mr. Deangelo did not listen – but this is the closest we get to an evaluative assessment. The child describes what we take to be inappropriate violence by an adult (throwing books, hitting on the back with a ruler), and he considers himself lucky to leave the class early, but Clifton does not make any explicit evaluation of his teacher's misbehavior. Typical of the stories that describe punishment violence, this child seems to recognize the practice as a fact of life. Escaping it is a matter of luck. The only critique we saw of punishment violence was that the grown-up was 'mean,' as Freddy tells us in Example 6.4.

EXAMPLE 6.4 Freddy, third-grade boy, Winterton Elementary, Memphis

EXAMPLE 6.4 FREDDY, THIRD-GRADE BOY, WINTERTON ELEMENTARY, MEMPHIS

When I was three years old I first went to dacare. The first thing I did was play with toys. The next day I met the assestant teacher. She was mean and I can prove it. She hit us with a belt when we came in from outside. But I'm glad that I faked crying. I couldn't wate for my guaguwation.

Freddy is remembering an event from his daycare, which he situates in the distant past – five years ago. Recognizing that (indeed, hoping that) this violence might not have actually happened in exactly the way Freddy describes it, we are nonetheless struck by the matter-of-factness with which Freddy recounts a teacher hitting children with a belt. He doesn't feel a need to tell us details that might help us understand why the teacher would do this. Freddy recounts the incident only to convince us of his assertion that the teacher was mean. Freddy reports that he faked crying, presumably to minimize the violence against him, and, like Clifton, he reports about his means to an escape (his graduation).

Stories are told when something report-worthy happens, and in this sense, our stories of punishment violence assure us that children did not see these events as so typical that they didn't bother to report them. Indeed, it was not unusual, as in the two stories above, for children to tell us about punishments that happened in previous grades, indicating that the events were salient enough to be remembered as report-worthy for a long time. Nevertheless, we were struck by the ordinariness the children seemed to ascribe to whoppings and whippings and beat-downs by parents, teachers, and principals. These punishments never provoked a story rich in the kind of moral analysis we saw in Example 1.2 from fourth-grader Warren, who told us that he "had a chance to consider" what he had done. Unlike Clifton and Freddy, Warren reported that he "thought about the boy and myself. I compared him to me, and really he isn't such a bad guy. When I really thought about it we were both wrong. I decided to be the better man and apologize." Warren used his narrative to do an evaluative critique of self and other. Children who wrote about punishment violence never did this. A description of a whipping by an adult seemed to obviate the need for the kind of reflective self-examination that Warren did.

"So he got suspended not me": Adults as Enforcers and Allies

Children sometimes reported about their own or their peers' resistance to adult authority, as we saw above. Sometimes, however, children wrote about occasions in which they embraced the rules and made strategic use of adult authority to induce compliance by their peers. There were stories in which children delight in the punishment justly rained upon their antagonists. There were stories in which the children confidently turned to adults to make amends when they have been wronged.

In Example 6.5, we see a child thinking strategically about how to use adult punishment to achieve his own ends.

EXAMPLE 6.5 DEMARKUS, SIXTH-GRADE BOY, IRONWOOD ELEMENTARY, MEMPHIS

One day last year at lunch Noble was checking me as usual. I got tired at it after about fifteen minutes so I checked him back. The reason I didn't tell was because the lunch lady Ms. Brown never listened to me. Noble got very offeded by my checking him and gave me a nasty look. later that day in the looker room he shoved me in a locker. I decided not to fight back so Noble would get suspended and not me. Noble got caught and was in trouble. As far me, I didn't recieve a scratch even though he still says he beat me up.

Demarkus describes the calculations he used in determining when to make use of adult enforcers. It's no use to tell the lunch lady, because "she never listened to me." Instead of reporting to Ms. Brown, Demarkus retaliated with more name-calling, which left Noble "very offended." Later, Demarkus again thinks strategically about how adult power might be used in his situation. The reason he gives for deciding "not to fight back" was so that "Noble would get suspended." Demarkus reports his success in manipulating this situation so that Noble "was in trouble," and he himself "didn't recieve a scratch." This author is able to make a coherent narrative, with ample attention to the reader's need to understand his own motives (he "got tired" of Noble's checking; he reported his "reason" for not telling on Noble in the first instance, and he gives us the basis for his decision in the second incident he reports). Demarkus is attentive to his antagonist's facial expression ("a nasty look") and his emotional experience ("Noble got very offeded"). With this level of narrative coherence and psychological mindedness, we might expect to see a sophisticated moral analysis, but the full extent of Demarkus' moral deliberations is a report of who did and did not get punished. As with the stories we considered above where children positioned the adults as adversaries, we find that reports of adult punishment seemed to suppress children's own moral voice, even when the child aligns the self with the adult.

Sometimes children presented themselves as fully justified in seeking the power of an adult to bring an antagonist in line. There are other occasions, however, in which seeking an adult is constituted as "tattling" or "telling on," a behavior that was clearly devalued by children and sometimes by adults. Candace struggles with this in Example 6.6.

EXAMPLE 6.6 CANDACE, THIRD-GRADE GIRL, COLLEGE ELEMENTARY, MEMPHIS

Once my friend Amiko didn't act like a friend. We were outside for recess. Amiko and I were playing tag. Well, she must have got the idea that if she hurts me she can make me do whatever she wants me to do. We didn't what to play tag anymore, so we had to think of something else to do. She said hide-and-go-seek. But I didn't what to play hide-and-go-seek. So Amiko took my hand and started scratching me! She had sharp nails so it really hurt. So I said "Okay, Okay"! That went on for a week. And everytime I thought about telling on Amiko, I kept saying to myself, "If I tell on Amiko then she won't be my friend anymore. I told my mom and she said "Candace, just do what's right." I couldn't take it anymore so I told on Amiko. She was mad for a few days, but finally I said "I don't like fighting with you"! So we made up and were friends agian. And Amiko, promised not to hurt me anymore.

The End

Candace tells about her struggle with a decision about whether to tell her teacher about her friend's abusive behavior. She orients to two norms here – a norm that gives the teacher responsibility for ensuring civility between the children, and a norm that denigrates 'telling on' as an offense that could end a friendship. Her indecisiveness about this dilemma led her to endure her friend's violent behavior for a week while she tried to decide whether to make use of adult authority. She discussed the matter with her mom, positioned as a consultant rather than as an enforcer in this story. We are not sure what the mom's "just do what's right" advice meant to Candace, but the mother seems to have expressed confidence in Candace's ability to resolve her dilemma.

> Write a true story about a time when a friend did not act like a friend. Tell everything you can remember about what happened from the beginning to the end. *If you need more room, you can use the back of this paper.*
>
> Once my friend ██████ didn't act like a friend. We were outside for recess ███ and I were playing tag. Well, she must have got the idea that if she hurts me she can make me do whatever she wants me to do. We didn't what to play tag anymore, so we had to think of something else to do. She said hide-and-go-seek. But I didn't what to play hide-and-go-seek. So ███ took my hand and started scratching me. She had sharp nails so it really hurt. So I said "Okay, Okay." That went on for a week. And everytime I thought about telling on ████ I kept saying to myself, "If I tell on ████, then she won't be my friend anymore. I told my mom, and she said "████ just do what's right." I couldn't take it anymore so I told on ████ she was mad for a few days, but finally I said "I don't like fighting with you". So we made up and were friends again. And ████ promised not to hurt me anymore.
>
> The End

EXAMPLE 6.6 Candace, third-grade girl, College Elementary, Memphis

Many children, like Candace, reported uncertainty about the appropriateness of "telling on." Sometimes, their reports described adults who were reluctant to get involved with the everyday spats that they expected children to handle without assistance. Fourth-grader Edward quoted his mother as saying "Just settle this" when he and his sister were arguing about which TV show to watch. Third-grader Penny told Mrs. Ronda that her friend Alyssa S had called her ugly, but the teacher, Penny reported, "said we need to work it out on our own." We suspect that adults feel uncertain about how to balance their responsibility to help children solve problems with their belief that children need to practice their own conflict resolution skills. This balance has undoubtedly tipped in the direction of more adult oversight of and intervention in peer conflicts as we have become increasingly concerned about bullying. Many anti-bullying programs include a component designed to overcome a culture of silence, not by encouraging children to report to adults, but by empowering bystanders to show empathy toward victims and to feel self-efficacy for defending them (Kärnä, Voeten, Little, Poskiparta, Kaljonen, & Salmivalli, 2011). Highly skilled classroom teachers monitor peer relations closely enough to be able to make sound judgments about which conflicts children should be allowed to struggle with, which conflicts require adult guidance or advice, and which require the full authority of adults who should enforce standards of acceptable behavior. Notice, however, that this requires attending to the developing social skills and fluctuating social relationships among twenty or thirty individuals, sometimes more. And promoting the development of healthy relationships is not generally taken to be the teachers' first priority. We stand in awe of those dedicated and talented teachers who manage to balance their responsibilities to teach academic content and skills with a commitment to nurturing a classroom community in which children get better and better at forming relationships and at managing the conflicts that are a part of human relationships. We argue in Part III of this book that a classroom practice of story-sharing and a focus on writing personal narratives can help teachers achieve this.

"I talked to my mom whose great at solving problems": Adults as Consultants

Candace positioned her teacher as an enforcer in her story, expecting her to put an end to Amiko's violence. Candace's mother, however, was positioned as a consultant, expected to give advice about how the conflict should be handled. Later in elementary school, we saw more and more children writing about situations in which they turned to adults to help them understand or resolve their problems. Two children in our Shenzhen sample wrote about the same incident, each of them giving somewhat different versions of their own role in the fighting, but both giving very similar accounts of the teacher's intervention.

EXAMPLE 6.7 LI QUAN, SIXTH-GRADE BOY, CHUNTIAN PRIMARY SCHOOL, SHENZHEN

Last Friday, we had PE class. I saw one classmate Zhang Jin-Yun playing on the slide, teacher told us, don't play on the slide, So I came up there and pushed him jokingly. After we came down, he hit my back really hard, I started to chase him, And then I was out of energy, I started doing something else. But he came to me and hit me several times, I was angry, chased him down. He ran to a sandpit and grabbed sand in his hand, and poured it on me. The sand went into my eyes, and my whole body turns yellow. I finally chased him down, and beat him up. But he came to me again and hit me several times, and ran away. I took his bag, stepped on it with my foot, He ran to me and slapped me harshly, and stepped on my bag. I couldn't catch him during the chase, so the only thing I can do was to tell the teacher. I came to teacher's office, and reported this to the teacher. Teacher asked me to find him, I came down, just saw him, So I asked him to go to the office, So I went to do my things. After ten minutes, one classmate asked me to go to the office. When got there, teacher wanted us to retell what happened, Then I found that I was wrong pushing him in the beginning, And I stepped on his bag, his glasses were in his bag, the glasses became blur because I stepped on the bag. In the end, the teacher reconciled us, we made up. Through this story, I found that I had many shortcomings, like I don't know the degree of seriousness when I make jokes, But he has faults too.

平日，每个人都可能会与别人发生矛盾。请回忆自己亲身经历的一次矛盾冲突，和同学，兄弟姐妹，朋友，或邻居的小朋友等都可以（和大人的冲突除外），无论发生在学校，家里，社区或别的地方都行。这个冲突可以是意见不和，争吵，误会，或相互动手等等。请如实写下事情的经过，包括你能记起的所有细节（如何开始，中间都发生什么事情，结果怎样，你的感受如何等等）。

上星期五，我们上体育课。我看到同学 ▮▮▮▮▮ 在滑滑梯上玩，老师说过，不准我们在滑滑梯上玩，我就上去开玩笑地推他一下。下去后，他一下子猛打我的背，我就开始追他，后来跑的没力了，又停下来做别的事。没想到他又打了我好几下，我愤怒了，追着他不放。他跑到沙池那里抓了一大把沙子，一下子撒在我身上，我的眼睛进了沙子，身上也变成黄色的了，我终于追上他，狠打了他一顿，没想到他又追上来又揍了我好几下，又跑了。我拿到他的书包，用力踩几脚，他跑过来使劲拍了我一巴掌，然后又踩我的书包。我追不上他，只好去告老师。

我来到老师办公室向老师报告了这件事，老师叫他上来，我下去，刚好看见他，就叫他去，我就去做自己的事了。过了五分钟，一个同学叫我上去老师办公室，到了老师办公室，老师叫我们俩对正，结果里发现是我推的那一下的错，而且我踩了他的书包，他的眼镜在书包里，被我踩得变得有点模糊了。最后，在老师的劝说下，我们又和好了。

通过这件事，我发现自身上的很多缺点，比如开玩笑不知轻重等等，但是他也有不对之处。

EXAMPLE 6.7 Li Quan, sixth-grade boy, ChunTian Primary School, Shenzhen

EXAMPLE 6.8 ZHANG JIN-YUN, FIFTH-GRADE BOY, CHUNTIAN PRIMARY SCHOOL

One day, during PE class, I was near by the corner of a slide, One classmate came by, and said, "teacher said we can't play on the slide, I'll tell teacher later." After hearing that, I walked up and down on the slide intentionally. My classmate was irritated by me, came and pushed me, I fell down on the ground. I rushed to hit him, and ran away, My classmate couldn't chase me down, stood at where I left, gnashed his teeth in anger. He tried to break my backpack, But couldn't find it, I stuck my tongue out And he couldn't do anything to me. My other classmate came over, and asked, "what was going on?" My classmate said, "where is his backpack?" He pointed me. That classmate took him to where my backpack was, he took my backpack hit and broke it. Because there was a glasses in my backpack, I came to him and beat him once, And he never touched my backpack again, instead he came to our teacher to help. Our teacher came to me and taught me a lesson. And asked me to make it up with him, in fact both of us had fault, we shouldn't be that impulsive, should think calmly, and solve the problems.

Although Li Quan seems at first to orient to the teacher as an enforcer ("I came to teacher's office, and reported this to the teacher"), both Li Quan and Zhang Jin-Yun describe a teacher who clearly takes a consultant role. Both report that the teacher "asked them" rather than "told them" what to do in this situation. Li Quan reports that the teacher wanted the boys to "retell what happened," and "through this story" he was able to see both his own shortcomings and those of his antagonist. Each of these young authors claims his own moral voice, establishing blame and considering what they should have done in the situation.

As we see in Figure 6.1, when children positioned adults as consultants in their stories, they were much more likely to take an evaluative stance than when they positioned adults as enforcers of standards. It may be that the rise in the tendency to see adults this way coincides with a rise in critical faculties. We saw in Chapters 3 and 4 that children tend to create challenges for themselves in domains of current developmental importance. When they are setting out to understand the obligations of friendship, they participate in practices that challenge loyalty and intimacy. When they are making early steps toward developing an identity, they participate in name-calling and insult practices that require them to defend a sense of self. When children chose to write about conflicts in which they positioned adults as consultants, we again saw them creating challenges for themselves in a key developmental domain. In the late elementary school years, many children are expending their capacity for moral evaluation, coming to understand themselves as participants in a system of rights and responsibilities that is not simply handed down to them. They take up the challenge of participating in the moral discourse of their cultural communities

平日，每个人都可能会与别人发生矛盾。请回忆自己亲身经历的一次矛盾冲突，和同学，兄弟姐妹，朋友，或邻居的小朋友等都可以（和大人的冲突除外），无论发生在学校，家里，社区或别的地方都行。这个冲突可以是意见不和，争吵，误会，或相互动手等等。请如实写下事情的经过，包括你能记起的所有细节（如何开始，中间都发生什么事情，结果怎样，你的感受如何等等）。

一天，在上体育课时，我在滑滑梯的一个角落，我的同学走过来，说："老师说不能玩滑滑梯，等一下我去告老师。"听到这番话，我就故意在滑滑梯上走上走下。同学被我激怒了，走过来推了我一下，我摔在了地上。我冲上去打了他一下，就跑了，同学追不上我，站在原地，咬牙切齿。他企图去砸我的书包，可是书包找不到了，我正朝他吐了吐舌头，可他就是奈不了我何。我们班的另一个同学过去，问："怎么了？"同学说："他的书包在哪？"他指了指我，那位同学把他带到我放书包的地方，拿起我的书包一顿砸、踢。因为书包里放着眼镜，我冲上去打了他一下，他并没有再动我的书包了，而是去找班主任来帮忙。

老师找我上去训话，并让我与他和好，其实大家都有错，不该这么冲动，要冷静思考，学会解决问题。

EXAMPLE 6.8 Zhang Jin-Yun, fifth-grade boy, ChunTian Primary School

(Miller & Goodnow, 1995; Turiel, 2002). If this is a potent area of developmental change, it is not surprising that children select conflicts to write about that include adults as consultants, and that they took on the challenge of evaluating those adults in a way that younger children did not.

More often than not, the adults in these stories come out looking pretty good. Child authors were especially appreciative of mothers, who were mentioned as consultants more often than other adults and were less often criticized than teachers or other school authorities. Nevertheless, we did see children making critiques in consultant stories that we did not see in the punishment stories. The most common critique children made when they positioned adults as consultants was that the grown-up was too busy, or was unwilling to help or to take the problem seriously. Sixth-grader Debra gave a barely coherent description of a peer group problem involving multiple insults with children taking sides and switching allegiance. She reported, "The next day every one got into a big cluique and I'm thinking 'Why won't our teacher help us?'" When fifth-grader Vivienne reported going to her teacher when a friend started a rumor that she was racist, the author reported that the teacher just said, "Well that's silly," making no effort to use the opportunity to help the children understand racism or to deal with inter-group conflict. In Example 6.9, we see an author report serious negative consequences of the adults' unwillingness to engage with the children to solve a problem.

EXAMPLE 6.9 GARRICK, FIFTH-GRADE BOY, IRONWOOD ELEMENTARY, MEMPHIS

Last year at my old school riverbrook I got into a fight with this arbino kid who was always messing with other people. sence he had eye had some problem he was always around the teacher. So he thouht he could get away from kid who were going to get him. Every time someone told the teacher about Nicolas she would say "well I haven't seen him do anything to you". That was because he did it every she turned her head. So we told the principle. She did nothing. So we began to take things in our own hands. One week the teacher asked me and him to help her with the science hall of fame project our class was doing. When the teach left he stated talking about family and stuff I ignored it. But when he hit me it was all over. I warned him to run before I get up he run right for the the principle office But I cought him and Beat him down.

This child reports multiple attempts by different students to elicit help from the teacher with antisocial behavior by a child with special needs. When the teacher dismissed the children's concerns, they went to the principal, who also "did nothing," as far as this young author could see. Garrick seems to have recognized that more than ordinary peer group sanctions were called for to solve the problem with Nicolas. We have to respect his wisdom in seeking assistance from first a teacher and then a principal to handle a problem that called for special sensitivity. When both of the grown-ups declined to address the problem, this sixth-grader and his friends began "to take the problem in our own hands." The result was violence against a child who was clearly facing serious challenges to his social adjustment. Children made critiques in consultant stories that we did not see in the punishment stories and we believe that a movement toward a consultant-like relationship with adults coincided with a move toward greater moral autonomy. We elaborate on our rationale for this interpretation in the following section.

How Researchers Have Described Adult Roles in Children's Conflicts

We have seen above that children most often positioned adults as enforcers, but that they became more likely to talk about adults as consultants as they moved into the fifth and sixth grades. We have also seen that child authors did not often evaluate the behavior of the adults they describe, except when they positioned the adults as consultants rather than as enforcers. Compared to stories that did not include reports of punishment violence, when children wrote about this type of violence in their stories, they were even less likely to evaluate and they almost never criticized the adults who meted out such punishment. In the sections below, we will consider how children's characterizations of the adults in their stories coincide with research on adult socialization behaviors.

Enforcers and Consultants as Authoritarian and Authoritative Parents

Over forty years of research on the ways parents try to socialize their children have been strongly influenced by a framework developed by Diana Baumrind (1971, 2013), whose observations and interviews of North American middle-class families in the late 1960s found that parenting practices of about 75% of families could be classified in three styles. Authoritarian parents valued obedience and they believed that strong and clear exercise of parental authority (often by use of coercion and harsh punishment) is required to make their children compliant with high expectations for appropriate behavior. Our 'adult as enforcer' stories seem to describe such adults. Permissive parents, by stark contrast, took a largely 'hands-off' approach, believing that most misbehavior is to be expected as a natural part of childhood and that it will be abandoned as the children get older. (Our authors did not write about interactions with adults that took this form.) A third parenting style that Baumrind called 'authoritative' was grounded in a collaborative approach, in which parents and children negotiate to establish consequences for violations of mutually agreed-upon rules for behavior. This type of parenting granted the child the freedom to voice discontent or frustration with parental decisions, the freedom to critique. When authors in our study described adults as consultants, the grown-ups looked a bit like these authoritative parents described by Baumrind.

Children's responses to these differences in socialization efforts have been studied extensively, looking at such child outcomes as academic performance (Areepattamannil, 2010), social, emotional, and relational success (Steinberg, Elmen, & Mounts, 1989), and performance on tests of moral judgment (Grusec & Goodnow, 1994). Most of these studies, especially those conducted with middle-class North American children, have shown that authoritative parenting produces children who are curious, sociable, and independent. By contrast, children whose parents took an authoritarian approach showed less self-control, less social competence, and had less academic success. (For thorough reviews of this research, see Baumrind, 2013; Bugental & Grusec, 2006; Parke & Buriel, 2006.) Although we did not have individual data about specific parenting styles used with the children in our samples, our finding that children who described grown-ups in the role of enforcers included less sophisticated moral analysis in their stories than children who described occasions in which they approached an adult as a consultant is consistent with findings that authoritarian as compared to authoritative behavior by adults suppresses moral development.

Research on the effects of corporal punishment on children has often shown that physical punishment suppresses both cognitive and social development (Benjet & Kazdin, 2003; Berlin, Malone, Ayoub, Ispa, Fine, & Brooks-Gunn, 2009.) A recent meta-analysis by Gershoff and Grogan-Kaylor (2016) found a link between spanking and increased risk for unfavorable child outcomes in the majority of studies included. MacKenzie, Nicklas, Waldfogel, and Brooks-Gunn (2011) found negative effects of physical punishment across ethnic groups and family circumstances. These authors noted a need for future research investigating the way children and parents make meaning of these disciplinary practices. Again, our data did not include information about which children were spanked or how often. What we did see, however, was how children used narrative, their most powerful meaning-making practice, to make sense of occasions in which they were subjected to violent punishment. What we saw was substantial impoverishment of the children's moral analysis when they chose to tell us about getting spanked or slapped or whooped.

How Children in Different Communities Described Adults

The communities in which we collected children's stories differed in many ways, including differences in the underlying philosophy that guided the approach to discipline and behavior 'management.' Of the six schools where children wrote stories for us, only two (the university-affiliated school and the ethnically diverse school in central Florida) took a constructivist approach to education and a clearly collaborative approach to discipline. This approach entailed teacher behavior that encouraged the children as collaborators, so that they agreed upon classroom rules and the children were encouraged to think of behavior management as a joint project requiring the cooperation of all class members. In one of these two schools there was a strong emphasis on emotion coaching, with a "safe zone" in each classroom, and with training for all staff (lunchroom staff, bus drivers, etc.) in disciplinary practices that emphasized self-control by each child rather than adult control of the children. In the other four schools there was considerably more variation by class, with some teachers taking a much more authoritarian approach than others. Three of those four schools made frequent use of corporal punishment, and even though two of them had peer mediation programs in place, there was a clear expectation that adults were in charge of maintaining order. The community center and the summer camp where we collected oral narratives all took a collaborative approach to discipline.

Early research that attempted to extend Baumrind's findings about the effects of authoritarian parenting to families in different countries and from different ethnic backgrounds raised the possibility that the negative effects of authoritarian parenting might apply primarily to middle-class North American families (Dornbusch, Ritter, Leiderman, Roberts, & Fraleigh, 1987), with recent immigrant families who used strict discipline and demanded obedience having children who did well academically (Chao, 2001). Important refinements to Baumrind's categories were prompted by studies of African American, "no-nonsense" parenting which combined high levels of parental control with high levels of nurturance and affection (Brody & Murry, 2001). As researchers in this area have produced conflicting results, sometimes affirming the advantages of authoritative parental behaviors across communities and sometimes affirming the cultural specificity of the negative effects of authoritarian styles (Sorkhabi & Mandara, 2013; Rudy & Grusec, 2006), it has become increasingly clear that we need to understand better how children make sense of the efforts their parents make to control them.

We found that children in settings where the adults engaged in more collaborative, consultative practices with children told more stories in which they positioned adults as consultants than did children in the schools that relied on more authoritarian disciplinary practices. Nevertheless, we saw children in the fifth and sixth grades, across the different communities, more likely to position the adults in their stories as consultants than did the third and fourth graders. On the cusp of adolescence, these older elementary school children may have shared more stories about adult consultants because these interactions were more in line with their strivings for autonomy (Ryan & Deci, 2000). In some cases, we saw these needs supported and encouraged by consultants (e.g., "I told my mom and she helped comfort me") and in others they were dismissed or ignored (e.g., "So we told the principle. She did nothing"). In each of our settings, when children told us about adults as consultants, they used their narratives to do more sense-making work, including more moral evaluation in consultant stories than in enforcer stories.

 Some early studies on the impact of corporal punishment found negative effects for middle-class European American children but not for children in economically distressed African American families (Deater-Deckard, Dodge, Bates, & Petit, 1996). Some scholars interpreted this research to mean that in cultural contexts in which physical punishment was an expected and culturally condoned part of parental practices, its impact on children would not be negative (Gershoff, Grogan-Kaylor, Lansford, Chang, Zelli, & Deater-Deckard, 2010). Consistent with this research and with reports that spanking rates in the US remain high (Child Trends Databank, 2015), the child authors in our studies virtually never criticized the harsh punishments of their parents and teachers. (The only exception to this were a few stories where a child considered it unfair that he got a beating while his sister did not, and a few stories, discussed above, in which the punishing adult was called 'mean.') Children seemed to accept corporal punishment as a legitimate practice, and this was true in all eight of the community settings where we collected data.

More recent, large-sample research on physical punishment, however, which has taken into account economic stress, parent education, and region of the country, has found a similarly negative impact of corporal punishment on children, regardless of race or ethnicity (Berlin et al., 2009; MacKenzie et al., 2011). In our research, we do not have the kind of data that could confirm the findings that children who are subjected to punishment violence are more aggressive, perform less well in school, or have poorer self-regulation skills. What we did see, however, was that in every community we studied, there were children who made narrative accounts of this kind of violence, and in every racial and ethnic group, when they produced these stories, they made reports without moral evaluation. They did not criticize the grown-ups who punished them, but they also did not engage in any evaluation of the behavior for which they were punished.

Conclusions

Developing their own moral voice, and becoming participants in the moral discourse of their own cultural community, may require children to step back from a view in which adults are the arbiters of right and wrong. At some point, maturity requires an acceptance of one's own moral authority. In early childhood, moral authority of parents and other adults is closely linked to their power over nearly every aspect of the child's life. As they come to make sense of a wide range of interpersonal conflicts, however, children will discover that moral authority and coercive power are not inexorably linked. This realization comes in halting steps. It may begin with the amusing recognition that the adults could be wrong. We saw children taking tentative steps toward evaluating the adults they put in their stories. They rarely ventured such evaluations when they told about adults giving commands or administering punishments. When they told about adults who gave advice or explanations or support or comfort, children were much more likely to take on the moral authority of authorship.

Children who contributed stories for our studies came from communities that differed in cultural practices pertaining to child discipline. Differences between school communities and family circumstances are certainly important, and much previous research has shown the influences of these variables on many developmental 'outcomes.' We found, however, more impressive similarities across samples than differences. We found stories about adults as enforcers dominating in all samples. We found a small number of stories of punishment violence in all samples and remarkable similarities across the community settings in the ways children reported such violence without evaluation. Children in all eight samples seemed to be moving with age toward a view of adults as people they should go to for support and council.

References

Areepattamannil, S. (2010). Parenting practices, parenting style, and children's school achievement. *Psychological Studies, 55*(4), 283–89. doi:10.1007/s12646-010-0043-0.

Baumrind, D. (1971). Current patterns of parental authority. *Developmental Psychology Monographs, 4*, 1–103.

Baumrind, D. (2013). Authoritative parenting revisited. In R. Larzelere, A. Morris, & A. Harrist (Eds.), *Authoritative parenting*. Washington, DC: APA Books.

Benjet, C., & Kazdin, A. E. (2003). Spanking children: The controversies, findings, and new directions. *Clinical Psychology Review, 23*, 197–224.

Berlin, L. J., Malone, P. S., Ayoub, C. A., Ispa, J., Fine, M., & Brooks-Gunn, J. (2009). Correlates and consequences of spanking and verbal punishment for low income White, African American, and Mexican American toddlers. *Child Development, 80*, 1403–20.

Bornstein, M. H., & Cheah, C. S. (2006). The place of "culture and parenting" in the ecological contextual perspective on developmental science. In K. H. Rubin & O. Boon Chung (Eds.), *Parenting beliefs, behaviors, and parent-child relations: A cross-cultural perspective* (pp. 3–33). New York, NY: Psychology Press.

Brody, G. H., & Murry, V. M. (2001). Sibling socialization of competence in rural, single-parent African American families. *Journal of Marriage and the Family, 63,* 996–1008.

Bugental, D. B., & Grusec, J. E. (2006). Socialization processes. In N. Eisenberg (Vol. Ed.), *Handbook of child psychology: Vol. 3. Social, emotional, and personality development* (pp. 366–428). New York, NY: Wiley.

Chao, R. K. (2001). Extending research on the consequences of parenting style for Chinese Americans and European Americans. *Child Development, 72*(6), 1832–43.

Child Trends Databank. (2015). *Attitudes toward spanking*. Available at: http://www.childtrends.org/?indicators=attitudes-toward-spanking.

Deater-Deckard, K., Dodge, K. A., Bates, J. A., & Petit, G. S. (1996). Physical discipline among African American and European American mothers: Links to children's externalizing behaviors. *Developmental Psychology, 32*, 1065–72.

Dornbusch, S., Ritter, P., Leiderman, P., Roberts, D., & Fraleigh, M. (1987). The relation of parenting style to adolescent school performance. *Child Development, 58*(5), 1244–57.

Gershoff, E. T., Grogan-Kaylor, A., Lansford, J. E., Chang, L., Zelli, A., & Deater-Deckard, K. (2010). Parent discipline practices in an international sample: Associations with child behaviors and moderation by perceived normativeness. *Child Development, 81*, 487–502.

Gershoff, E. T., & Grogan-Kaylor, A. (2016). Spanking and child outcomes: Old controversies and new meta-analyses. *Journal of Family Psychology, 30*(4), 453–69.

Grusec, J. E., & Goodnow, J. J. (1994). Impact of parental discipline methods on the child's internalization of values: A reconceptualization of current points of view. *Developmental Psychology, 30*, 4–19.

Kärnä, A., Voeten, M., Little, T. D., Poskiparta, E., Kaljonen, A., & Salmivalli, C. (2011). A large-scale evaluation of the KiVa antibullying program: Grades 4–6. *Child Development, 82*(1), 311–30.

MacKenzie, M. J., Nicklas, E., Waldfogel, J., & Brooks-Gunn, J. (2011). Corporal punishment and child behavioural and cognitive outcomes through 5 years of age: Evidence from a contemporary urban birth cohort study. *Infant and Child Development*. Published online in Wiley Online Library (wileyonlinelibrary.com). doi:10.1002/icd.758.

Miller, P. J., & Goodnow, J. J. (1995). Cultural practices: Toward an integration of culture and development. In J. J. Goodnow, P. J. Miller, & F. Kessel (Eds.), *Cultural practices as contexts for development* (pp. 5–16). San Francisco, CA: Jossey-Bass.

Parke, R. D., & Buriel, R. (2006). Socialization in the family: Ethnic and ecological perspectives. In W. Damon & N. Eisenberg (Eds.), *Handbook of child development: Vol. 3. Social, emotional, and personality development* (6th ed., pp. 463–552). New York, NY: Wiley.

Rogoff, B. (2003). *The cultural nature of human development.* Oxford: Oxford University Press.

Rudy, D., & Grusec, J. E. (2006). Authoritarian parenting in individualist and collectivist groups: Associations with maternal emotion and cognition and children's self-esteem. *Journal of Family Psychology, 20*(1), 68–78.

Ryan, R. M., & Deci, E. L. (2000). Self-determination theory and the facilitation of intrinsic motivation, social development, and well-being. *American Psychologist, 55*(1), 68.

Sorkhabi, N., & Mandara, J. (2013). Are the effects of Baumrind's parenting styles culturally specific or culturally equivalent? In R. E. Larzelere, A. S. Morris, & A. W. Harrist (Eds.), *Authoritative parenting: Synthesizing nurturance and discipline for optimal child development* (pp. 113–35). Washington, DC: American Psychological Association.

Steinberg, L., Elmen, J. D., & Mounts, N. S. (1989). Authoritative parenting, psychosocial maturity, and academic success among adolescents. *Child Development, 60*, 1424–36.

Turiel, E. (2002). *The culture of morality: Social development, context, and conflict.* Cambridge: Cambridge University Press.

7

"LITTLE GIRL, I WAS NOT TALKING TO YOU!"

Taking on Gender in Middle Childhood

> but I said my Mom told me Never hit a girl and she hit me but I don't hit her I
> called my sister Blue foot and it was a cat fight
>
> *Keshaun, sixth-grade boy, Connors Elementary, Memphis*

Much of the previous research that has looked at gender in middle childhood has primarily asked questions about the differences between girls and boys. In what ways do girls and boys behave differently or perform differently or exhibit different propensities or capacities? Studies of peer aggression and peer relationships have been especially attentive to the possibility of gender difference and dozens of studies seeking to document these differences (or to dispute them) have provided us with plenty of fascinating reading (see a review by Rose & Rudolph, 2006). This stream of research is all the more fascinating because of the 'now you see it, now you don't' quality of many gender differences. In the first part of this chapter, we report on what we learned when we looked for gender differences in the stories children told us about their conflicts. How did stories by girl authors differ from stories by boy authors, and what can we conclude from those differences?

The more closely we looked for differences between stories by boy and girl authors, the more we came to understand that the gender-differences question might be diverting our attention from questions about the way gender was functioning in our stories. We came to a greater appreciation of the arguments of such feminist scholars as West and Zimmerman (1987) and Hare-Mustin and Maracek (1994) who encouraged us to focus on *how* and *when* gender came to be salient in day-to-day interactions. The second part of this chapter is an examination of what children *did* with gender in their stories about conflict. Here we see how and when children take on gender – in both senses of the expression 'take on.' Sometimes we see them adopting or embracing or enforcing gender; sometimes we see them dismantling or resisting or critiquing the gender system. We consider when children made gendered identity claims, and what they had to say about romance, sexuality, and the gendering of opportunity. The 'how did girls differ from boys?' question gets transformed into 'how does gender come into play in children's stories?'

Comparing Girls' Stories to Boys' Stories

When we looked for differences between stories authored by girls and those authored by boys, we were sometimes able to identify differences consistent with stereotypes about gender that tend to be dominant in current public discourse in North America.[1] For example, boys were more likely than girls to write about physical violence and to write about more severe or dangerous physical violence. This difference was statistically significant in most (although not all) of our samples. Girl authors in some samples (but not all) were more likely than boys to write about aggression that previous researchers have called relational or social (Crick, Casas, & Nelson, 2002; Underwood, 2003). These incidents concerned deliberate exclusion, gossip, and other efforts to hurt someone by damaging their social relationships as we described in Chapter 4. Girls and boys did not differ, on the other hand, in the tendency to produce stories that reported instances of name-calling or other verbal insults.[2]

Our gender-of-author comparisons were sometimes consistent with previous research (Buckner & Fivush, 1998; Reese, Haden, & Fivush, 1996) and with culturally dominant stereotypes in which girls (at least in some contexts[3]) are more attentive than boys to the emotional and relational contexts that give their stories meaning. In some of our samples boys gave significantly fewer reports of their own or others' emotions or mental states, and were less explicit in making moral evaluations than were girls. (These findings have been presented in Walton & Brewer, 2001 and Walton, Harris & Davidson, 2009.) Examples 7.1 and 7.2 present stories that exemplify these findings, the first by a girl author who writes about a dispute involving social aggression and the second by a boy who reports a physical fight.

EXAMPLE 7.1 TANYA, SIXTH-GRADE GIRL, IRONWOOD ELEMENTARY, MEMPHIS

One afternoon alot of my friends and I were at the library. Every thing was going just fine until a girl name Amber started to talk about me. I did not care because she was just playing little girl games and I don't play thoese any more. My best friend Jessica was standing over there getting the detail so she could come and tell me. Every thing she said reflected right back on her. The next day we were at school and amber was acting all hard and like she was mad at me. I did not care because she was playing little girl games When we went to lunch she told some other girls some thing about me. When she finished she said now don't you feel stanky. I said no and we began to argue. Later on that day she started to act like she was my friend and all but I was still mad so I did not talk to her. The next day I was no longer mad at herso we were friends and cool again.The only reason I was her friend again is becaus I did not want to play her little girl games.

EXAMPLE 7.2 VINCENT, SIXTH-GRADE BOY, IRONWOOD ELEMENTARY, MEMPHIS

One day (for no obvious reason) I went up to my little brother and kicked him in the knee cap! Then the little punk kicked at me "its on now!," I said walking toward him I felt like Tyson while I was beating the :)@# out of him, (except he left with his ears) Looking at his mangled body on the ground I almost felt bad, then I remembered I was emotionless I kicked him again and walked off laughing. brother is obviously a die hard person. cause he had the nerve to bite me. I pushed him and he tripped over my shoe and hit his head on the wall. POW "ooops . . . ." I said slowly walking away, because I saw smoke coming out of his ears, (which means his mad) and I was gone. Thats pretty much how it ended. I left him alone and he left me alone.

Tanya's story presents a peer relational drama in which she reports five times about her own emotions (denying twice that she cared, denying that she felt stanky, and reporting being mad and not mad), once about the emotion of her antagonist ("still mad"), and once about the antagonist's speculation about Tanya's feelings ("Don't you feel stanky?"). Tanya's evaluative tone is inescapable; she expresses her disdain for "little girl games" and her belief that gossiping reflects badly on the gossiper ("everything she said reflected back on her"). She contrasts "acting like a friend" with being a friend. At least part of what this sixth-grader wanted us to know about "what it is like to be a kid these days" is that negotiating friendship is complex and morally challenging.

By contrast, Vincent's story explicitly rejects the consideration of emotion and moral sensibilities. He claims (though not without a detectable irony) to "almost feel bad" about the harm hc has caused, until he "remembered I was emotionless." Vincent was a sixth-grader in 1998, a year after boxer Mike Tyson was disqualified for biting off part of Evander Holyfield's ear in a highly publicized heavyweight championship fight. With considerable literary skill, Vincent makes allusion to this event to add sarcasm and humor to his story. We have little doubt about this author's *ability* to assess the moral significance of his actions or to consider the internal states of his antagonist. He does, in fact, recognize his brother's "nerve" and he reports that his decision to walk away from the fight was based on his assessment of his brother's anger (the "steam coming out of his ears"). The author is, however, performing a kind of masculinity in this story – a kind of masculinity that glorifies violence and denigrates empathy. Stories such as this, by a sixth-grader with notable literary skills, make us see that the differences we observe between boy and girl authors in the tendency to report about internal states, to speculate about motives, and to ascribe moral significance to action may have less to do with a difference in the astuteness of girls and boys, and more to do with their understanding of how the behavior of boys and girls should be described.

As we read through story after story, we could not escape the obvious fact that most girls wrote (as did Tanya) about conflicts with other girls, and most boys wrote (as did Vincent) about conflicts with other boys (Walton, Harris, & Davidson, 2009). This was not surprising, since elementary school playgrounds and lunchrooms tend to be gender-segregated (Leaper, 1994; Thorne & Luria, 1986). We did, however, find ourselves curious about the 23% of stories by girl authors that described boy aggression and the 19% of stories by boy authors writing about girl aggression. When we looked at our stories according to the gender of the antagonists rather than the gender of the author, we were struck by a powerful feature of the way gender works. We found that boy and girl authors are very similar in the ways they depict gender. Tanya's story in Example 7.1 is typical of how girl authors wrote about social aggression. Note how similar it is to Anton's story in Example 7.3.

EXAMPLE 7.3 ANTON, FIFTH-GRADE BOY, IRONWOOD ELEMENTARY, MEMPHIS

One day I came over my friend house. She was watching tv, and she was mad for some reason. I asked her what is wrong. She said nothing. She said one of my classmates said that I called you ugly. I told her that I did not say that. She wasn't ugly, she just had a attitude all the time. Everytime I tried to tell her what is right she get mad. So I guess she did not understand what I meant. She wanted to fight me but I refuse. So I explained it to her. She was happy that I told her she was pretty. I told her she need to stop having a attitude. I told her that do not listen to what other people say I was glad she trusted me. Know everytime I tell her what's right she does not get a attitude. I wonder why did she trusted me.

Anton tells a story in which relationship trouble is caused by the 'he-said-she-said' typical of social aggression (she said a classmate said he said she was ugly). He is attentive to the emotions and cognitions of his friend ("she was mad," "she was happy," "I guess she didn't understand"), and he recognizes a need to explain her emotional state ("I asked her what was wrong"). His story includes efforts to explain to his friend "what is right" and ends with his own musings about the mystery of interpersonal trust.

Although this fifth-grader was certainly not aware of the gender issues he raised in this story, he has constructed a prototypical tale of the making of a lady. A feisty girl who "has a attitude all the time" and gets mad when this boy tries to "tell her what is right" is positioned as the source of trouble in this story. The girl "wanted to fight," but the boy refused. He "told her she was pretty" and that "she need to stop having a attitude" and that she should "not listen to what other people say." Anton is a bit mystified about why this worked so well ("I wonder why did she trusted me"), but by the end of the story, the girl has come into compliance with gender expectations: "everytime I tell her what's right she does not get a attitude." Anton's attention to his friend's thoughts and emotions suggests that differences between girl and boy authors do not reflect a difference in capability but instead emerge from the way in which children of any sex engaged with the gender norms circulating in their cultural contexts (Leaper, 2000).

It is not prudent to conclude from our data that boys were more violent and less attentive to psychological mindedness or to the moral implications of aggression than girls were; boys' stories were like this primarily when they were portraying boys as aggressors, and when they did not write about social aggression. When boys told stories about girl aggression, their stories were as psychologically minded as were the girls' stories when the girls were telling about girls. When the girls told about boy aggressors, they also tended to avoid enriching their stories with reports of emotions and mental states. Compare Anton's story to Example 7.4, written by a fourth-grade girl.

EXAMPLE 7.4   EVIE, FOURTH-GRADE GIRL, CONNORS ELEMENTARY, MEMPHIS

Once one afternoon I was takin my brothers to our daycare bus and this little boy starts hitting my brother then my brother punches him back. So his cousin, Davis, decides to call me a B. Then, he starts pulling on my brother's backpack while he was getting on the bus. My bus driver told the two boys to leave us alone.

Evie describes the physical aggression of boys, and similar to the boy authors describing boy physical aggression, she fails to offer explanations, to report about emotional or mental states, or to suggest motives. She makes no moral assessments. Evie is probably capable of the moral analysis and attention to internal states that we see in Tanya's story and in Anton's; she just saw no need to include those details in this account of boy aggression. Story-telling is a discourse practice that specializes in highlighting a culturally non-canonical (and thus report-worthy) event, and in making it understandable, using the 'common-sense' explanatory systems of the culture (Bruner, 1990; Labov, 2006). The process of 'becoming a native' in any cultural setting is a process of coming to share with others a set of expectations about what behaviors and events are culturally valued, about what needs to be explained, and about what will count as an explanation (Bem, 1993). In Evie's world, the aggression of boys requires no explanation.

Girl authors, when they wrote about boys, sounded very much like boy authors. Boy authors, when they wrote about girls, sounded very much like girl authors. Because girls usually wrote about conflicts with other girls, their stories typically included all the moral and psychological work that goes along with explaining girl aggression. Because boys usually wrote about conflict with other boys, their stories were generally neglectful of this analysis. If we had only looked at the gender of the authors, or if we had only looked at the 79% of the stories in which children wrote about same-gender conflicts, we would have missed an important feature of our data and would have made deeper ruts in the path that leads many people to interpret the behavior of girls as more emotionally and relationally astute than the behavior of boys. Our data, in fact, provide evidence that elementary school boys are just as capable as girls of being attentive to the emotions, thoughts, and motives of the actors in their stories.

This is consistent with Niobe Way's (2011) work whose interviews of middle school boys found them highly attuned to the nurturing of deep friendships that involved sharing thoughts and feelings. Way found that these highly relational and emotionally attentive middle school boys became more distant as they moved into high school. Although they expressed a strong longing for the emotional closeness of their earlier relationships, they came to see that kind of closeness as a threat to their masculinity. Similar to the boys Way studied, our boy authors were not lacking an understanding of motivation or emotion. They were not unable to evaluate or to assess the moral significance of their conflicts. They were, however, unlikely to use these skills when they described conflicts with other boys.

This important insight shows us that narrative accounts are a critical part of the discursive production of gender. Children gender the actors in their stories as they make decisions about how those actors should be described, about what aspects of their behavior should be noted and what aspects should be taken for granted, about what requires explanation and what should be backgrounded in a narrative account. Gender comes into being as stories are told about the behavior of actors. Members of a cultural community decide which behaviors are report-worthy, which behaviors must be explained, and which situations or experiences will count as an adequate explanation for various behaviors. They make these decisions as they share stories about their own experiences.

Sometimes their decisions are aligned with broad cultural norms – norms that are widely shared and presented in myths and folk tales, in cartoons and advertisements, and in all manner of mass-media messages (including highly publicized athletic misconduct). But an elementary classroom or playground is its own miniature cultural community. The narrative accounts children give of their experiences in these settings will sometimes reflect those broad cultural norms, but sometimes they will not.

What Children Do With Gender in Their Stories

As soon as we put to rest the question about whether the girls were different from the boys in our stories, we awakened a sleeping giant of a question. How did children use (and ignore) and enforce (and resist) gender in their stories? How did gender come into children's stories about their own conflict? What did they *do* with gender?

Our first questions were pretty straightforward: How often did children label themselves or other actors in their stories with gendered terms? In some ways this is a simple metric of how relevant gender was to the children. At the very least, it is an indicator of how relevant gender was in accounts of conflict. What we found when we asked this question may be a little surprising for those of us who have come to see gender as a pervasive category that organizes almost all human interactions. Almost 40% of our stories (39.3%) described a conflict without mentioning the gender of any participant and without invoking any gender norm or gendered identity.[4] Children were less likely to write genderless stories as they moved from third to sixth grade. A full 67.8% of the third-graders' stories were genderless, whereas only 30.8% of the sixth-graders failed to report about gender. Boys were more likely than girls to ignore gender (50.8% versus 37.4%), and children in better-resourced schools ignored gender more than did children in economically challenged neighborhoods (65.5% versus 30.7%).

Gender is an important social category – important to social scientists, educators, and parents. In all our years of looking at children's stories about their conflicts, we have asked many questions, and no matter what the focus of our analysis, we always checked to see whether the girls and the boys were different. It is rare to find a published study of elementary school children in which the authors fail to mention whether the girls and boys differed. When student investigators worked with our data, the first questions they thought about asking were often questions about gender. Given the pervasiveness of gender as a category of interest to the grown-ups, we think it is striking that about 40% of the time, children's stories ignore it. As we have done more and more work to understand how children understand gender, we have tried to keep in mind that it is not unusual for them to do nothing at all with gender. It is easier to analyze and to write about what children do than about what they do not do, but it is important to keep in mind that the gendering of conflict may be more important or more often important to us than to the children.

In the 60% of our stories in which children did attend to gender, we examined *how* gender came into the story. Sometimes children simply reported the gender of characters and said nothing else about it. Sometimes gender was the focus of the dispute. What function did reports of gender play in children's stories? Below we discuss prominent themes that emerged when children put gender in their stories about conflict.

Making Gender Claims or Just Marking Gender

Interestingly, our authors were much more likely to report about the gender of other characters than they were to make gender claims about themselves. In a full 97% of the 1,553 stories that reported gender, the author reported about the gender of another character. When children reported their own gender, they were always making an important point in their story. Not so when they reported the gender of another character. Authors regularly introduced a character as a girl or a boy when gender seemed irrelevant to the rest of the story; they could have easily said 'kid' or 'classmate.' The pragmatics of communication in English often require that we mark gender. Syntax requires us to do it if we use a singular pronoun (he, she, him, her), and pragmatic rules urge us to do it in many other situations. There is just something slightly odd about saying 'My parent dropped me off early this morning.' You would ordinarily be expected to say whether it was your mother or your father. The singular 'sibling' has an odd ring to it in most ordinary usage; better to say whether you are talking about your sister or your brother.

There are situations in which a gender-neutral term can be used without sounding odd. 'This kid on the playground was bossing everyone around' sounds just fine – no need to say whether it was a girl or boy. This is because the author is making age ('kid' is marked for age) the salient feature, and so gender can be ignored. 'Someone from Ms. Jones' class came over to our table' is OK because the fact that the actor was from another class is the salient feature and it trumps gender. 'A person came over to our table' would be a little odd in ordinary conversation. 'A grown-up came over to our table' would be acceptable, because it allows the author to feature age, not gender. Ordinary usage in most of our language communities requires us to specify gender unless there is another feature of identity that we want to make more prominent. Our data have led us to believe that children pick up on these sophisticated pragmatics between third and sixth grade, so we see a significant increase in 'gratuitous' reports of gender with grade. Older children are more likely than the younger ones to report gender when it plays no role in the story. They tend to comply with a pragmatic rule asserting that gender must be marked unless another identity feature is specified. Increasing compliance with this feature of ordinary usage is part of what makes gender more salient as children move through the elementary school years.

Although only 3% of the stories that reported gender reported the author's own gender, these forty-seven identity claims were especially interesting. Almost all of these were made by boy authors. Masculinity was problematized in children's stories in ways that femininity was not. Consider Example 7.5 by a boy who recounts his experience of a broken leg as a gender accomplishment.

EXAMPLE 7.5 Zack, fourth-grade boy, Winterton Elementary, Memphis

EXAMPLE 7.5   ZACK, FOURTH-GRADE BOY, WINTERTON ELEMENTARY, MEMPHIS

One day in the past every one was calling me a sisae because I would not climb the tree. But that day I was afraid of heights and I was afraid I was going to get hurt. So one night it took me at least 45 minutes to get over my fears. That same night I finally climbed the tree. Once I got to a thin branch I knew I was in bad shape. I got to a thin branch. I fell and broke my leg. I went to the hospital. So they checked it out. It wasn't that bad so I had to were a cast and I stayed in the hospital for at least 2 days. My mother said was going to be allright. The Doctor gave me some medicine for the pains. Once I got home I had to take the medicine because I was walking on it. In 2 or 3 weeks my leg got better it was still hurting a little bit but it was mother realy. After that they did not call me a sisae.

Zack's story gives us a taste of just how difficult it is to establish oneself as adequately masculine. The author makes sure we know that his identity as a sissy was a problem on "one day in the past." He assures us that his fear of heights was something that came on "that day," and he recounts his valiant effort "to get over my fears." The broken leg is not the point of this story; Zack orients to a cultural trope about overcoming one's fears, and demonstrating to his antagonists that he should not be called a sissy. He uses minimizers to talk about the injury ("It wasn't that bad," "It was still hurting a little bit") and with an amazingly Freudian 'slip of the pen,' he tries to tell us that it was really nothing, substituting 'mother' for 'nothing.'

Much attention in both academic research (Brown & Gilligan, 1993) and best-selling books (Pipher, 2005) has been given to the ways that the gender system wreaks havoc on the development of girls in adolescence. Less attention has been paid to such theorists as Chodorow (1989) and to researchers such as Devine, Gilligan, Miczek, Shaikh, and Pfaff (2004) and Way (2011) who point out that significant harm may be done to the development of boys because they are asked to accomplish gender early in childhood. Considerable suffering may be required to avoid being a 'momma's boy,' however foundational the relationship with the mother may be. The assurance of his mother that he "was going to be allright" made it into Zack's story, along with reports about the hospital stay and the pain medication, and then, an intrusive and accidental reference to mother crept in, just when Zack was trying to establish that broken legs are really nothing for a masculine boy who will not be called a sissy again.

Zack was not alone in tying claims of masculinity to violence and to "taking it." A fifth-grader, Paxton, for example, described being jumped by some boys from the projects, and then assured his reader that "It dosen't make me a weec boy, It makes me a man From the beaten I tock." Rarely, a boy attempted to resist establishing masculinity through violence or through an ability to be 'tough,' and when Warren in Example 7.5 tried to claim a more positive kind of masculinity, it didn't go well.

EXAMPLE 7.6 WARREN, FIFTH-GRADE BOY, IRONWOOD ELEMENTARY, MEMPHIS

One day when I was on the blacktop playing basketball a boy took my basketball and kicked it. I was already having a bad morning so I called him a punk. As a comeback he checked my mother. So I checked his whole family twice. He was ticked off then so he tried to dislocate my jaw. I let myself go then I mean I went ballistic on him. We were to toe to toe for about a minute. My friends pulled me away right when he kicked me. After I had a chance to consider what I had done, I got angrier because I had loss. I though about the boy and myself. I compared him to me, and really he isn't such a bad guy. When I really thought about it we were both wrong. I decided to be the better man and apologize about checking his family. When I went over there I heard him bragging about he could grind me into meat.

After an impressive moral analysis (discussed in Chapter 1), with careful consideration of the role he and his antagonist played in this conflict, Warren decided that he could assert masculinity, and "be the better man" by apologizing. Sadly, this attempt to overturn the violence–masculinity connection was met with derision. Warren's prosocial, peace-maker construction of masculinity is going to face real challenges in his cultural community.

Although gendered identity claims were very interesting, they were relatively rare in our data, and they were made only by boys. So what *else* did children do with gender? When they were not just marking gender gratuitously, or attempting to convince us of their own masculinity, children often reported about threats to a gendered identity.

Making Identity Threats and Enforcing the Gender System

Name-calling was described in 818 of the U.S. stories that included reports of aggression by children. Of these, seventy-four (9%) reported insults that called into question the antagonist's gender appropriateness or used gender in some way to threaten identity. In Barrie Thorne's (1993) ethnography of children in two elementary schools, she described a set of activities she called borderwork. Borderwork involved girls and boys playing together in ways that strengthened a gender divide. Girls-chasing-boys and other 'boys against girls' games exemplified borderwork. The name-calling incidents reported in our stories that were gender-relevant almost always functioned to enforce gender stereotypes, underlining the distinction between masculine and feminine, making deviations from these socially risky, and denigrating the female side of this dichotomy.

We have already seen, in the examples above, some of the borderwork that is accomplished by gendered insults. Tanya rails against the "little girl games" that her antagonist is playing. Vincent refers to his brother as a "little punk," a gendered insult only used in our sample against boys. Anton decries the unladylike "having and attitude," an accusation leveled only against girls in our sample. Evie reports being called a "B," a gendered insult so potent that the children in our sample declined to spell it out, sometimes referring to it as "the B word" or writing "b★★ch." Zack's quest to prove his masculinity is motivated by being called a "sisae," an insult so disturbing that it causes him to risk a major injury. Warren identifies his antagonist as a "punk," and the antagonist escalates this by "checking my mother." Our examination of the gendered insults in our sample led us to two major conclusions: gendered insults primarily denigrate femininity; and gendered insults make gender nonconformity risky.

Defaming the Feminine

When fifth-grader Cassie wrote, "I don't want those females in my conversation," the word 'female' is dripping with derision – even coming from the pen of a girl! The single most common gendered insult reported in our stories was 'little girl' used as a form of address. Authors quoted themselves and their antagonists saying such things as, "Little girl, I was not talking to you!" or "Little girl, you better keep my name out of your mouth," or "Little girl, don't lay your hands on my sister." 'Little boy' was used in this way only once in nearly 3,000 stories. We found ourselves worried about what it might mean to recognize yourself as a member of the category 'little girl' when the category name is an insult. We searched in vain for other membership categories that functioned in this way, and found only the word 'nigger,' used similarly, and that was used only twice. It is difficult to avoid the conclusion that 'girl' is a devalued identity among the children in the elementary schools we visited.

The gendered insults reported in our sample included slut, prostitute, hooker, queen, gay, and the general 'your momma,' which functioned as a shorthand for a set of familiar taunts that either alleged that your mother is so ugly, so poor, or so promiscuous. It is immediately obvious, reviewing this list, that gendered insults denigrate the feminine. 'Punk' is the only insult that called into question the value of masculinity. Over forty years ago, feminist scholar Robin Lakoff (1975) noticed that English includes a much richer vocabulary for the disparagement of women, and especially for vilifying female sexuality than for defaming men or masculinity. Perhaps we should not be surprised to see this pattern of vocabulary usage emerging in elementary school.

Not only did we find that name-calling was used most frequently to malign girls and women and femininity, but even when gendered insults were used against boys, the two most common ways to do it were to insult their mothers or to call them girls or sissies or gay. All of this is consistent with our finding reported above that only boys make gendered identity claims. For girls, claiming femininity would be claiming a quality of the self that is frequently devalued in their cultural communities. These findings are consistent with a recent study by Braun and Davidson (2016) in which children tended to devalue feminine characteristics in favor of masculine characteristics when expressing their preference for potential classmates.

Making Gender Non-Conformity Risky

When children reported gendered insults in their stories (and we remind ourselves that this happened in only 9% of the stories), the insults were largely used to reproduce and enforce inequality. This was most strikingly true on the twenty-one occasions in which children told about accusations of homosexuality. We do not know how our young authors understood such words as 'gay,' 'faggot,' or 'lesbian,' but we can see that they understood such words to be especially troubling. For example, the third-grader below was unable to remember the name that has been used to accuse her, but she understood it to be demeaning.

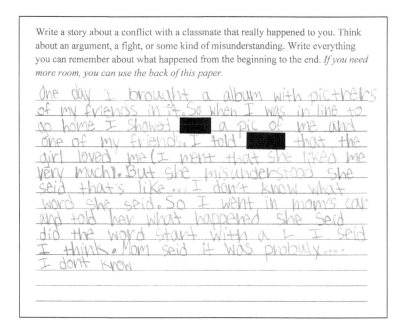

EXAMPLE 7.7 Beth-Ellen, third-grade girl, College Elementary, Memphis

EXAMPLE 7.7   BETH-ELLEN, THIRD-GRADE GIRL, COLLEGE ELEMENTARY, MEMPHIS

One day I brought a album with pictrers of my friends in it. So when I was in line to go home I showed Aine a pic of me and one of my friends. I told Kelli that the girl loved me (I ment that she liked me very much). But she misunderstood she seid that's like . . . I don't know what word she seid. So I went in mom's car and told her what happened she seid did the word start with a L I seid I think. Mom seid it was probuly . . . I don't know

Although Beth-Ellen seems to want us to understand this feature about 'what it is like to be a kid her age,' she can't remember the word that Kelli used or that her mother gave her, and her story just trails off into an admission of not knowing. She does, however, mount a defense against an accusation of lesbianism, which she makes as a parenthetical aside to her reader, "I ment that she liked me very much." Beth-Ellen's initial assertion of love from a friend has been problematized, and she seems to get the message that love between girls is unacceptable. Adler and Adler (1998) found pre-adolescents making such accusations as these as a way of asserting social dominance, and in some of our stories (such as Yolanda's story in Example 7.8 below) this may indeed be a motive. We believe, however, that this kind of name-calling primarily functioned to enforce gender conformity. Beth-Ellen, we predict, will be more cautious in the future about expressing her affection for same-sex friends. Whatever children take it to mean when their classmates call them gay, their stories reveal that such accusations are a serious threat to their social well-being. Examples 7.8 and 7.9 present two different reactions to such threats.

EXAMPLE 7.8   YOLANDA, SIXTH-GRADE GIRL, CONNORS ELEMENTARY, MEMPHIS

A Conflict

Close to the end of the year I had humongus probelm. Two people are involed in this probelm. One girl hollered out that I was gay. Then her and her other friend started to say hay gay. So they just keap messing with me. The way they were messing with me is by calling me out of my name. I just got tired of htem and told Mr. Bennett. Chay talked to him. After that they still were acting and doing things to me. They also had alot of people thinking I was gay. They tried to keep me from going on a School Trip. I am a good student I come to school and get my lesson. These are some more of the things they said eat the poo-poo, swing there hair in my face and pushing other people on me.

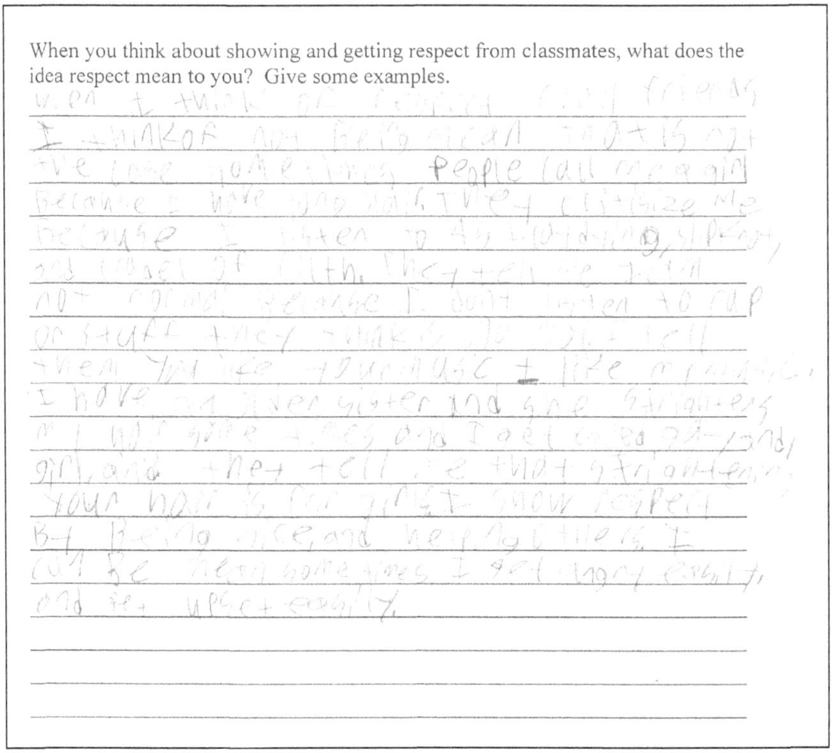

When you think about showing and getting respect from classmates, what does the idea respect mean to you? Give some examples.

EXAMPLE 7.9 Forrest, fifth-grade boy, College Elementary, Memphis

EXAMPLE 7.9 FORREST, FIFTH-GRADE BOY, COLLEGE ELEMENTARY, MEMPHIS

When I think of respect from friends I think of not Being mean that is not the case sometimes People call me a girl because I have long hair. They criticize me Because I listen to As I lay dying, slipknot, and cradel of filth. They tell me I am not normal Because I dont listen to rap, or stuff they think is normal. I tell them you like your music, I like my music. I have an older sister and she strightens my hair some times and I get called gay and, girl, and they tell me that stightening your hair is for girls. I show respect By Being nice, and helping others. I can Be mean sometimes, I get angry easily, and get upset easily.

Both Yolanda and Forrest are experiencing social exclusion and rejection from peers, and their difficulty is related to gender non-conformity. Yolanda identifies being called gay as a "humongus problem," and indeed, she describes behavior of her classmates that includes not only name-calling and gestures of humiliation ("swing there hair in my face"), but attempts at exclusion from a school activity ("They tried to keep me from going on a School Trip"), and physical violence ("pushing other people on me"). She describes herself as "a good student" and her story does not reveal any insight she may have about why her classmates are mistreating her. Unlike Zack, who had an idea of what he needed to do when accusations of gender non-conformity were leveled against him (he had to get over his fears and climb that tree), Yolanda turns to her principal for assistance, and she reports that his attempt at intervention did not improve her situation.

Unlike Yolanda, whose physical appearance and personal presentation offered no obvious clues that she would be taunted by classmates as 'gay,' Forrest was immediately identifiable to even a casual observer as a gender rebel. Forrest describes his long hair and the straightening of his hair, and strategically implies that these features of his appearance are similar to his preference for music. Others "criticize" him and tell him he is "not normal," but Forrest is not buying "what they think is normal." Forrest obliquely (making use of a double negative) accuses his antagonists as lacking respect and as "Being mean." (It is not always the case that they show respect by not being mean.) Compared to Yolanda, whose story makes no moral assessment of her tormenters, and no speculation about their motives, Forrest seems to have constructed a defense that allows him to preserve a sense of his own agency. He construes his choices as falling in the realm of differences in preference that ought to be respected. Still, it is worth noting that Forrest more easily defends his choice in music than his choice in hairstyles. He ends his story with a self-affirmation ("I show respect By Being nice, and helping others"), but this is followed immediately by a heartbreakingly honest admission that he can sometimes be mean, and a recognition of his own painful reactivity to his situation ("I get angry easily, and get upset easily").

One final comparison between Yolanda's and Forrest's stories focuses our attention on narrative skill. Yolanda's account begins with an introduction that orients us to the concern at hand (the "humongus problem"), telling us when it happened (toward the end of the previous school year) and who was involved. She establishes a pretty clear chronology of events, up until the intervention by the principal fails to improve the situation. From this point, the narrative falters. Yolanda lists additional behaviors of her classmates, interrupting that with two sentences about herself ("I am a good student I come to school and get my lesson"), and then listing more of the taunts she has endured. She is not able to construct an ending to her story. She does not claim an authorial voice that would allow her to evaluate her tormenters or to make sense of her own suffering.

Forrest's story, by contrast, neglects to set the reader up with a time and place, or to give us a chronology of events. He writes entirely in the simple present tense, telling us about things that regularly happen, not things that happened at a point in time. However, Forrest is able to use a remarkable set of literary devices to make his experience meaningful. He frames the story at the beginning and end with statements about respect, and this orients us to the idea that when people criticize him and tell him he is not normal, he experiences this as their failure to respect his choices. He juxtaposes the choices he makes about how to wear his hair with his preferences about music. As an author he claims the authority to reject what others "think is normal." He positions himself as a person who can make his own choices and who respects the choices of others ("you like your music, I like my music"). This author is using the power of narrative to make sense of what is happening in his social world. This is a power that Yolanda did not wield.

We have seen above that children use gendered insults in a way that seem to enforce hetero-normative behaviors and to make gender non-conformity socially risky. If it is a humongous problem to be accused of homosexuality in elementary school, we are sorry to report below that it is scarcely easier to be accused of heterosexual attraction or romantic interest of any sort. Consistent with Adler and Adler's (1998) findings, our children often reported 'liking' as a secret, and the betrayal of those secrets exposed both the liker and the liked to ridicule.

Heterosexual Pairings and the Dawning of Romantic Adventure

As children move from middle childhood into early adolescence, they typically enter a social world that includes expectations for romantic heterosexual pairings. A number of researchers concerned with adolescent development have recognized these expectations as a threat, especially to the development of girls and young women (Holland & Eisenhart, 1990; Lees, 1991; Tolman, 1994). These authors critique a construction of romantic love that values girls and women primarily for their beauty and for their heterosexual desirability, that affords agency to men (with ladies waiting to be chosen), and that discourages "attitude" or fortitude in girls and women. Popular concern that sexuality and the gender system are introduced to our children at ever younger ages led the American Psychological Association to create a task force in 2007 to study the sexualization of girlhood (American Psychological Association, 2007). These authors made astute criticisms of the media portrayals of sexuality that children consume and of the sexualized portrayals of children in popular culture, but they did not consider the way children construe their own experience with romance and with the dawning of romantic interest.

When our children wrote about their experiences of conflict, they selected conflicts that focused on romantic themes sixty-eight times (about 2.6% of the U.S. stories). Some of these stories validated concerns that the entrance into romance entails a loss of agency for girls. Notice how Morgan's desire is discounted in Isaac's story in Example 7.10.

EXAMPLE 7.10   ISAAC, FOURTH-GRADE BOY, CONNORS ELEMENTARY, MEMPHIS

I remember that me and Kevin got the fight becouse this gril name Morgan said she liked me but she liked Kevin so me and him got mad at each other so I said kevin I don't want to fight you becoues your my best friend I don't want to fight you If you want to go with Morgan go with her I an't stopping you so let shake hands and be friend.

Although Isaac reports that Morgan said she liked him, he claims the authorial power to assert that she actually liked Kevin. Isaac orients to the importance of friendship and claims twice in his story that he does not want to fight with his friend Kevin. He gives Kevin permission to "go with Morgan" if he wants to, and he proposes that they shake hands to seal this deal. There is no evidence that Isaac considers Morgan's wishes to be relevant in this matter. Our stories of romance included occasions when "all the girls sat down and waited for a boy to ask them to dance" and occasions when girls insulted one another by calling into question their romantic desirability, as when fourth-grader Temika reported that she told her antagonist, "That's why Anthony Harris don't want you no more." Sometimes, children's stories about their entrance into romance appeared to be appropriating a gender system that belittled girls much as the gendered insults did. These were not, however, the most prominent features of our stories of romance.

Many of our stories about romance were written by girl authors who resisted being positioned in a romantic discourse. Sometimes, girls like fourth-grader Xandria declined involvement in romance by claiming that they are too young: "I told him I don't like you because we is to young my mother taught me good thing." This defense against the gender system may be effective for a little while longer, but claims of immaturity introduce their own problems.

For a few of our girl resisters, like Hannah in Example 7.11, romance was just seen as an annoyance.

EXAMPLE 7.11   HANNAH, SIXTH-GRADE GIRL, COLLEGE ELEMENTARY, MEMPHIS

It all started when my friend Lucia had a crush on a boy. He had it too. Lucia and him told each other but kept it a secret but the dominos droped and basicly the hole grade new about it. That was only the first problem. Lucia kept on passing notes to me while I was working on math problems about problems she had with this boy. The notes started pileing up and I got anoyed. I told her if she has that many problems just break up or at least stop comeing to me from problems. She broke up a week later at a "pep rally?" and ever since then she complained to me about I was the one who broke them up It got quite annoying especaly since she sat right behind me and the boy right in front. I just stopped talking to her. That was the beginning of 6th grade and now we are at seperate schools. My friend who goes to the same school said she still talks about me and calls me names. At the beginning we were friends now she just uses me.

Hannah's story presents Lucia as a friend who seems to enjoy the intrigue and drama of romantic problems. Hannah, on the other hand, positions herself as a person who resents having her work on her math problems interrupted. If romance entails "that many problems," our no-nonsense author suggests that

---

Write a story about a conflict with a classmate that really happened to you. Think about an argument, a fight, or some kind of misunderstanding. Write everything you can remember about what happened from the beginning to the end. *If you need more room, you can use the back of this paper.*

It all started when my friend ▮▮▮▮ had a crush on a boy. He had it too ▮▮▮▮ and him told each other but kept it a secret but the dominos droped and basicly the hole grade new about it. That was only the first problem. ▮▮▮▮ kept on passing notes to me while I was working on math problems about problems she had with this boy. The notes started piling up and I got anoyed. I told her if she has that many problems just break up or at least stop comeing to me for problems. She broke up a week later at a "pep rally" and ever since then she conplained to me about I was the one who broke them up. It got quite annoying especaly since she sat right behind me and the boy right in front. I just stopped talking to her. That was the beginning of 6th grade and now we are at seperate schools. My friend who goes to the same school said she still talks about and calls me names. At the beginning we were friends now she just uses me.

EXAMPLE 7.11 Hannah, sixth-grade girl, College Elementary, Memphis

Lucia "just break up." And as an alternative to that, Lucia should at least stop annoying Hannah with the passing of notes about the matter. So far, at least, the entrance into hetero-normativity is not enough to divert this sixth-grader from the STEM subjects!

Sometimes, romance was presented as trivial or unimportant, especially in comparison to friendships between girls.

EXAMPLE 7.12   KAREN, FOURTH-GRADE GIRL, CONNORS ELEMENTARY, MEMPHIS

I got in to a argument with my cousin Elizabeth and Luna. First, A boy come to our school and both cousins liked him. Second, They say they was in love with him. Third, I said he was ugly and they got mad at me. Forth, they curse me out and told my parents that I curse them out witch I don't use because my mom said that will not get you any where. Fifth, we knew the boy didn't make any diffrence so we apologize to each other. and we didn't let that come into our friendship. Sixth, we didn't even reconize him but they still had a crush on him. Seventh, we started to play and be happy.

Karen presents her conflict as having resulted from her failure to join in with the romantic adventure of liking or being "in love with" a new boy in school. Not only does she decline to participate, she expresses her opinion that the boy was ugly. This provoked cursing and false accusations and it might have been disastrous to Karen's relationship with her cousins, except that (according to our author) the girls "knew that the boy didn't make any diffrence." Karen was one of several authors whose story explicitly prioritized friendship over romance ("we didn't let that come into our friendship"), or explicitly criticized other girls who neglected friends in favor of boyfriends ("I couldn't believe it, I mean she already promiced to go with us!").

Although our girls who wrote about romance seemed to be unanimous in their opinion that friendship is more important than romance, they did not all construe romance as a threat to friendship. Indeed, many of our romance stories exemplified a kind of romantic intrigue or romantic adventure that seemed to support friendship. Girls shared (and sometimes betrayed) secrets about their romantic attraction. They served as emissaries for one another, delivering declarations of affection and trying to learn whether romantic interests were reciprocated. They offered support to each other in the face of rejections or betrayals. These girls, unlike Hannah, and similar to the college students that Holland and Eisenhart (1990) described as educated in romance, may have been distracted from doing their math problems, but they were not stripped of agency. In their writing about conflicts involving romance, they positioned themselves rarely as objects of desire, and often as instigators.

When we read through the full set of romance stories in our data set, we come away less worried about the gendering of elementary school children than we were when we read the set of stories that included gendered insults. Whereas children wrote about gendered insults in ways that seemed to enforce the gender system (sometimes harshly), children's writing about romance encouraged us to imagine that they will act out gender in new ways on a new stage. Sometimes they will decline to play the gender roles their society offers; sometimes we predict that they will take the roles, but they will play them in new ways. This encouraging conclusion was even more strongly reinforced when we read what children had to say when they were explicit about gender equality.

Explicit Challenges to the Gender System

In thirty-two stories the children explicitly invoked a gender rule. In nine of these stories the author put the rule in the voice of an authority (e.g., "Her mom came up and said yall don't need to be fighting like little boys," or "My mom told me never hit a girl so I didn't hit her"). In all but one of these occasions, the author affirmed the rule and the gender difference was endorsed. However, when children explicitly brought up rules about gender using their own authorial voice, they were often advocating for gender equality or fairness. Our most powerful example of a child taking on gender injustice was a story by a seventh-grader from one of our after-school samples. Children in our after-school programs told their stories, rather than writing them, so Minnie's story in Example 7.13 is transcribed from an audio recording. We let Minnie edit the transcript to make sure the story stands just as she wanted us to have it. The story was quite long, and she began by telling us how her teacher came to be dismissed in the middle of the school year, leaving her class with a string of substitute teachers. We pick up her story at this point.

EXAMPLE 7.13 MINNIE, SEVENTH-GRADE GIRL, MEMPHIS[5]

Some days we ain't have no subs. And then one day, this man named Mr. Marshall, He said he was gonna be our sub till she come back. And if he ever miss a day, then we know what class to go to. But, now days, all he do is take up for the boys. Because, he think they're better. And I told him, "neither one of us is better than, uh, the other." And he said, "Well, I think boys are best," and I said, And I said, "they may be in one way, but girls, they're best too in another way. Neither one of us is perfect." And he said, "I know that, but I just like boys best cause the girls, they get hot and they in their dresses, so nasty." And I told him, "well some girls don't like that cause we have to dress proper and keep our body covered." And then I said, "boys, they, sometimes they get outta hand, sometimes they do that stuff. Cause, some boys, they have problems at their houses. And, uh, it's somethin' they're goin' through, like that." And then we just sit down and talked for a long time. And he tried to understand girls more better. And then he started to talk to us and just take up for each, each and every one of the students. Because he knows it was not fair what he was doin'. And that was the end of that discussion.

How impressive that this seventh-grader is willing to confront her teacher about his unfair treatment of the girls in his class. Minnie begins her story by accusing her teacher of unfairness ("all he do is take up for the boys") and by speculating about his opinion ("Because, he think they're better"). After this, she gives us a turn-by-turn report of her conversation with Mr. Marshall, using direct and indirect quotation. We come to have confidence in the accuracy of her report, partly because of her use of quotation, and partly because of the reasonableness of her own position and the balance of her presentation. When Mr. Marshall declares that "boys are best," Minnie partly concedes the argument ("they may be in one way"), a strategy that advances the conversation without escalating the argument. She makes the indisputable point that "Neither one of us is perfect," which elicits an acknowledgment of partial agreement from her teacher ("I know that, but"). Mr. Marshall's next assertion that he "just like boys best cause the girls, they get hot and they in their dresses, so nasty" would leave many full-grown women flabbergasted, we believe. How could we expect a thirteen-year-old girl to formulate a response to this? Has this teacher accused Minnie and her female classmates of sexual inappropriateness? Minnie reports that her own response reminded the teacher that not all girls are improperly dressed and that boys sometimes "get outta hand." She goes on to explain that when boys "do that stuff" it is because they are going through difficulties at home. Minnie is seeking to win fair treatment for the girls in her class, but she does not neglect to express her empathy for the boys as well. At this point in Minnie's story, she abandons her strategy of direct quotation, and summarizes, "we just sit down and talked for a long time." She reports that Mr. Marshall made an effort to understand the girls. Minnie has positioned herself as a reasonable person with the right to expect fair treatment, and with the persuasive power to motivate changes in her condition. However much the gender system has come down on Minnie, it has not succeeded in diminishing her understanding of fairness or the power of her voice.

Conclusions: Taking on Gender and Taking on the Gender System

In this chapter, we have asked ourselves two questions: What can children's stories about conflict tell us about how they are taking on (in the sense of adopting) gender? What can their stories tell us about how they might take on (in the sense of resisting) the gender system? We didn't ask children to tell us about gender; we asked them to tell us about conflicts. We didn't ask them to defend an identity that we could characterize as masculine or feminine. We told them we wanted to learn what it was like to be a kid their age, and we asked them to tell us about their conflicts. When they explicitly positioned themselves and their peers vis-à-vis gender norms, or when they spontaneously chose gendered themes as the source of their conflicts, we attempted to hear what they wanted us to learn about how gender gets acted out in their world.

First, we came to recognize that elementary school children were paying attention to gender and were 'doing gender' in their narrative accounts *sometimes*. Children included some kind of gendered report in their stories about 60% of the time. Almost 60% of those stories that did report gender *only* reported the gender of someone in their story, without making anything of this report in the story. This left us with 621 stories, just under 25% of the U.S. sample, in which child authors *featured* gender in their stories. We have vacillated in our interpretation of this '25% gender' finding. We did not ask the children to tell us anything about gender; we asked them only to tell us about their conflicts. If a full quarter of the time they chose to tell us something about gender, this shows us their work to take on gender in their cultural community was pretty salient to them. At the same time, we remind ourselves, 75% of elementary children's stories of conflict had nothing to say about gender, and that is an impressive majority. Gender is only one of many cultural meaning systems that children are taking on in middle childhood.

Our initial efforts to determine whether the girls' stories differed from the boys' stories led us to replicate a recognizable feature of sex differences research in middle childhood: if you look for culturally condoned gender differences, you can generally find them in some settings and in some circumstances. In some of our samples boys wrote more violent stories than girls did and in some of our samples girls were more attentive to the motivations and emotions of the actors in their stories than boys were. Closer examination, however, led us to conclude that this was only true when girls wrote about girls and when boys wrote about boys. We found boys to be as psychologically and morally astute as girls were; however, both boys and girls tended to neglect such analysis when they wrote about boys. We have come to the conclusion that gender 'comes into play' for our children in some contexts, but it is very much backgrounded most of the time.

When we moved, in the second part of this chapter, to close readings of stories in which gender came into play, we learned about some of the mechanisms that enforce dominant understandings of gender. We found that boys made claims of masculinity, backed up with reports of violence or of a 'tough-guy' ability to 'take it.' Girls did not make similar claims of femininity. In fact, 'little girl' and 'female' were used as insults. When gender was used in name-calling, it was nearly always the female that was denigrated. One of the ways that the gender system appears to be enforced in elementary school is by gendered teasing and insults – insulting boys for being girl-like and insulting girls (or 'your momma') for being the wrong kind of female. The single most potent of the gendered insults seemed to be an accusation of homosexuality or gender non-conformity. Children recounted suffering the taunts of peers who called them 'gay,' and it was clear that failing to conform to gender norms was socially risky among our authors.

Although children appeared mostly to be colluding to reproduce gender inequality when we looked at identity claims and identity threats, when we looked at their stories of romance we found a little groundswell of resistance to culturally stereotypical notions of agentive, desiring males and passive, objectified females. Both girls and boys tended to prioritize same-sex friendship over romance, and girls wrote about romance in ways that affirmed their own agency and desire.

Finally, our examination of gender in our children's stories has underlined the importance of narrative skills in middle childhood. It is in the creation of personal narratives that children create a self. They become actors with agency and responsibility for their own behaviors and for the outcomes of their behaviors, primarily as their experiences get 'storied.' It is in creating stories of their own experience, in being the authors of their own experience, that they take on gender. Some of them try on gender and find that the fit is satisfactory. Some of them struggle to make themselves out to be adequately 'masculine' for an audience that understands masculinity in terms of violence and toughness. Some of them struggle to reject being positioned in devalued gender categories. There are some stories in our sample in which children *take on* the gender system, resisting versions of masculinity or femininity that do not suit them. When elementary school children narrate their own conflicts, they sometimes *take on* gender, and our take on their stories leads us to be hopeful that the children will come out stronger and the gender system will come out weaker on account of the battle.

Notes

1 All of the findings reported in this chapter are based on analyses of the stories collected in our seven U.S. samples. Children in Shenzhen may have been similar in their orientation to gender, but we were not confident that the categories we coded to identify appropriation and resistance to gender norms were functioning similarly in this very different cultural context.

2 The difference between boys and girls in severity of violence reported may be more complex than this. When children wrote stories that reported *only* physical aggression, we did not observe differences between boys and girls. However, when boys wrote stories that included name-calling, they were much more likely than girls to describe more severe violence. These identity threats were more likely to be paired with physical aggression in stories by boy authors than in stories by girls.

3 Consistent with previous research that has been attentive to social class and ethnicity (Zalot et al., 2007), we found that differences between boy and girl authors were non-significant in the more socio-economically stressed neighborhoods.

4 We counted any person descriptor that includes gender as part of the definition, such as mother, aunt, waitress, boy, man, slut, sissy, Mr., girlfriend, and so on. Because English does not allow a gender-neutral singular pronoun to refer to people, we did not include pronouns in this analysis. We did not include proper names, although those are sometimes reliable indicators of gender.

5 Minnie attended an after-school program in Memphis serving youth living in a high-poverty, predominantly African American community. We collected data from fourteen children in that program, but we did not describe their data in Chapter 2 because we did not use those stories in any of our analyses except for this example in 7.13.

References

Adler, P. A., & Adler, P. (1998). *Peer power: Preadolescent culture and identity*. New Brunswick, NJ: Rutgers University Press.

American Psychological Association, Task Force on the Sexualization of Girls. (2007). Report of the APA Task Force on the Sexualization of Girls. Retrieved from http://www.apa.org/pi/women/programs/girls/report-full.pdf.

Bem, S. L. (1993). *The lenses of gender: Transforming the debate on sexual inequality*. New Haven, CT: Yale University Press.

Braun, S. S., & Davidson, A. J. (2016). Gender (non)conformity in middle childhood: A mixed methods approach to understanding gender-typed behavior, friendship, and peer preference. *Sex Roles: A Journal of Research*.

Brown, L. M., & Gilligan, C. (1993). Meeting at the crossroads: Women's psychology and girls' development. *Feminism & Psychology, 3*(1), 11–35.

Bruner, J. S. (1990). *Acts of meaning*. Cambridge, MA: Harvard University Press.

Buckner, J. P., & Fivush, R. (1998). Gender and self in children's autobiographical narratives. *Applied Cognitive Psychology, 12*, 407–29.

Chodorow, N. J. (1989). *Feminism and psychoanalytic theory*. New Haven, CT: Yale University Press.

Crick, N. R., Casas, J. F., & Nelson, D. A. (2002). Toward a more comprehensive understanding of peer maltreatment: Studies of relational victimization. *Current Directions in Psychological Science, 11*(3), 98–101.

Devine, J., Gilligan, J., Miczek, K. A., Shaikh, R., & Pfaff, D. (2004). Youth violence: Scientific approaches to prevention. Prologue. *Annals of the New York Academy of Sciences, 1036*, ix–xii.

Hare-Mustin, R. T., & Maracek, J. (1994). Asking the right questions: Feminist psychology and sex differences. *Feminism & Psychology, 4*(4), 531–7.

Holland, D. C., & Eisenhart, M. A. (1990). *Educated in romance: Women, achievement, and college culture*. Chicago, IL: University of Chicago Press.

Lakoff, R. (1975). *Language and woman's place*. New York, NY: Harper and Row.

Labov, W. (2006). Narrative pre-construction. *Narrative Inquiry, 16*(1), 37–45.

Leaper, C. (1994). Exploring the consequences of gender segregation on social relationships. *New Directions for Child and Adolescent Development, 65*, 67–86.

Leaper, C. (2000). The social construction and socialization of gender during development. In P. H. Miller & E. Kofsky Scholnick (Eds.), *Toward a feminist developmental psychology* (pp. 127–52). Florence, KY: Routledge.

Lees, S. (1991). *Sugar and spice: Sexuality and adolescent girls*. London: Penguin.

Pipher, M. (2005). *Reviving Ophelia*. London: Penguin.

Reese, E., Haden, C. A., & Fivush, R. (1996). Mothers, fathers, daughters, sons: Gender differences in autobiographical reminiscing. *Research on Language and Social Interaction,* *29*(1), 27–56.

Rose, A. J., & Rudolph, K. D. (2006). A review of sex differences in peer relationship processes: Potential trade-offs for the emotional and behavioral development of girls and boys. *Psychological Bulletin, 132*(1), 98.

Thorne, B. (1993). *Gender play: Girls and boys in school.* New Brunswick, NJ: Rutgers University Press.

Thorne, B., & Luria, Z. (1986). Sexuality and gender in children's daily worlds. *Social Problems, 33*(3), 176–90. doi:http://dx.doi.org/10.2307/800703 176-190.

Tolman, D. L. (1994). Doing desire: Adolescent girls' struggles for/with sexuality. *Gender & Society, 8,* 324–42.

Underwood, M. K. (2003). *Social aggression among girls.* New York, NY: Guilford Press.

Walton, M. D., & Brewer, C. L. (2001). The role of personal narrative in bringing children into the moral discourse of their culture. *Narrative Inquiry, 11*(2), 1–28.

Walton, M. D., Harris, A. R., & Davidson, A. J. (2009). "It makes me a man from the beating I took": Gender and aggression in children's narratives about conflict. *Sex Roles, 61,* 383–98.

Way, N. (2011). *Deep secrets: Boys' friendships and the crisis of connection.* Cambridge, MA: Harvard University Press.

West, C., & Zimmerman, D. H. (1987). Doing gender. *Gender & Society, 1*(2), 125–51.

Zalot, A. A., Jones, D. J., Forehand, R., & Brody, G. (2007). Self-regulation, aggression, and conduct problems among low-income, African American youth from single mother homes: The moderating roles of perceived neighborhood context and child gender. *The Journal of Black Psychology, 33,* 239–59. doi:10.1177/0095798407302569.

8

"FROM THAT DAY ON I BECAME MORE RESPONSIBLE"

Creating the Self and Re-Creating Culture in Middle Childhood

> I told Mr. Morris the hold truth and nothing but the truth. He still gave me three licks and gave him two.
>
> *Barry, sixth-grade boy, Connors Elementary, Memphis*

A fascinating thing about examining stories by children is the opportunity it gives us to see a new generation 'picking up' culture and using it to create themselves. As they made narrative accounts of their conflicts, children appropriated bits and pieces of the discourse that surrounds them. Sometimes they did this awkwardly and with clearly limited understanding of the words and phrases they use. Sometimes they did it with remarkable insight or delightfully imaginative twists. Just as they 'took on' gender in both senses of the phrase (described in Chapter 7), we saw them taking on other cultural commitments – sometimes adopting and sometimes resisting expected practices and meanings. This process is at the heart of cultural change: as children select the cultural meanings and practices they need to create themselves, they inevitably change the cultural communities they enter (Briggs, 1992).

William Corsaro (1992) spent many years studying peer interactions among preschool children, and his sensitive and thoughtful work with these observations led him to propose a process of enculturation he called interpretive reproduction. As these young children interacted with one another, their play incorporated themes and practices they observed in the world around them. It became increasingly clear to Corsaro, as he steeped himself in worlds created by preschoolers, that these children were not just absorbing culture as they engaged in serious and fanciful play. They were in a constant process of embellishment, elaborating on themes, juxtaposing scripts and scenarios from the world they observed, and recombining things to suit the most pressing needs of the moment. Our work with the narratives of children six to ten years older than Corsaro's preschool participants found them similarly engaged in interpretive reproduction. They picked up scraps from the language feast around them, finding just the morsels they needed to form the meat of their argument, or to spice up their tale.

One of our greatest pleasures in reading and listening to children's stories about their conflicts stemmed from the regularity with which they borrowed from the cultural practices and meanings that surrounded them, putting them to their own uses as they defended themselves or accused one another or just speculated about the meaning of their experience. From the very first story we presented, we have been quoting children quoting culture. Daria's story in the Introduction was framed by allusions to the classic children's story of the "big bad wolf." We have seen in every chapter children using culturally recognizable similes, metaphors, and idioms (e.g., "these two thoughts were like angel and demon in my head," "the domino dropped," "they were just skin and bones," "she would act like a queen at ressice and think she would rule the fort"). They used popular expressions from recent movies or music (e.g. "she aks like a Dramaqueen," "now we are cool"). They describe rituals and cultural practices (e.g., "swear her to secrecy," "coming up in my face," "went to peer mediation"). Children situate themselves in a cultural context when they make stories about their experiences. They position themselves as certain kinds of characters, with distinctive voices, and in doing this they create their very selves in relation to the people around them (e.g., "I was playing with my 'go through fire and water' brother").

Most research on identity development has focused on adolescence, and much of it has been grounded in Erik Erikson's theory, in which the primary task of adolescence is to navigate a personality crisis that will result in either the achievement of identity or role confusion (Erikson, 1950). Erikson's theory was grounded in a psychodynamic approach, in which the struggle for identity was located deep in the individual psyche. Many researchers who built on his work took a cognitive-constructivist approach, focusing on identity as a largely cognitive accomplishment – the achievement of self-understanding (e.g., Moshman, 1998). This line of research often studied the development, in adolescence, of political, religious, and other ideological commitments that guide lifestyle choices (Marcia, 1966; Berzonsky, 1989). Recent writing by Phillip Hammack (2008) has integrated both the psychodynamic and cognitive-constructivist approaches with current work in narrative and discursive psychology, defining identity as "ideology cognized through the individual engagement with discourse, made manifest in a personal narrative constructed and reconstructed across the life course, and scripted in and through social interaction and social practice." This rich definition of identity informed our understanding of the stories of middle childhood, partly because these stories make up the raw material individuals will use to construct versions of the life story that will manifest an identity, and partly because the identity-forming processes that Hammack described are clearly emerging before adolescence. When children create themselves as characters in their own stories, they are beginning the work that will be referred to in adolescence as identity development.

In the first section below, we look at ways that conflict narratives show children 'engaging with discourse,' using their stories to claim a cultural identity. We see them appropriating culture in two major ways, first by alluding to master narratives recognizable in their cultural communities (Bamberg, 2004), and second by incorporating a polyphony of voices (Bakhtin, 1981). Next, we see the dawning of an authorial voice, as children show an awareness of self and a developing meta-awareness of the discursive nature of self-making. Finally, we see the dawning of children's awareness of the social, political, and economic issues that situate them in historical time and sociological place. We show how children struggle with, resist, and make alterations in the discourses that get incorporated in their stories. We see that the interpretive reproduction of culture does not result in the replication of culture. Children creating stories are creating new ways of interpreting experience, and this constitutes cultural change.

"I am nothing like those people": Claiming a Cultural Identity

When we asked children to write about a conflict, we did not instruct them further to let us know what kind of a person they are or want to be. Nevertheless, many of them took the recounting of a conflict as an opportunity to claim an identity. Consider the story in Example 8.1 by a Memphis fifth-grader.

EXAMPLE 8.1 PAXTON, FIFTH-GRADE BOY, CONNORS ELEMENTARY, MEMPHIS

I got into a Argument with my Cousin. I told him I didn't want to Fight my black race. we all are Family. We discuss things out and we both apolijize. This really happen. Now That we are cool, I watch his back, He watch my back. One Day I was coming home From School I got Jumped by Some Rosewood park boys From The Projects. They Thought They could Tell everybody What to do. Oh Yes I got a but kicking. But I seel am not afraid of Them. It dosen't make me a weec boy, It makes me a man From the beaten I tock axually I sleeped better That night feeling happy because I know I am Saved.

Paxton begins his story with an identity claim that situates him in a family – his argument is with his cousin. In his next sentence, Paxton identifies himself with a racial group, "my black race." His third sentence affirms the importance of both race and family: "we are all Family." As he assures us that his argument with his cousin was resolved, Paxton makes a subtle claim to a kind of 'street-worthiness.'

He and his cousin "are cool" and they watch each other's backs. Here he is using a metaphor that identifies him with a street culture – an identity that is problematized in the next part of his story. As he tells us about getting 'jumped' as he walked home from school, Paxton establishes another feature of his identity in opposition to an 'other.' He is not one of those 'boys from the Projects.' In Paxton's neighborhood in the 1990s, government-subsidized housing was referred to as "Housing Projects," and Paxton's family was financially better off than those who lived in Rosewood Park public housing. Paxton reports getting "a but kicking" from these boys, but he wants to reject the identity he fears his reader will ascribe to him because of this. "It doesn't make me a weec boy," Paxton asserts. In fact, he claims the identity "a man," based on his ability to take a beating. Before he ends this story, Paxton makes one more identity claim, telling us that he knows he is 'saved,' and thus claiming membership in a religious community, where 'getting saved' is a ritual of personal commitment and acceptance. In a 121-word story about "a conflict that really happened to you," this child made seven identity claims. The opportunity to make a narrative account of one's own experience is an invitation to work on the creation of an identity.

Paxton's identity claims can be understood further through an integrative model of child development proposed by Cynthia García Coll (García Coll & Szalacha, 2004). This model expands on ecological models of child development with the fundamental assumption that children's cognitive, emotional, and behavioral development is shaped profoundly by their social position. Features of the school and neighborhood environments and experiences with racism and segregation in a stratified social structure will both promote and inhibit aspects of development. The unique experiences and interplay among these derivatives of social stratification for children of color lead to unique pathways of child development and identity creation. Paxton attended a school that served a predominately African American, economically disadvantaged population, and was disturbingly under-resourced compared to the public schools located in more affluent neighborhoods ten miles up the interstate. Paxton's school and neighborhood contexts were inhibiting in the sense that they provided him with limited resources and academic preparation (he critiques his school in a later written account provided in Example 8.6), but they may have promoted strong social support, as relationships with "Family" and other members of his "black race" may have buffered him from negative influences and discriminatory experiences with mainstream society. No doubt, Paxton's experiences with exclusion, racism, and discrimination in various environmental contexts shaped his burgeoning understanding of his identity as a young, African American male in Memphis in the late 1990s; his written account of a conflict experience gives us a glimpse into this understanding.

In a close analysis of conversation between five young adolescent boys, Michael Bamberg (2004) found them strategically telling stories and using those stories to position themselves as certain kinds of characters, affirming their alliance with forms of masculinity and claiming moral commitments. We saw children five years younger similarly creating and defending identities for themselves in written narratives, both by alluding to master narratives and by incorporating voices from their cultural communities.

"I finally realized the difficulties Lubu experienced when he fought the three heroes": Appropriating Master Narratives

Children's work of creating identities for themselves sometimes seemed to be a very natural and unselfconscious side effect of using the language they know to tell about their experiences. When Paxton writes "I watch his back He watch my back," we have no reason to think that he deliberated about whether to use this expression or whether to say, more literally, "now we protect each other." But Paxton was clearly strategic in his presentation of self. When he writes, "it doesn't make me a weec boy," we see that Paxton is considering what his reader is likely to think. He knows that there are two interpretive frames, two master narratives in his cultural community – one that establishes manhood by being strong enough to overcome adversaries, and one that establishes manhood by being tough enough to 'take it.' A master narrative is a plotline or a thematic umbrella that is common and easily recognizable in a cultural community (Bamberg, 2011). Twenty-first-century North Americans and indeed citizens of many countries where Hollywood movies are exported are familiar with stories about super heroes who take on monstrous evils and emerge victorious. In contrast to that, we know stories about heroes who endure the 'slings and arrows of outrageous fortune' with dignity and perseverance, emerging with honor. Paxton is deliberate in directing his reader to the second of these master narratives – the cultural interpretation that supports the identity he is choosing for himself.

We saw children making use of master narratives and counting on their readers to see the connection between the experiences they recounted and the tales they referenced. When Shenzhen fourth-grader, Yu Bingyin, told about a property rights dispute with her desk-mate, she reported that he said, "You crossed the 38th parallel," alluding to the line of demarcation between North and South Korea. The establishment of the 38th parallel as a line to divide two Korean states ended a bitter war three generations earlier, and this child author counts on her readers' understanding of this as she seeks to explain her own conflict. Another Shenzhen boy, Hsu Enlai, wrote, "I was fighting alone. I finally realized the difficulties Lubu experienced when he fought the three heroes. But it was better as some people come to my side later, it's easier to be the 'five heroes on the langya mountain'." This author has appropriated two classic battle stories. The first story was from the *Romance of Three Kingdoms*, a fourteenth-century classic in Chinese literature. It portrays a battle between the powerful warrior Lubu, who finally fell to the three heroes Liu, Guan, and Zhang. Counting on his readers to understand these allusions, Hsu Enlai contrasts this with the story of the five heroes who fought against a Japanese attack under the leadership of the Communist Party between 1937 and 1945. When authors appropriated the classic stories, the history, and the master narratives of their communities, they were taking ownership of a cultural identity.

"You don't allways get what you whant, even if you try really hard": Appropriating a Polyphony of Voices

When fourth-grader Zaire describes her friendship with Tramecia, she writes, "we go together like sock with shoe, like chip with dip, like koolade with the flavor." Her words go straight from the page to the reader's ear, and those readers who have had an opportunity to spend much time with African American girls in the southern United States will quite probably experience at least two distinct movements of their shoulder as we read "KOOLade with the FLAvah!" Zaire used her narrative to express a part of her identity, to situate herself in a socio-historical cultural community. As children achieved their own narrative voice, we heard the polyphony of voices that Mikhail Bakhtin (1981) held to be critical to what it means to be a self. We argue that children begin to construct their identities as they select from the polyphony of voices around them, doing a similar kind of embellishment as Corsaro described in preschoolers' play.

Among the polyphony of voices children borrowed as they made a place for themselves in a cultural community were several that they quoted to claim authority. The clearest marker of the elusive literary quality we call voice is also the most literal: the use of direct and indirect quotation. In a sample of 689 stories we examined for this, we identified 3,427 instances of reports about speech (Walton & Walton-Wetzel, 2013). Only sixty-four of those stories included no occasions of any type of talk about talk, and only twenty-four of 451 children failed to include any reported speech in any of their stories. Clearly, when children wrote about interpersonal conflicts, talk about talk was pervasive.

We classified talk about talk in children's stories into six types: direct quotation (e.g., So after school she asked me "why are you getting an attitude?"), indirect quotation (e.g., So after school she asked me why I was getting an attitude), mixed quotation (e.g., So after school she asked me why am I getting an attitude), putative voicing (e.g., She should have asked me to stop), reports of speech acts (e.g., We discussed it out), and reports of non-speech (e.g., So I wouldn't speak to her for the rest of the day). In addition to counting each of these types of reported speech, we gave each story a score for the number of distinct types used. We noted *whose* speech appeared in the children's stories: adults, children, the self, and generalized others which included "someone" or "everyone" or "anyone." We used these counts to create a variable that would indicate how many distinct types of voices the child incorporated in the story. For example, if an author attributed speech to the self, to a child other, and to an adult other, that story had three 'voice types.' If the story also included speech attributed to a generalized other, it had four. As children got older, they produced more distinct forms of reported speech, and they included more distinct voices in their stories. When children reported about speech in their stories, they were strategic, more often selecting direct quotation when they quoted their own voice or the voice of an adult. Close examination of this showed that often children used direct quotation when they positioned the speaker as an authority figure. Note, for example, how Evalie used quotation in Example 8.2.

EXAMPLE 8.2   EVALIE, FIFTH-GRADE GIRL, IRONWOOD ELEMENTARY, MEMPHIS

It was when my friend and I got real mad because she got real mad because she said that in theren that it has fish poop and pee in it. I said NO and she said yes and we started arguing. So I went home and asked my mother She said no silly Where did you get a Idea like that I said one word "Vicky" then left I went upstairs. I called Vicky and said "My mom said that there is no pee or poop in the rain." She said your point and after that I hung up in her face.

Since Evalie's story is focused on a dispute over one statement, it is surprising that the author's first report of the statement in question is a barely understandable indirect quotation. When she writes, "she said that in theren that it has fish poop and pee in it," what 'she' said seems confused. When Evalie switches to direct quotation, reporting her dispute with Vicky, however, her meaning is clear: "I said NO and she said yes." Although she does not choose to use correct punctuation here, she does distinguish the authority of her own "NO" from Vicky's 'yes' by the use of capitals. Evalie uses direct quotation again (also without punctuation) when she reports her mother's response to her question about Vicky's claim: "No silly Where did you get an idea like that?" Then, Evalie makes use of quotation marks, bringing her antagonist's name into the story with accusatory force: "Vicky." Most importantly, though, she uses near-perfect grammatical quotation when she tells us that she told Vicky, "my mom said that there is no pee or poop in the rain." In terms of denotational content, this report is merely a reproduction of the confused report that opened the story. Vicky's speech is being rephrased and negated. This time, though, the author has avoided any incoherence, despite the fact that she is working with a more complex construction, triply voiced (I-[write]-that-I-said-that-my-mom-said). This difference between the two formal 'takes' on the same content is related to Evalie's claiming of authority in her story. At the beginning of her story, Evalie uses indirect quotation to report speech by another child that she is disputing. In the middle, she uses direct quotation of an adult to support her own belief. At the end, she embeds an indirect quote of the adult authority in a direct quote of her own voice. This establishment of her own authority is delivered with grammatical and orthographical correctness.

Evalie's story is a good example of the way that learning to write about one's own experience entails development that goes much beyond the learning of correct punctuation and grammatical form. As children add literacy skills to their cultural toolkit, they start using those tools, imperfectly at first, to create themselves. They take authority over their own experience. In Chapters 5 and 6, we saw how this authority gave many children moral agency. Here, we see a child take ownership of her own knowing. This is entirely consistent with Bruner's ideas, summarized in Chapter 1, that narrative requires both a moral and an epistemic stance. Below, we will also see evidence that child narrators take a cultural stance.

When children brought speech into their stories in the form of dialogue, as Evalie did, we easily coded whose voice was incorporated. Sometimes, however, the author claimed authoritative voices without direct or indirect quotation. When sixth-grader Barry asserted that he told his principal "the hold truth, and nothing but the truth," we recognize that he was lending credibility to his account by quoting a part of U.S. courtroom practice. Children similarly incorporated language of their Holy Scriptures or worship liturgy (e.g., "let those who have ears, hear!"), and in Shenzhen, we were able to identify official language that our Chinese readers heard as language of the state (e.g., "If you use your brain, think about solutions, any difficulty will be overcome and the door to victory will open, and dreams will come true").

Children borrowed freely from folk wisdom and common proverbs when they wanted to legitimize their own behavior or critique the behavior of an antagonist. Authors in Shenzhen were especially fond of this device, exhorting the reader that "It takes two people to fight but one to stop." "One should not treat others in ways that one would not like to be treated." "One should have the courage to admit their mistakes." "Sometimes success is only a matter of time." But children from our U.S. samples also appropriated proverbs and adages, such as third-grader Jeremiah from Memphis who, after describing the disappointment of not winning the prize he had expected, wrote: "The moral of this true is: You don't allways get what you whant, even if you try really hard." Then, thinking about what his readers would need to know, he added an addendum to the bottom of his page: "PS. Crying won't help either."

One common way that children claimed authority was by using the official language of school or church or state. When third-grader Chad said, "so me and him decided to breathe," we could hear the instruction that was a part of the social-emotional learning focus of the Orlando school he attended. When Neko said "I just used my walking feet," we could hear the voice of the staff at the Wellness Center where she attended KidsTalk sessions. Staff training there exhorted teachers and volunteers to avoid making negative commands (such as "Don't run") in favor of positive, if slightly odd ones (such as "find your walking feet"). One Memphis fifth-grader complaining about an antagonist who pushed her out of her chair on Good Friday wrote, "This is not the way we should act, especially on a holy day." A Shenzhen child wrote of her antagonist, "She does not demonstrate any collective spirit." When children picked up this kind of vocabulary in their stories, they aligned themselves with school or church or community center, or state, and they borrowed the authority of those institutions.

"This is my story and it's 100% true": Identity as Self-Awareness

We saw Paxton's strategic use of an authorial voice to influence his reader's ideas about the kind of person he was. "This really happen," he assures us, addressing the reader directly. The researchers from the gated college across town, who have expressed an interest in what it's like to be a sixth-grader these days, just might not believe that boys like Paxton and his cousin are capable of 'discussing things out,' negotiating mutual apologies, establishing a mutually supportive relationship. Paxton is thinking about what his readers probably believe about him, and he wants to set us straight. When an author spoke *as an author*, this constituted an additional layer of stance-taking. In addition to positioning the self vis-à-vis the other characters in the story (e.g., "those boys from the projects"), these authors positioned the self vis-à-vis an imagined reader.

As children exercise their authorial voice and begin incorporating multiple speech forms in their stories, what Bakhtin (1981) called a 'layering of voices,' they are developing meta-awareness, an awareness of the process of story-telling (Walton & Walton-Wetzel, 2013). Children made meta-narrative comments in 27.3% of their stories. These included statements that addressed the reader directly using an imperative form or a second-person pronoun (e.g., "Guess what!" "You won't believe what he did"), statements that labeled parts of the narrative or spoke about the story as a story (e.g., "Here's what happened next," "The end. Non-fiction"), and statements that made a self-conscious reference to the self as an author or narrator ("I don't want to say what she said but it was bad," "So, on I go with my story"). Meta-narrative comments increased with the grade of the author, and the children who 'went meta' in their stories wrote stories that were reliably judged by readers to be more literary than the stories that did not include these comments. The 'meta' stories were more likely to include dialogue, and they exhibited more psychological mindedness.

Our efforts to pin down the elusive quality we might call literary voice or authorial voice took us through many iterations of many coding schemes. We counted a variety of literary devices (e.g. emphasis markers, colloquialisms), we attempted to identify especially expressive vocabulary (e.g., 'perished' or 'bellowing'), we asked readers to make ratings on a Likert scale. We tried to get a handle on the quality of good writing that makes us feel we have a relationship with our favorite authors, that makes us recognize the undeniable style that distinguishes Faulkner from Hemingway (Humphrey, Walton, & Davidson, 2014). Sometimes, when we read a child's story, we experienced an undeniable sense that we were getting to know a real person. Compare Examples 8.3 and 8.4.

Write a story about a conflict with another
kid that really happened to you. Think
about a fight, an argument or some kind of
misunderstanding. Write everything that
happened from the beginning to the end.

One day ... I was playing inside
with my sister and my friend
my friend said I did something I
really didnt do. When we started to
my little sister went outside to
my home, I came to make it up and
tell her what was happening. Soon
she came out with my ... and my
... what happened so I ... ...
Finally she asked ... I only did what I
didnt do ... I said "no" and she sent
my old friend home. She told her
mom ... what happened and I wasnt
aloud to play with her for the
rest ... the summer.

EXAMPLE 8.3   Wendy, fourth-grade girl, Magnolia Springs Elementary, Orlando

EXAMPLE 8.3   WENDY, FOURTH-GRADE GIRL, MAGNOLIA SPRINGS ELEMENTARY, ORLANDO

One day when I was playing inside with my sister and my friend my friend said I did something I didn't really do. When we started to fight my little sister went upstairs to my mom's room to wake her up and tell her what was happening. Soon she came out with my mom and my mom asked what happened so I told her. Finally she asked if I really did what I didn't do so I said "no," and she sent my old friend home. She told her mom what happened and I wasn't alowd to play with her for the rest of the summer.

EXAMPLE 8.4   YVONNE, FIFTH-GRADE GIRL, MAGNOLIA SPRINGS ELEMENTARY, ORLANDO

One time in 4th grade My friend Angel and I, Were sitting at our own private desk doing our work. Now We are like best friends So we both wanted to sit together like every one does. So We asked are teacher Ms. hendrix to get a big table and let us sit together. When Ms. hendrix finaly got our desk we wilingiy Moved are stuff over to our new desk. After We were all settled and ready and rollen we were Just so happy and overjoyed because we got to sit by eachother. That wonderful satisfaction went one for about 2 ½ Months before...... [turn of page] After that 2 ½ months The battle began. Angel and I were just bellowing back & fourth. Then finally Ms. hendrix finally got Fed-up with it and Just Moved us to separate sides of the classroom. Well that's My story and it's all a 100% true!

Both of these stories describe adult intervention in a conflict between two friends. Wendy's story is strong in the mechanics of writing – it is high in clarity, and almost completely free of errors in spelling or conventions of punctuation. The author incorporates the voices of her friend and her sister with reports of speech acts; she uses indirect quotation to report her mother's speech, and perfectly grammatical direct quotation to report her own denial. Wendy does not, however, incorporate the features of style that contribute to a strong authorial voice. By comparison, Yvonne's story is rife with errors of spelling, capitalization, and punctuation, but what a vibrant young person comes off the page! She and Angel are not just at their desks – they are at their "own private desks." They don't just move – they "willingly move." They are not just settled, they are "ready and rollin." They were not simply happy, they were "just so hapy and overjoyed" and they experienced "that wonderful satisfaction." Their teacher didn't get annoyed, she "got fed up." The two friends didn't yell at each other – they were "just bellowing back and forth." Yvonne's use of the focusive 'like' in "we were like best friends" connects her to a teenage girl speech style (Dailey-O'Cain, 2000). Yvonne's awareness of herself as an author is demonstrated by her use of a page turn to emphasize the turning point of her story, and by her final meta-narrative comment to the reader. Self-awareness, attention to the way the self is perceived

Write a story about a conflict with another
kid that really happened to you. Think
about a fight, an argument or some kind of
misunderstanding. Write everything that
happened from the beginning to the end.

One time in 4th grade My friend ████████
and I were sitting at our own private desk
doing our work. Now we are like best friends
████ both wanted to sit together like
every one does. So we asked are teacher
████████ to get a big table and let us sit
together. when ████ finally got our desk
we willingly moved are stuff over to our
new desk. After we were all settled and
ready and rollen we were just so happy and
over joyed because we got to sit by each other.
That wonderful satisfication went one
for about 2½ Months before......

After that 2½ months The battle began.
████████ and I were just bellowing back +
fourth. Then finally ████ finally got
Fed-up with it and just moved us to seperate
sides of the classroom. Well that's My story
and it's all a 100% true ☺

EXAMPLE 8.4 Yvonne, fifth-grade girl, Magnolia Springs Elementary, Orlando by others, and explicit attempts to manipulate those perceptions are famously a part of the adolescent experience (Harter, 2012). We saw the beginnings of this in stories of middle childhood, as children like Yvonne demonstrated awareness of themselves as authors of their own experience.

"Respect should be given everywhere to create an equal society": Children's Take on Society

As children made themselves characters of one type or another in their own stories, they also characterized their cultural communities, sometimes making astute observations about the nature of the social world and their relationship to it. Bamberg (2004) described how storytellers accomplish narrative identity by positioning themselves in three ways. With level 1 positioning, authors take a stance vis-à-vis the other characters in the story. We saw Paxton, in Example 8.1, position himself in contrast to "those Rosewood park boys from the projects." Bamberg noted that while storytellers do this, they must also be aware of their relationship to the hearer of the story. When authors leave the 'story time' and speak directly to the reader in the present time, as when Paxton assured us "This really happen," they are doing what Bamberg called level 2 positioning. They 'go meta,' demonstrating an awareness of the process of story-telling. It takes considerable narrative skill to accomplish this, attending to both the events in the story time and the reactions in the telling time. Between 25% and 33% of elementary school children in our samples showed clear evidence of the ability to do level 2 positioning in their stories.

Bamberg's third level of positioning was rarer among the elementary children who wrote stories for us. This requires taking a stance vis-à-vis the master narratives or the broader discourses that are in play in a larger cultural community. When Li Na in Example 2.2 suggested, "She is just spoiled. She meant no harm," Li Na was having a voice in a current cultural discourse in China about 'spoiled little emperors' resulting from a 'one-child' policy, that had resulted in a generation of children with four grandparents all to themselves. Fifth-grader Feng Jin-Yun made a similar analysis of his antagonist: "Maybe he is spoiled at home. In society, a person like him is doomed to be useless."

Sometimes, children's society-level critiques showed an awareness not only of local concerns, but of global issues. A Shenzhen sixth-grade girl, Guo Ding-Ke, added her voice to a global discourse about the perils of environmental pollution when she criticized a classmate: "He said he spent two yuan on transportation every day as if he was so rich! Now everyone leads low carbon dioxide lifestyle. He still advocates high carbon dioxide life style!" We saw a similar critique of cultural practices or cultural values in several stories from our university-affiliated elementary school and from our KidsTalk sessions that served primarily professional-class families. Sometimes children in these samples mentioned brand names that they presented as important markers of status. Twice among those 'brand-name' stories, authors problematized this kind of materialist snobbery, as when a fifth-grader quoted her classmate, "Just because you wear Coach sneakers that doesn't mean you're better than me."

Stories in which children took a political or ideological stance were rare in our sample, but it is noteworthy that they were not absent. A third-grader, born in 2008, when Barack Obama was elected to the U.S. presidency, was participating in a KidsTalk session during the 2016 presidential campaign. She interrupted the storyteller to exclaim, "I'm sad about that white man for president." One of the other children responded: "Yeah, he's going to make us all be cleaners." This child, attending a "college preparatory" charter elementary school in Memphis, serving nearly 100% African American children from a low-income, high-poverty neighborhood, probably had little understanding of economic policy or political platforms, but she had some awareness of the fragility of her chances for going to college and moving into the professions. She wanted to become a teacher ("if my singing career doesn't work out"), and she had some sense of the possibility that the results of a presidential election might affect her chances.

As we saw in Chapter 6, children rarely criticized their teachers in their stories, but they occasionally made implicit critiques of the educational system. A Memphis fifth-grader described her progress in gymnastics (learning to do back-bends and handsprings), and expressed a desire to learn to work on the uneven bars and the parallel bars, but, she reported, her school did not have enough money for this equipment. When we asked Paxton to write another story about a conflict six months after he wrote the story that opened this chapter, he made an astute critique of the effectiveness of his school (see Example 8.5).

EXAMPLE 8.5   PAXTON, FIFTH-GRADE BOY, CONNORS ELEMENTARY, MEMPHIS

I almost fell 2nd grade but I passed. My teacher said you might fell. when I got my report card in the summer it said promoted to third grade. I was happy In 3rd grade It was easy to me but I passed with C's and B's. This part I'm telling You is trueful. Ms. Milton was teacher that that didn't teach well, but she was smart. I had c's and D's, and A's. I mostly had B's and A's going down the row on my card. When my report card was mailed. It had C's and D's. I had a d in soc studies, science, and math. She passed me for nonthing. I knew I was supposed to fell. but she passed most of uswith bad grades She couldn't teach Thats why I dont have the skills for 5th Grade.

The system of assigning grades appears to be a bit opaque to Paxton. He reports that he had "C's and B's" in the third grade. Then in the fourth grade he reports, "I had c's and D's, and A's. I mostly had B's and A's going down the row on my card." He doesn't seem to think that there is a clear connection between his report card and his performance. What he does understand is that he does not now "have the skills for 5th Grade," and that he should have failed fourth grade. He attributes this to be the shortcomings of a fourth-grade teacher who was smart, but "didn't teach well."

We never cease to be impressed in this era in which children's literacy skills are constantly assessed, and often fail to meet strict standards, that the stories written in a half hour by elementary school students are so enlightening. As children position themselves in local and global contexts, they embrace, resist, and critique their cultural communities.

Conclusions: Creating the Self/Creating the Future

The analyses we have presented here suspend the elementary school story-makers we studied between the playful interpretive reproduction that Corsaro described in preschool children and the identity quest that Hammack described in adolescence and beyond. Like the preschoolers, the children we studied embellished their stories with metaphors and idioms and a variety of voices borrowed from the various cultural communities that intersected with theirs. Like the adolescents, they positioned themselves as certain kinds of characters, attending to the stance they were taking vis-à-vis the researcher who would read their stories, and occasionally entering into a broad cultural discourse. While elementary-aged children's identity is very much in the early stages of development, we are convinced that the cognitive and socio-cultural struggles to achieve a sense of identity are not just an adolescent and adult project. The participants in our studies have made a respectable start.

It is apparent that when they narrate stories of personal conflict, children are taking in culture. But they are not regurgitating culture. These young authors are preparing to become change agents and creators of the future. Sixth-grader Manny has plans to "make my own help program to help people that do drugs and violence (And I will call the program Stay Drugs and Violence Free)." We have hopes that Guo Ding-Ke will grow up to create policies and practices that will support a "low carbon dioxide life-style." Children prepare to do this recreating and transforming their cultural communities as they borrow from the polyphony of voices and manipulate master narratives to serve their own aims. This is a narrative project, and as they undertake it, on the cusp of adolescence, they are simultaneously creating themselves.

References

Bahktin, M. (1981). *The dialogic imagination*. (C. Emerson & M. Holquist Trans.). Austin, TX: University of Texas Press.

Bamberg, M. (2004). "I know it may sound mean to say this, but we couldn't really care less about her anyway": Form and functions of "slut bashing" in male identity constructions in 15-year-olds. *Human Development*, 47(6), 331–53.

Bamberg, M. (2011). Who am I? Narration and its contribution to self and identity. *Theory & Psychology, 21*(1), 3–24.

Berzonsky, M. D. (1989). Identity style conceptualization and measurement. *Journal of Adolescent Research, 4*(3), 268–82.

Briggs, J. L. (1992). Mazes of meaning: How a child and a culture create each other. *New Directions for Child and Adolescent Development, 58*, 25–49.

Corsaro, W. (1992). Interpretive reproduction in children's peer cultures. *Social Psychology Quarterly, 55*(2), 160–77.

Dailey-O'Cain, J. (2000). The sociolinguistic distribution of and attitudes toward focuser *like* and quotative *like*. *Journal of Sociolinguistics, 4*, 60–80. doi:10.1111/1467-9481.00103.

García Coll, C., & Szalacha, L. A. (2004). The multiple contexts of middle childhood. *Future of Children, 14*(2), 81–97.

Erikson, E. (1950). *Childhood and society.* New York, NY: W. W. Norton.

Hammack, P. L. (2008). Narrative and the cultural psychology of identity. *Personality and Social Psychology Review, 12*(3), 222–47.

Harter, S. (2012). *The construction of the self: Developmental and sociocultural foundations.* New York, NY: Guilford Press.

Humphrey, R., Walton, M. D., & Davidson, A. J. (2014). "Im gonna tell you all about it": Authorial voice and conventional skills in writing assessment and educational practice. *Journal of Educational Research, 107*(2), 111–22.

Marcia, J. E. (1966). Development and validation of ego-identity status. *Journal of Personality and Social Psychology, 3*(5), 551–8.

Moshman, D. (1998). Identity as a theory of oneself. *Genetic Epistemologist, 26*(3), 1–16.

Walton, M. D., & Walton-Wetzel, J. A. (2013). Reported speech and the development of narrative voice in middle childhood. *Narrative Inquiry, 23*(2), 388–404.

PART III

Applying the Lessons Learned From Children's Stories of Conflict

9

ORAL STORY-SHARING PRACTICES AND THE HEALTHY CLASSROOM COMMUNITY

> and then I talked to her. When I started talking, I told her how I felt.
>
> *LaToya, fourth-grade girl, Connors Elementary, Memphis*

Throughout Part II we described how much rich psychological and moral analysis children do when they share stories about their own conflict experiences. We have seen their willingness to share with one another and with researchers their take on what it's like to be a kid these days, and their take on the world around them. Any notions we may have had that childhood is a carefree time have been replaced with a deep respect for the courageous work that children do – to form friendships that involve communication and trust (as well as fun and liking), to begin the work of forming (and defending) identities as people with moral agency, to claim a voice in the polyphony of voices that surround them – and to do all of that while they manage conflicts with their peers and siblings, parents and teachers. We have argued throughout this book that the human practice of creating and sharing narrative accounts is critical to the social, emotional, and moral development of these children. In this chapter, we describe an oral story-sharing practice, and we look closely at how the encouragement of a narrative culture might enhance student development and classroom communities. We argue that such a practice is especially impor- tant for appropriately managing the inevitable conflicts that emerge in middle childhood, for promoting student engagement, and for encouraging an inclu- sive classroom community.

Around the time we began collecting written narratives as part of a violence prevention program, we also began to organize story-sharing circles in afterschool programs, in community centers, and sometimes in summer camps. We gathered six to eight children in a circle, with one or two college students. At each session, we suggested a story prompt, and each child was given a turn to tell his or her own story about the prompt. "Tell about a time you or someone you know got lost," "Tell about a time you fixed something." "Tell about a time somebody got blamed for something they didn't do." "Tell about a time you went on a trip." "Tell about a time something was really unfair." Appendix E includes a list of all the prompts we have used over twenty years of KidsTalk sessions, organized by topic. We passed around a 'story stick,' and the only rule was that everyone must listen to the storyteller who had the stick. No child was required to tell a story, and some children were hesitant, sharing a story only after attending several sessions without speaking. Most children enjoyed the activity, however. KidsTalk facilitators participated in a simple two-hour training session, so that they knew how to handle difficult situations that arose occasionally, and so that they had an opportunity to discuss ethical responsibilities. The primary responsibility of the facilitator was to give each storyteller undivided attention. No correcting, no challenging, minimal prompting. (Appendix F includes instructions for KidsTalk facilitators.) The fact is, most children love to tell about their experiences. They love to have an adult who is genuinely interested in what has happened, and after a few sessions, most of them show signs of enjoying the stories told by the other children in their circles.

Most of the KidsTalk sessions we run are not for research purposes. Students in a developmental psychology class and students on our research team benefit from opportunities to hear children telling about their lives in their own words, and the afterschool programs and community centers where KidsTalk is implemented find it to be a valuable addition to their programming. For nine months, during the 2005–6 academic year, however, we got permissions from parents and from the staff at a Community Wellness Center to study the stories children told. We were pleased to find that over the nine months children's stories got more sophisticated in many ways. The more sessions children participated in, the more their stories included causal links between events, the more attention they gave to internal psychological states of both the self and other actors in the story, and the more their stories incorporated assessments of the events and behaviors described. These findings were replicated ten years later, when we saw similar improvements with practice over the eight weeks of a summer camp. Remember that KidsTalk facilitators only listened. They responded with appropriate emotion and with genuine interest, but they did not prompt the children with "how did that feel?" or "why do you think she did that?" Children began including in their stories more internal state reports, and more moral evaluations, not because they were asked to do this. Practice just made them better story-tellers, and these features of a landscape of consciousness were part of a good story in their cultural communities.

More surprising than the gradual improvement of children's stories as they participated in KidsTalk was the impact that KidsTalk had on the children who had not attended. We compared the first three stories told by children who began KidsTalk during the first three months to those of children who dropped in during the second trimester, to those of children who did not participate until the third trimester of program implementation. We found that the very first stories of children who began participation later were more attentive to a landscape of consciousness and to moral assessment than were the first stories of the children who began when KidsTalk was new. KidsTalk not only gave children practice in making better and better stories, it created a 'story-sharing culture' in the Wellness Center. The staff of the center, in response to the enthusiasm the children expressed for telling their stories, even outside of KidsTalk sessions, added a 'story table' to activities that children could select in the quiet-play room. Children chose to play board games, to work on art projects, to read or do homework – and some of them chose to write their stories. The staff asked us for prompt suggestions, and started posting a new prompt each week at the story table. They started designing prompts that supported their own educational programming. "Tell about something that happened when you were home alone" was the prompt at the table when home-alone safety was the focus of the week's lessons. "Tell about a time you tried a new food" was the prompt during 'good nutrition' week. Once the nine-month study was over, the center director asked us to provide KidsTalk training for all the child-life specialists, and we have been doing this regularly. They recognized that the creation of a community in which individuals are encouraged to share their stories with each other was altogether supportive of their mission to promote good health behaviors.

As we watched children participate week after week in story-sharing circles, we became increasingly aware of how their stories influenced one another. In a session in which the children were prompted to "tell about something that happened in a big storm," the first child told what was clearly an important family story about a flood that destroyed her grandmother's home. The next child did not tell about a storm; he told about a time his grandmother had to go to the hospital. What followed was a sharing of grandmother stories. The children wanted to tell one another about what their grandmothers were like, and this was more interesting to them than stories about storms, perhaps because it was more identity-relevant. Children wanted to share stories about what was important to them.

In addition to sharing stories that were thematically similar, children emulated the literary devices that their peers used when they shared personal stories. In one KidsTalk session, an especially expressive child told the story in Example 9.1.

EXAMPLE 9.1 VAIDA, FIFTH-GRADE GIRL, COMMUNITY WELLNESS, MEMPHIS

One time I was outside and I was with my sister and my sister and I went to the park and we played a lot and lot and lot of times and I saw my class walking to the park and I hid away from them because they saw me and I didn't want them to see me because they will come and tell me that Ms. Black said, "Don't ride to the park," because I will get in trouble and I did it anyway and I got in trouble and I was right by my teacher. After she came to get me I was definitely in trouble and I was not right by my teacher and my mom took me over my grandma's house and I went to use the restroom so she said "No" but I went anyway and I went to the park with my friends and they asked me what was I doing and *I said "nothing"* and we played a lot and lot and lot of games and my mother told me "No" after all so me and my sister never did it again and ever ever ever ever and ever again. So, I did it one more time and I never ever ever ever ever did it again because I was punished because I did it. I was punished because I disobeyed her and I wasn't supposed to disobey her, she told me not to do it but I did it. I had to clean up a lot and lot and lots and lots of times and clean up my room and wash the dishes and sweep and mop the floor and clean my cat's litter box and my dog's and my puppy's and my rat's.

A couple of stories later, a child told a story about her brother, who got in trouble "a lot and lot and lot and lot." Another child made his friend promise to "never ever ever ever do that again." By the end of the week, we were noticing the use of this engaging oratory device in conversations the children had with one another around the center. We are not inclined to dismiss this as an uninteresting example of children imitating one another. We believe that we were observing how the regular sharing of stories creates local culture – culture writ small – in which ideas, themes, and literary tropes are propagated through friendship groups. This, we believe, is how children come to share interpretive repertoires and explanatory systems – some of them aligned with the cultural communities familiar to their grown-ups, and some of them quite distinct from anything that the grown-ups in their world would use or recognize. Maybe Vaida had heard the expression "a lot and lot and lot" used in her family or in her community, but we think it is unlikely that an adult would say this. Vaida probably attended a church where she regularly recited "to God be the glory forever and ever. Amen." We suspect that she extended this bit of liturgical oratory. We also suspect that the grown-ups took no notice of the fact that the children had developed a fondness for the repetition of quantifiers. This is a trivial enough example, but we argue that it is an example of the very ground-floor creation of culture we discussed in Chapter 8 – culture created by children as they do the playful embellishment and recombination of the symbols and meanings in the world around them. Further, it reveals the social nature and the connection-enhancing power of story-telling.

As children participate and engage in this practice together, they are developing a sense of belonging and identity within their community; but, as "a lot and a lot and a lot" and "again and again and again and again" reveal to us, children are not simply regurgitating the narrative practice modeled to them by adults. Through this shared, social activity, children are also changing the practice, creating a new practice that suits them (Miller & Goodnow, 1995).

After so many years of focusing on the stories children told in KidsTalk sessions, our attention has only recently been drawn to the way children respond to one another's stories. We do not have video records of our story-sharing sessions, but when we listened to the audio files of KidsTalk sessions at the FLASH summer camp, we were struck by an impression that children became increasingly considerate of one another's stories as the summer progressed. Much work remains to be done to determine whether this impression holds up to careful observation and systematic analysis. Ongoing research by Monisha Pasupathi and her colleagues at the University of Utah has focused on the effects of listeners on story-tellers (Pasupathi & Billitteri, 2015). Their work has found that more attentive listeners promote more elaboration and attention to the landscape of consciousness in story-tellers. We admire the ethnographic research of Peggy Miller and her colleagues with preschool children in families, giving careful attention to paralinguistic features of communicative exchanges (Miller, Fung, Lin, Chen, & Boldt, 2012) and we are eager to see future research develop more analytic procedures that can capture the back-channel encouragement (or disapproval), the call-and-response-type affirmations that children provide for one another, and the rolling of eyes and other non-verbal expressions of disapproval or disdain. After all, when stories are told, they are told to someone, and it seems important to understand the impact of story-telling on the listener in addition to the storyteller. This is a rich area for future research.

Recent research on social-emotional learning has focused on the development of classroom activities that promote the creation of compassionate communities and nurture children's social-emotional well-being (Greenberg & Harris, 2009). While a primary goal of schools is preparing children to succeed academically, there is broad agreement that success in life also requires that children engage in socially skilled, respectful, and safe ways of interacting with parents, teachers, peers, and community members (Weissberg, Durlak, Domitrovich, & Gullotta, 2015). Further, as schools and communities become increasingly multicultural with racially, ethnically, and economically diverse students, it is more important than ever that children learn to maintain healthy, productive relationships with individuals from different backgrounds. The Collaborative for Academic, Social, and Emotional Learning (CASEL) is an organization developed to help establish evidence-based social-emotional learning as an essential part of preschool through high school education (see www.casel.org). One of the five core competence domains recognized by CASEL is social awareness (Weissberg & Cascarino, 2013).

This domain includes "the ability to take the perspective of those with different backgrounds or cultures and to empathize and feel compassion" (Weissberg et al., 2015, p. 6). In the following sections of this chapter, we argue that a story-sharing activity similar to KidsTalk can support many of the goals of social-emotional learning programs, promoting the development of a peaceful classroom, an engaging classroom, and an inclusive classroom community.

Story-Sharing and the Peaceful Classroom

In 1998 we began our work as part of a violence prevention program organized by the MidSouth Peace and Justice Center, and a major insight achieved in our first year of regular meetings with representatives of a dozen community organizations devoted to non-violence was that our goal should not be to suppress conflict. A peaceable classroom is not a classroom in which there are no conflicts. We have learned from education theorists including Jean Piaget (1932/65), John Dewey (1916/2004), and Jerome Bruner (1996) that children do not grow and learn, and indeed, humans do not thrive without conflict. We are challenged to create deeper and more effective understanding when our expectations are violated. Such violations provoke us to reconcile differences between the way things are and the way we think they should be. In the social domain, this almost always involves interpersonal conflict. We came to believe more and more deeply that our classrooms should be places where conflict is respected as an important part of social life, and where children learn to do conflict well. We met initial resistance from educators when we argued that peer conflicts are absolutely critical to social, emotional, and moral development. Their reluctance is understandable: teachers have important work to do, and interpersonal conflicts between children interrupt math or history or science lessons. Most of the teachers who participated in our research, however, were ultimately persuaded that their academic work is supported when their children have the skills they need to resolve conflicts peacefully. Effective conflict resolution skills in children are more beneficial than efforts to suppress conflicts by teachers.

When conflicts happen between peers, children should have the opportunity to 'tell their side of the story.' Some disputes concern fundamental disagreements about what happened – about the sequence of events and the causal connections between them – and we saw that the ability to construct such chronologies is a fundamental part of narrative coherence that increased with practice. More often, however, conflicts erupt because of misunderstandings about the motives or intentions of other actors. In these cases children need to be able to explain their reasons and motives. In Example 4.5 in Chapter 4, Brandi described a conflict in which she and her friend, Cameron, got to the gym "kinda late" and saw their friend, Kito, playing with another girl, Sheena. Brandi and Cameron apparently didn't notice when Sheena left the gym so Kito, now alone, "thought we were trying to avoid her and ignore her." Brandi had to be able to explain to Kito that they thought she was still playing with Sheena. Resolution of the conflict required her to understand that her own thoughts and interpretations were relevant to establishing the meaning of her behavior as antisocial. We saw that KidsTalk participants gradually included more descriptions of their own thoughts, emotions, and motives as they got more and more practice with telling stories. Communicating one's own intentions, and explaining how one's own motives are aligned with the general good, is critical to negotiating peaceful resolution to conflicts.

As a classroom community gradually comes to establish its own moral order, children not only need to have the opportunity to tell their side of the story, they need to know that this kind of accountability will be expected of them. A peaceful community is one in which each member is afforded moral agency, and we saw throughout Part II of this book that story-tellers claim moral agency as they position themselves as good guys or bad guys in their own stories. Ageliki Nicolopoulou's work with preschool children showed that children move with narrative practice from stories that described actors behaving in the world, to stories describing agents whose behavior is linked to intentions and other mental states, to stories describing persons with character traits and full mental representations (Nicolopoulou & Richner, 2007). When children are expected to make themselves the protagonists in their own stories, they claim a position in the moral order and are challenged to take moral responsibility for their own behavior.

Story-Sharing and the Engaged Classroom

Learning is not always fun, especially for the children whose experience includes repeated failure feedback. But we believe our children should be happy in school. They will be more fully engaged in activities they enjoy. KidsTalk has been an optional activity in most of the settings where we have implemented it. In some afterschool settings, it was one of the activities available during the 'quiet homework time.' Children were supposed to finish homework first, but some of them snuck into KidsTalk to avoid those worksheets they had to do. In one setting children could choose to come to story-sharing or to play board games, sit in the reading beanbags, or work at the art table. Different settings offered different options, but we found many children eager to participate in every community center or afterschool program where it was offered. We did not fully understand, however, how much children enjoyed this simple opportunity to share their experience with others until we implemented KidsTalk at the FLASH summer camp. Fifteen minutes before KidsTalk was about to begin each day, an announcement was made over the camp loudspeaker. We were astonished to see children rushing to get dried off from the water-slide, closing down their activities in the computer room, and leaving the basketball court or the gymnastics floor to come join our circles.

Story-making and story-sharing is a primary form of entertainment among humans in a variety of cultural contexts (Kyratzis, 1999; Engel, 1995; Nicolopoulou, 2002). People who can tell a good story are fun to be around because good stories are fun to hear. We saw in Chapter 3 that sharing stories or "just talking" is a frequently mentioned friendship activity. Story-sharing happens among children in middle childhood, whether or not the adults facilitate the practice. We believe, however, that there is much to be gained by making time and space to support this activity in classrooms. When children get better at telling their own stories and at listening to their classmates' stories, they are developing friend-making skills. A classroom practice of story-sharing may also enhance children's sense of engagement because it feels good to share a personal story and to be heard. When we share the joys and sorrows of our past experiences with an attentive audience, sympathetic listeners may celebrate and laugh with us or cry with us. And, more than that, when others listen to our story, it means that some aspect of our self is acknowledged and accepted. The Pasupathi and Billitteri (2015) findings of the effect of attentive listening on story-tellers, described previously, support this claim. No doubt being heard contributes to children's sense of belonging within the classroom community. Classrooms in which children have a sense of belonging and feel connected to the other children are classrooms in which children are engaged in learning, and academic progress is enhanced by healthy peer relationships (Osterman, 2000).

As classroom narrative practice bolsters children's sense of belonging and connection, it can also support children's developing reading skills. To support young readers' ability to attach their own experiences to what they are reading (i.e., text-to-self connections), teachers can incorporate story-telling activities into their classroom reading instruction. Whitney Chatterjee, a fourth-grade teacher in Charleston, South Carolina, has developed a classroom practice that harnesses the power of personal story-telling in the service of reading instruction and in the development of critical thinking skills. Noting the difficulty that many children have in achieving the advanced reading skills of making inferences and applying prior knowledge to their current learning in independent reading, she developed *The Reader's Toolkit* (2016), a set of tools (given to each child in a 'toolkit') that make these skills concrete for children and allow young readers to apply them in a very personal way. During classroom reading exercises, when students make a text-to-self connection, they pull out a paper clip with their picture glued to it from their toolkit and attach it to the page where they made a connection (see the paperclip example and other examples of these reading tools in Appendix F). Students then share their personal story with the rest of the class. Just as they know that a paper clip attaches one piece of paper to another, they come to realize that their own personal stories attach to those of the characters or the information in a book. This simple but powerful activity keeps children engaged by using a tangible object and it draws them into a narrative community by giving them the opportunity to share (and to listen to) personal stories that are related to course material. This is the very essence of engaged learning.

Story-Sharing and the Inclusive Classroom Community

Teacher encouragement for story-sharing may be especially valuable for children who are likely to be left out or for children who face challenges with communication or social skills. KidsTalk-like classroom activities can give such children opportunities to practice skills that will facilitate their integration in the classroom community and will help them develop the skills that support friendships.

In classroom settings that are enriched by cultural diversity among the students, teacher-facilitated story-sharing may be especially important for two reasons. First, the perspective-taking skills that story-sharing promotes are even more important when students come from widely different backgrounds (Abrams, Rutland, Palmer, & Purewal, 2014). The more children share stories, the more they understand one another, learn from one another, and form connections to one another. A second reason to emphasize story-sharing in diverse classrooms pertains to the connection between oral narratives and literacy development (Cooper, 2005). We noted in Chapter 8 how African American children in the U.S. South bring narrative performance skills that are developed in rich traditions of front porch (or front stoop) story-telling, and much work has described the variety of narrative forms and dynamic improvisational skills that are highly valued in these communities (Bloome, Katz, & Champion, 2003; Green, 2002). Recent research with preschoolers has shown that the link between oral narrative and literacy skills may be especially strong for African American children (Gardner-Neblett & Iruka, 2015). Skillful teachers recognize the narrative skills the children bring to the classroom as a strength, and they give the children opportunities to use that strength as a springboard to writing and to a love of other academic pursuits. Less skillful teachers, we fear, may see these remarkable narrative performances as disruptions to classroom practices, and this disapproval may be a hindrance to the development of a positive teacher–child relationship.

It is not only African American children who benefit from story-telling at home, however. Indeed, many immigrant families and ethnic communities similarly nurture narrative traditions (Cline & Necochea, 2003). Further, research documents the importance of family narrative in fostering resilience for children (Bohanek, Marin, Fivush, & Duke, 2006; Fiese et al., 1999; Fivush, Bohanek, Robertson, & Duke, 2004). Children benefit when families tell stories, and especially when several family members collaborate to tell stories. When teachers provide opportunities for sharing these stories, this may promote an inclusive school environment for children and their parents. Families of recent immigrant children and parents whose own literacy skills are limited or who face a language barrier in communicating with school staff may not feel welcomed and may sometimes feel intimidated by teachers and by an unfamiliar school system (LaRocque, Kleiman, & Darling, 2011; Kavanagh & Hickey, 2013). Research is clear that family involvement is important for children's success in school, and immigrant parents care deeply about their children's education; but it is often difficult for them to know how to be involved. When teachers and school administrators recognize and celebrate these oral narrative skills, they may set children up to be more successful with writing and reading, and they may help parents to be more involved in the children's education in the process. We consider the connections between narrative and literacy more closely in Chapter 10.

Conclusions and Recommendations

Our twenty-five years of listening to children in KidsTalk settings in schools, in afterschool programs, in summer camps, and in community centers have convinced us that there is much to be gained by establishing a regular practice of story-sharing between children. KidsTalk-like story circles can be implemented in different ways, consistent with the aims and constraints of various classrooms and programs. We have a set of four recommendations for making KidsTalk maximally beneficial over a wide range of settings:

1. Develop prompts that request stories relevant to ongoing programming and curriculum. For example, if the classroom is implementing a bullying prevention program, the children can be invited to tell stories about a time someone was bullied. This will almost certainly result in the sharing of stories that report genuine pain and struggle for some children, and it will give both the adults and the other children opportunities to understand and to respond to that pain. If the lesson for the day is about fractions, ask children to tell about a time they had to divide something up. When children are encouraged to share their personal experiences, their learning becomes personal. This is the defining feature of engaged learning.
2. Formulate and implement curriculum that addresses the concerns raised by children in their stories. The themes that arise and the topics that dominate children's stories can serve as guides for programming and interventions. If the adults are listening to children's stories, they may learn about what events in the news have captured the children's imaginations (and should probably be discussed with some adult guidance). For example, after Hurricane Katrina struck New Orleans and many displaced families came north to Memphis, we heard children telling very confused stories about broken levees. It became clear that most of them did not know what a levee is, how it works, and how it might fail to work. An attentive and creative teacher who recognized this could integrate various lessons with what the children needed to know about their own safety. In Memphis, a field trip could allow

children to see levees on the Mississippi River and this could be integrated with lessons in history, social studies, science, literature, and music. Such lessons could help translate children's moral concerns into moral action.

3. Quote material from the children's stories. When adults listen to children, they are in a position to strengthen children's voices. A thoughtful teacher can use the children's own words to encourage the child's development. For example, when Samuel is teasing a child who made a bad grade, his teacher can say, "Stop being mean to your classmate," or she could instead say, "I remember that story you told about helping Ralph after he fell during freeze tag. I know you are a really kind person." The latter affirms Samuel's good character and encourages him to make his own decision to stop teasing his classmate.

4. Encourage children to gather stories in their families, and treat these stories as treasures. We found that it was not uncommon for children to tell stories about their families, regardless of the prompt. If we asked about a conflict with a classmate, we would often get a child telling about a conflict with a sibling or cousin. If one child in a session did this, it was very likely that we would have sibling conflicts all around. Children want to tell stories about what is most significant to them, and their family life often fits that bill. When we honor family stories and story-telling traditions, we are showing respect for the child's home and the family's wisdom. This can help form links between children's sense of belonging in the classroom and their participation in larger social contexts (Hammack, 2010). Further, the practice of listening to the diverse experiences and perspectives of others is a way to create an inclusive classroom climate, especially in classrooms that are enriched by ethnic diversity (Lee & Quintana, 2005).

In any context where adults are designing programs to promote healthy development among children, listening to children's voices should be a central practice. Children's experiences are constantly changing with technological, social, and political evolution. It is one thing for adults to provide opportunities for children; it is an even better thing for those opportunities to be grounded in the lived experiences and concerns of those same children. Through the simple act of listening to children's stories, we can gain a better understanding of their daily experiences and be better equipped to meet their needs in the most relevant ways. In addition to helping us understand the needs of children, narrative practice encourages children's developing understanding of themselves and their communities. Providing constructive opportunities for children to voice their experiences and concerns through narrative encourages their process of making meaning of those experiences. These narrative practices serve to strengthen children's voice so that they can more effectively participate and shape the social, moral, and civil discourses of their communities.

References

Abrams, D., Rutland, A., Palmer, S. B., & Purewal, K. (2014). Children's responses to social atypicality among group members: Advantages of a contextualized social developmental account. *British Journal of Developmental Psychology, 32*(3), 257–61. doi:10.1111/bjdp.12053.

Bloome, D., Katz, L., & Champion, T. (2003). Young children's narratives and ideologies of language in classrooms. *Reading & Writing Quarterly: Overcoming Learning Difficulties, 19*(3), 205–23. doi:10.1080/10573560308216.

Bohanek, J. G., Marin, K. A., Fivush, R., & Duke, M. P. (2006). Family narrative interaction and children's sense of self. *Family Process, 45*(1), 39–54.

Bruner, J. S. (1990). *Acts of meaning.* Cambridge, MA: Harvard University Press.

Bruner, J. S. (1996). *The culture of education.* Cambridge, MA: Harvard University Press.

Cline, Z., & Necochea, J. (2003). My mother never read to me. *Journal of Adolescent & Adult Literacy, 47*(2), 122–6.

Chatterjee, W. (2016). *The reader's toolkit.* Unpublished manuscript.

Cooper, P. M. (2005). Literacy learning and pedagogical purpose in Vivian Paley's "storytelling curriculum". *Journal of Early Childhood Literacy, 5*(3), 229–51. doi:10.1177/1468798405058686.

Dewey, J. (1916/2004). *Democracy and education: An introduction to the philosophy of education.* London: Macmillan.

Engel, S. L. (1995). *The stories children tell: Making sense of the narratives of childhood.* New York, NY: W.H. Freeman.

Fiese, B. H., Sameroff, A. J., Grotevant, H. D., Wamboldt, F. S., Dickstein, S., Fravel, D. L., . . . & Seifer, R. (1999). The stories that families tell: Narrative coherence, narrative interaction, and relationship beliefs. *Monographs of the Society for Research in Child Development, 64*(2).

Fivush, R., Bohanek, J., Robertson, R., & Duke, M. (2004). Family narratives and the development of children's emotional well-being. In M. W. Pratt & B. H. Fiese (Eds.), *Family stories and the life course* (pp. 55–76). Mahwah, NJ: Lawrence Erlbaum Associates.

Gardner-Neblett, N., & Iruka, I. U. (2015). Oral narrative skills: Explaining the language-emergent literacy link by race/ethnicity and SES. *Developmental Psychology, 51*, 889–904. doi:10.1037/a0039274.

Green, L. (2002). A descriptive study of African American English: Research in linguistics and education. *International Journal of Qualitative Studies In Education, 15*(6), 673–90. doi:10.1080/0951839022000014376.

Greenberg, M. T., & Harris, A. R. (2009). Nurturing mindfulness in children and youth: Current state of research. *Child Development Perspectives, 6*(2), 161–6. doi:10.1111/j.1750-8606.2011.00215.

Hammack, P. L. (2010). Narrative and the cultural psychology of identity. *Personality and Social Psychology Review, 12*(3), 222–47.

Kavanagh, L., & Hickey, T. M. (2013). "You're looking at this different language and it freezes you out straight away": Identifying challenges to parental involvement among immersion parents. *Language and Education, 27*(5), 432–50.

Kyratzis, A. (1999). Narrative identity: Preschoolers' self-construction through narrative in same-sex friendship group dramatic play. *Narrative Inquiry, 9*, 427–55.

LaRocque, M., Kleiman, I., & Darling, S. M. (2011). Parental involvement: The missing link in school achievement. *Preventing School Failure, 55*(3), 115–22.

Lee, D, C., & Quintana, S. M. (2005). Benefits of cultural exposure and development of Korean perspective-taking ability for trans-racially adopted Korean children. *Cultural Diversity and Ethnic Minority Psychology, 11,* 130–43.

Miller, P. J., Fung, H., Lin, S., Chen, C-H., & Boldt, B. (2012). How socialization happens on the ground: Narrative practices as alternate socializing pathways in Taiwanese and European-American families. *Monographs of the Society for Research in Child Development,* 77(1, Serial No. 302). Boston, MA: Wiley-Blackwell.

Miller, P. J., & Goodnow, J. J. (1995). Cultural practices: Toward an integration of culture and development. *New Directions for Child and Adolescent Development, 67,* 5–16. doi:10.1002/cd.23219956703.

Nicolopoulou, A. (2002). Peer-group culture and narrative development. In S. Blum-Kulka & C. E. Snow (Eds.), *Talking to adults* (pp. 117–52). Mahwah, NJ: Erlbaum.

Nicolopoulou, A., & Richner, E. S. (2007). From actors to agents to persons: The development of character representation in young children's narratives. *Child Development,* 78(2), 412–29.

Osterman, K. F. (2000). Students' need for belonging in the school community. *Review of Educational Research, 70*(3), 323–67.

Pasupathi, M., & Billitteri, J. (2015). Being and becoming through being heard: Listener effects on stories and selves. *International Journal of Listening, 29*(2), 67–84.

Piaget, J. (1932/65). *The moral judgment of the child.* London: Routledge & Kegan Paul.

Weissberg, R. P., & Cascarino, J. (2013). Academic + social-emotional learning = national priority. *Phi Delta Kappan, 95*(2), 8–13.

Weissberg, R. P., Durlak, J. A., Domitrovich, C. E., & Gullotta, T. P. (2015). Social and emotional learning: Past, present, and future. *Handbook of social and emotional learning: Research and practice.* New York, NY: Guilford.

10

BEYOND LITERACY SKILLS

Story-Writing Facilitates Social, Emotional, and Moral Development

> So we never fighted again. p.s. Thank you for making me write this.
>
> *Paige, third-grade girl, Winterton Elementary, Memphis*

In Chapter 9, we discussed the importance of an oral story-sharing culture, and how KidsTalk sessions gave children opportunities to tell stories to each other. However, most of our work has been with written narratives in school settings, and what we have learned leads us to argue for the importance of a narrative writing practice for children in elementary school. Children are expected to learn to write in elementary school, and many teachers include daily writing assignments so that children can practice the skills that will be important for their long-term academic success. Our work suggests that it is not just important that children write. It is important that they write about their own experiences. We fully recognize, however, that classroom teachers may be reluctant to add activities that distract from the English Language Arts standards being assessed. In this chapter, we argue for the inclusion of a narrative writing practice in elementary school classrooms that celebrates and builds on children's authorial voice. Following that, we review a set of Common Core writing standards and suggest classroom practices that follow from our research findings, arguing that narrative writing activities will serve these standards as they simultaneously promote social, emotional, and moral development.

Narrative Writing and the Celebration of Authorial Voice

We believe that teachers can focus on personal narrative writing in their classrooms without sacrificing their other educational goals and mandates. Specifically, we propose that teachers pay attention to an important component of authorship, something we call authorial voice, and use this as a springboard for building other writing skills, including mechanics. What we are proposing is in alignment with what many good teachers are already doing, which is appreciating and building on that personal style of writing that communicates the author's stance toward events reported and the author's relationship to the audience. We described authorial voice in Chapter 8 and Appendix D describes our coding of such story features as *expressiveness* (e.g., "I surprised him with that bag of hot flamin chips"); *meta-narrative comments* (e.g., "Well that's my story and it's all 100% true!"); *emphasis markers* (e.g., "I got sooo mad"); and *cultural voice* (e.g., "We started to fight by talking trash").

Regan Humphrey (2013) provided a compelling case for and concrete example of the inclusion of authorial voice in *The Author's Toolkit*. In this toolkit, she acknowledges the likelihood that children who come from communities with rich narrative traditions – who are often of low socio-economic status – enter school equipped with a strong authorial voice. Teachers can view this voice as an academic asset, using it as a foundation for other writing skills. Minimal research has explored this topic, but previous work has shown the benefit of using culturally diverse literature in the classroom for empowering and building on children's authorial voice. Further, this literature can be used to enhance children's understanding of story structure, while it fosters cultural awareness and appreciation (Bryant, 2005; Heller & McLellan, 1993; Rasinski & Padak, 1990). Incorporating engaging poetry with a strong authorial voice in reading and writing instruction can help to increase other indicators of children's voice, such as repetition, rhyme, and onomatopoeia (Certo, 2004; Kovalcik & Certo, 2007). Drawing on this previous work, we propose that integrating multicultural literature with a strong authorial voice in English Language Arts would capitalize on children's existing strengths and use them to build other reading and writing skills. As we discussed in Chapter 9, KidsTalk revealed to us that children's authorial voices grow stronger in an environment that celebrates story-telling and provides ample opportunities to share narratives of all kinds. This argument is consistent with the writings and practice of master teacher Vivian Paley, who has long advocated for the recognition of children's authorial voice through a classroom narrative practice (Paley, 1990, 1997, 2004). We believe that explicit instruction in the development of authorial voice in children's writing could be especially effective for building other writing skills.

It is no secret to anyone involved in elementary education that writing assessments used in the US during the No Child Left Behind era and those recently developed in response to Common Core standards have attended primarily to the mechanics of writing, reflecting a focus on organization and writing conventions, such as appropriate use of punctuation, capitalization, sentence formation, and spelling. We fear that an emphasis on writing mechanics at the expense of other literary features that add color and entertainment to children's writing not only limits children's writing competency (and interest in writing!) but also dismisses authorial voice. In a short-term longitudinal study, we found that teachers were more attuned to the mechanics of writing (*clarity* and mastery of *conventions*), and that teacher ratings of academic skill were based on mechanics more than on features of authorial voice. On the other hand, when we asked classmates about which children were the best students, their ratings of academic skill were predicted by authorial voice (Humphrey, Walton, & Davidson, 2014). We fear that some teachers' nearly exclusive attention to the mechanics of writing may actually discourage the development of authorial voice, even in children whose narratives show exceptional flair. It is possible that exclusive training in literacy mechanics may drown out vibrant authorial voices and our findings lead us to fear that some teachers may actually squelch this important feature of children's writing, just by failing to recognize it when they see it. In the section below, we describe how the inclusion of narrative writing prompts in elementary school classrooms can encourage authorial voice and other mechanical skills that align with writing standards defined by the Common Core.

Narrative Writing and the Promotion of Literacy Skills in Alignment With Common Core State Standards

At the time of this publication, forty-two states in the US, the District of Columbia, four territories, and the Department of Defense Education Activity (DoDEA) have adopted Common Core State Standards. As an example, we present the key writing standards regarding *Text Types and Purposes* in fourth grade according to the Common Core. Children are expected to: (1) Write opinion pieces on topics or texts, supporting a point of view with reasons and information; (2) Write informative/explanatory texts to examine a topic and convey ideas and information clearly; and (3) Write narratives to develop real or imagined experiences or events using effective technique, descriptive details, and clear event sequences (http://www.corestandards.org/ELA-Literacy/W/4). The fourth-grade Common Core narrative writing sub-standards are presented in Table 10.1.

Elementary school teachers' inclusion of narrative writing prompts in their classrooms can both encourage authorial voice and meet these Common Core writing standards. Prompts can be framed so that children are asked to think and write about everything they can remember from the beginning to the end of the story. This encourages them to orient their reader to a situation and to organize an event sequence that unfolds naturally (W.4.3A), as well as providing a conclusion that follows from the event (W.4.3E). As we discussed in detail in Chapter 8, when children described their conflict experiences in writing, they appropriated a polyphony of voices to make a place for themselves in a cultural community and to convey and make sense of the positions, cognitions, emotions, and motives of themselves and others in their stories. This meant that when children wrote about interpersonal conflicts, talk about talk was pervasive, and many children's stories incorporated "dialogue and description to develop experiences and events or show the responses of characters to situations" (W.4.3B). Incorporating narrative prompts about "a time you had a conflict with another kid/sibling/friend" or "a time you

TABLE 10.1 Common Core fourth-grade narrative writing standards*

CCSS.ELA-LITERACY.W.4.3	Write narratives to develop real or imagined experiences or events using effective technique, descriptive details, and clear event sequences
CCSS.ELA-LITERACY.W.4.3A	orient the reader by establishing a situation and introducing a narrator and/or characters; organize an event sequence that unfolds naturally
CCSS.ELA-LITERACY.W.4.3B	Use dialogue and description to develop experiences and events or show the responses of characters to situations
CCSS.ELA-LITERACY.W.4.3C	Use a variety of transitional words and phrases to manage the sequence of events
CCSS.ELA-LITERACY.W.4.3D	Use concrete words and phrases and sensory details to convey experiences and events precisely
CCSS.ELA-LITERACY.W.4.3E	Provide a conclusion that follows from the narrated experiences or events

Note: * http://www.corestandards.org/ELA-Literacy/W/4.

helped someone (or someone helped you)" into classroom writing instruction gives children practice with describing the experiences of protagonists and antagonists in conflict and helping situations. Children's responses to these prompts can also provide teachers with insight into children's peer relationships inside and outside of the classroom *while* the children are practicing important literacy skills.

Narrative prompts can be coordinated with other curriculum goals in ways that may help children become more personally engaged with science and math curricula. In two Memphis elementary and middle schools, college science students ran sessions we called KidsTalk Science. Children were asked to tell, and then to write stories about, "a time you were very curious," "a time you followed instructions exactly," and "a time you observed something closely or noticed something for the first time." These and similar prompts were designed to help students recognize in themselves skills and dispositions valued in math and science. In writing such stories, children practiced writing skills through attention to the sequence of events that unfolded in their stories (W.4.3C), while also making a personal connection to scientific methods and concepts. "Tell a story about a time someone did something unhealthy" can be used to encourage students to attend to concrete words, phrases, and sensory details to convey experiences and events precisely (W.4.3E); simultaneously, such a prompt allows for the inclusion of cultural voice, as when fifth-grader Roosevelt shared, "Then, my brother showed me his big ol' bag of candy."

Beyond the explicit academic writing standards that can be enhanced through narrative writing, writing about personal experiences supports the development of important social-emotional skills. These are critically important to human development, and, as we discussed in Chapter 9, they are recognized as essential for building socially competent, responsible, and compassionate human beings

(Weissberg, Durlak, Domitrovich, & Gullotta, 2015). Recognizing their importance for children's development, a growing number of states in the US have developed and adopted a set of social-emotional learning (SEL) standards for children in school (Collaborative for Academic, Social, and Emotional Learning, 2015). Yet social-emotional skills are not generally recognized as the primary aim of elementary education, and they are not skills that get assessed explicitly in the high-stakes, standardized tests that often determine teacher evaluation and school funding. Some educators and researchers have argued convincingly, however, that these skills are implicitly embedded in Common Core standards for English Language Arts and Mathematics (Elias, 2014). Using the fourth-grade writing standards as an example, we can see that the ability to support one's point of view with reasons and information when writing an opinion piece requires a child to understand the perspective of herself and others, the ability to write an informative or explanatory piece that conveys ideas and information clearly requires strategic thinking and metacognitive skills, and the ability to develop real or imagined experiences with descriptive details requires an extensive emotion vocabulary and the ability to recognize, label, and evaluate the emotions of oneself and others.

In the following sections, we discuss the effectiveness of a narrative writing practice in nurturing children's social-emotional development in three domains: facilitating healthy peer adjustment, promoting emotional competence, and encouraging a participation in a moral discourse.

Narrative Writing and Social Adjustment With Peers

In Chapter 9, we discussed several ways that sharing oral narratives can facilitate healthy peer relationships in a classroom. But most of our data have examined written, not oral narratives, and in two of our samples (College Elementary and Magnolia Springs) we were able to gather data about peer adjustment along with children's written narratives. In Chapter 4 we reported that our assessments of the children's narratives were related to peer rejection. We were surprised to find that children who wrote stories about peer rejection were more psychologically minded and more attentive to their own and others' motives, and they were less lonely, less disliked, and less victimized than children who wrote about other kinds of conflicts. At College Elementary, we were able to follow children over two school years, and we found that narrative skills (reports of motives, coherence, and moral concerns) in year one predicted peer adjustment (peer reports of victimization, disliking, and self-reports of loneliness) in year two, even after year one peer adjustment was statistically controlled (Davidson, Walton, Kansal, & Cohen, 2016). If we take two children with similar peer rejection difficulties in year one, we can predict that the child with the stronger narrative skills will be less disliked and less victimized by classmates, and will report less loneliness in the following school year than the child with poorer narrative skills. This is important support for our argument that narrative skills are friend-making skills. There has been considerable success in the last decade in establishing classroom practices that minimize bullying and peer victimization (Saarento & Salmivalli, 2015; Salmivalli & Poskiparta, 2012), but these programs have found that it is much easier to protect a child from peer victimization than to help the child experience acceptance and liking from classmates. We can't easily make children *like* each other, and the personal qualities that make a child vulnerable to rejection may be difficult to change. We have good reasons to believe, however, that narrative practice may be a path to acceptance for some rejected children.

All of the benefits of a story-sharing practice we described in Chapter 9 may be especially difficult to realize for some children. In KidsTalk sessions over the years, we have seen a minority of children sit quietly for multiple sessions before they find the courage to share a story. We believe that a written narrative practice could be especially beneficial for such children. If story-sharing is, as Bruner (1990) argued, and as we have shown in every chapter of Part II, the primary way that humans come to understand one another, then children who have limited story-sharing opportunities are likely to lag behind their classmates in their ability to create culturally recognizable interpretations of events, to make reasonable inferences about the internal states and the motives of actors, and to make moral assessments that are defensible in their cultural community. For these children, it may be especially important to give them opportunities to write their stories. Free of the immediate gaze of others, and without the fear of being challenged as they create their account, the same social-cognitive skills can emerge with practice. The practice in writing accounts of their own experience may give such children the extra skill and confidence they need to be prepared to interpret behavior *in situ*.

Below, we consider a classroom practice of writing and then sharing stories. This practice may make it easier for shy or rejected children to find a voice in their classroom community, partly because they have a chance to make sense of their experience without interruption and partly because the structure of the sharing can serve as scaffolding. These sharing events may facilitate the development of empathy and compassion among all the children in a classroom.

Narrative Skills and Emotional Development

There is a tendency of many grown-ups to cling to a romantic view of childhood as a happy, carefree time. We want our children to be protected from the serious problems of the world, and we certainly do not want them to suffer. However well intentioned this 'carefree innocence' discourse may be, it ignores the reality that children do suffer and struggle as they make their way through ordinary mishaps and serious losses that are a part of every childhood. When we encourage children to write about their own experiences, they will sometimes write about painful or even tragic situations, and some researchers have argued for caution in eliciting personal narratives about difficult experiences from children (Fivush, Marin, Crawford, Reynolds, & Brewin, 2007; McLean, Breen, & Fournier, 2010). Recently, we had one anonymous journal reviewer argue that it is dangerous to ask children to write about their conflicts in a classroom situation; that this should only be done under the supervision of a trained clinician. In Chapter 5, we reviewed evidence refuting this position, and we believe it is seriously mistaken. Children should not have to protect their grown-ups from knowing that they have suffered fear and rejection and betrayal. We saw in Chapter 5 that a small minority of children did write about very violent or very tragic situations requiring special attention by qualified guidance counselors, and we were grateful that professional care was available to those children. But many more children wrote about significant pain that did not require clinical intervention, but did deserve the attention of caring adults. Consider Example 10.1.

EXAMPLE 10.1 Jenny, fifth-grade girl, Winterton Elementary, Memphis

EXAMPLE 10.1   JENNY, FIFTH-GRADE GIRL, WINTERTON ELEMENTARY, MEMPHIS

My grandfather was my most favorite Grandfather (who was my Mom's Dad) he had a very kind & sweet loving voice. I would usually visit him for the summer sometimes. I would always do things with him. HIS name is Rick Roberts who is married to my grandmother Sadie Roberts. I have loved him so much. So one day he was sick. I said, "Grandpa what's the matter are you okay? He said don't worry I'm alright don't worry about me old people should get sick. Now lets take a walk. So we did. We talked & he said something I'll never forget he said: Jenny you know I love you very much. Well I'm really sick & I might die but never forget me cause we love each other & lets never forget how much we love each other. I said: OK Grandpa But you know I'll always love you no matter what. The next two weeks he died. I know that he loves me & I love him very much.

When Jenny was invited to write about her own experience for researchers who wanted to know what it is like to be a fifth-grader nowadays, she used the opportunity to make a beautiful memorial to her grandfather. Her story had the power to make members of our research team remember the loss of their own grandparents. We felt privileged to share this sweet sadness with a child. When teachers invite children to write their stories, they will occasionally get stories like this, and we believe that this will strengthen their connections to their students and their ability to guide their students' learning. Jenny was not invited to share her story with her classmates, but we believe that such sharing would be healthy. *Children Full of Life* is a 2003 Japanese documentary film, directed by Noboru Kaetsu. The filmmaker followed a fourth-grade teacher in Kanazawa, Japan. Mr. Kanamori's students wrote in notebooks and each day three students shared their story with the class. The film captures a day when Ren reads a story about his grandmother's death. His story evoked tears from some of the other students, and Mr. Kanamori gently but courageously guided the children as they shared feelings of loss. This led to a painful revelation by a classmate, Mifuyu, about the death of her father several years earlier. We see the other children struggle to express their compassion for Mifuyu and to connect this compassion with their own experiences of loss. By the end of the school year, we see Mifuyu proudly sharing a picture made by her father before he died. She is finally able to tell stories about her father, and her classmates are able to support her. Sometimes the sharing of stories entails the sharing of suffering, even for children. When we invite children to participate in this sharing, even when it is painful, we are inviting them to become more full-fledged participants in a human community. We are giving children the opportunity to listen to the struggles and joys that others are experiencing, and to understand that the challenges they go through, while meaningful and difficult, are not completely unique. With a continued practice of authoring and listening to others' stories, children become more self-aware and more socially aware, and this awareness is important for emotion regulation, self-management, and the maintenance of positive relationships (Weissberg et al., 2015).

Narrative as Moral Discourse

In each of the chapters of Part II, we saw impressive moral evaluative work that children did when they created narrative accounts of their own conflicts. In Chapter 3, we saw how children worked to figure out the obligations of friendship, struggling with violations of expectations for exclusivity and loyalty. In Chapters 4, 5, and 6, we saw them considering the motives of perpetrators and making both critiques and justifications of the behaviors they described (and we noted with concern those occasions in which this moral analysis seemed to be suppressed). In Chapters 7 and 8, we saw evidence of children beginning to exercise their own moral voices as they 'took on' gender norms and other cultural identity commitments. Throughout the book we have compared stories in which children take a strong moral stance to those in which they do not. Table 10.2 summarizes these findings.

We have identified three underlying reasons for the suppression of moral voice in the stories described in the right-hand column of Table 10.2: violence is too commonplace, violence is too closely aligned with dominant discourses, or the child's narrative skills are inadequate (Walton, Harris, & Davidson, 2009). First, when aggression (and especially serious physical violence) is commonplace, it is less report-worthy. Narrative form, as we have seen, requires us to explain the non-canonical. When violence is so commonplace as to be expected, children don't attempt to explain it. This happened in neighborhoods experiencing high levels of violent crimes. It may also be part of the reason for suppressed moral reasoning by children in families that use punishment frequently and as a primary socialization technique (Gershoff, 2002).

Second, in cultural communities in which a dominant discourse or master narrative provides a rarely disputed explanation for violence, child authors do not need to do an extensive moral analysis. This, we believe, is why the violence of girls, but not the violence of boys, was explained and evaluated by both girl and boy authors. A dominant 'boys will be boys' discourse makes the aggressive

TABLE 10.2 Strength of moral stance in children's conflict narratives

Authors take a strong moral stance when they describe:	Authors describe conflict with a weak or absent moral stance when they describe:
Social aggression or mild to moderate physical aggression	Severe or life-threatening violence
Child physical aggression	Adult physical aggression, especially if occurring in the family
Physical aggression or violence that is out of the ordinary in their community	Community violence, violent crime, where exposure is frequent
Adults positioned as consultants, advisors	Adults positioned as enforcers, especially with physically violent punishment
Girl aggression	Boy aggression

behaviors of boys less noteworthy and less morally puzzling than the aggressive behaviors of girls (Walton et al., 2009).

Finally, we believe that moral stance is sometimes weak or absent because the author does not possess the narrative skills required to make moral sense of the conflict described. Consistent with this interpretation is the fact that moral voice and the expression of moral concerns increased with age in our samples. As children got more practice in writing narratives, they included more moral analysis. There are some stories, however, that will overwhelm the story-making capacities of all but the most gifted authors. Traumatic violence is traumatic partly because it is so difficult to make sense of it. We believe that children who wrote stories about traumatic violence, and especially serious violence in the child's own family, failed to express a moral stance because such violence overwhelmed the young authors' moral stance-taking abilities.

In Chapter 5 we discussed the extension of Jamie Pennebaker's (1997) Expressive Writing Paradigm to elementary school children, reviewing evidence for the benefits of having children write about difficult personal experiences. Previous research has shown benefits in domains of physical well-being (including improvement on several measures of fitness and health), emotional health (including reduction in internalizing symptoms), and social acceptance (including reduced aggressive behavior). Here we suggest that this kind of writing practice may also produce benefits in the moral domain, and that these benefits may be realized most importantly for the children whose life experiences include the events described in the right-hand column of Table 10.2.

In sum, the evidence we've provided from our own research on story-writing practices in elementary schools suggests that it is not just important that children write. It is important that they write about their own experiences; as they do, they will gain important social, emotional, and moral competencies that nurture the development of compassionate and healthy human beings.

Conclusions

With rigorous writing standards in place for elementary school students and assessments of writing primarily focusing on mechanics in evidence-based writing responses, we are sympathetic to teachers' reluctance to focus on personal narratives and authorial voice. However, we strongly believe and our research supports that a complete and accurate picture of students' writing skills must include an attention to both mechanics and the largely neglected construct of authorial voice. Narrative writing that incorporates an engaging voice is not mutually exclusive with mechanically precise text-dependent writing; rather, the former can be used as a springboard for building the latter in elementary school classrooms. With the many demands placed on teachers in the current assessment-obsessed school environment, we understand that classroom teachers may be reluctant to add activities that distract from the standards that will be assessed. Yet our research supports the belief that incorporating narrative writing and story-sharing activities into daily English Language Arts instruction will both promote grade-level literacy skills and facilitate children's social, emotional, and moral development.

References

Bruner, J. S. (1990). *Acts of meaning*. Cambridge, MA: Harvard University Press.

Bryant, S. A. (2005). In consideration of Latino children: A sociocultural perspective of literacy skills development using Literature Circles. *Colombian Applied Linguistics Journal, 7*, 108–29.

Certo, J. L. (2004). Cold plums and the old men in the water: Let children read and write "great" poetry. *The Reading Teacher, 58*, 266–71. doi: 10.1598/RT.58.3.4.

Collaborative for Academic, Social, and Emotional Learning (2015). *Identifying K-12 standards for SEL in all 50 states* [Table]. Retrieved from http://www.casel.org/state-scan-scorecard-project.

Davidson, A. J., Walton, M. D., Kansal, B., & Cohen, R. (2016). Narrative skills predict peer adjustment across elementary school years. *Social Development*.

Elias, M. J. (2014). Social-emotional skills can boost Common Core implementation. *Phi Delta Kappan, 96*(3), 58–62.

English Language Arts Standards – Writing – Grade 4. (n.d.). Retrieved from http://www.corestandards.org/ELA-Literacy/W/4.

Fivush, R., Marin, K., Crawford, M., Reynolds, M., & Brewin, C. R. (2007). Children's narratives and well-being. *Cognition and Emotion, 21*(7), 1414–34.

Gershoff, E. T. (2002). Corporal punishment by parents and associated child behaviors and experiences: A meta-analytic and theoretical review. *Psychological Bulletin, 128*(4), 539–79.

Heller, M. F., & McLellan, H. (1993). Dancing with the wind: Understanding narrative text structure through response to multicultural children's literature (with an assist from HyperCard). *Reading Psychology: An International Quarterly, 14*, 285–310.

Humphrey, R., Walton, M. D., & Davidson, A. J. (2014). "Im gonna tell you all about it": Authorial voice and conventional skills in writing assessment and educational practice. *Journal of Educational Research, 107*(2), 111–22.

Humphrey, R. (2013). The author's toolkit: Cultural voice as a springboard for other literacy skills. *Tennessee Reading Teacher, 4*.

Kovalcik, B., & Certo, J. L. (2007). The poetry café is open: Teaching literary devices of sound in poetry writing. *The Reading Teacher, 61*(1), 89–93.

McLean, K. C., Breen, A., & Fournier, M. A. (2010). Adolescent identity development: Narrative meaning-making and memory telling. *Journal of Research on Adolescence, 20*, 166–87.

Paley, V. G. (1990). *The boy who would be a helicopter: The uses of storytelling in the classroom*. Cambridge, MA: Harvard University Press.

Paley, V. G. (1997). *The girl with the brown crayon*. Cambridge, MA: Harvard University Press.

Paley, V. G. (2004). *A child's work: The importance of fantasy play*. Chicago, IL: University of Chicago Press.

Pennebaker, J. (1997). Writing about emotional experiences as a therapeutic process. *Psychological Science, 8*(3), 162–6.

Rasinski, T. V., & Padak, N. D. (1990). Multicultural learning through children's literature. *Language Arts, 67*, 576–80.

Saarento, S., & Salmivalli, C. (2015). The role of classroom peer ecology and bystanders' responses in bullying. *Child Development Perspectives, 9*, 201–5.

Salmivalli, C., & Poskıparta, E. (2012). KiVa antibullying program: Overview of evaluation studies based on randomized controlled trial and national rollout in Finland. *International Journal of Conflict and Violence, 6*, 294–302.

Walton, M. D., Harris, A. R., & Davidson, A. J. (2009). "It makes me a man from the beating I took": Gender and aggression in children's narratives about conflict. *Sex Roles, 61*, 383–98.

Weissberg, R. P., Durlak, J. A., Domitrovich, C. E., & Gullotta, T. P. (2015). Social and emotional learning: Past, present, and future. *Handbook of social and emotional learning: Research and practice*. New York, NY: Guilford.

11

"IT IS OKAY TO HAVE CONFLICTS, THE MOST IMPORTANT THING IS TO KNOW HOW TO SOLVE CONFLICTS"

The Critical Role of Conflict Narratives in Human Development

> I looked at the sky, why the sky is so blue, clouds are so white, the birds are so cheerful, people are so complex, could it be?
>
> *Zhu Ying-Ke, sixth-grade girl, ChuTian Primary School, Shenzhen*

Throughout this book, we have seen evidence that when children tell or write stories about their own experiences with interpersonal conflict, they do impressive analysis that reveals much about their social, emotional, and moral development. We showed in Part II that the study of their stories can give us insights about important features of their lives: about how they create and maintain friendships, about the social aggression that threatens those friendships, about how they understand and cope with physical aggression ranging from mild offenses to severe violence, about how they understand adults' efforts to socialize them, and about how they 'take on' gender and other cultural commitments. Listening to children's stories is advantageous to us – at least to those of us who seek a fuller understanding of human development. In Part III, we have so far argued that creating and sharing narratives about their conflict experiences is beneficial to the children as well – facilitating social, emotional, and moral development while meeting academic demands. In this final chapter, we consider how this might work. How is it that narrative practices bring about these positive outcomes for children? Figure 11.1 presents a schematic description of the process, and Zhong Lin-Lin's story illustrates the process in Example 11.1.

EXAMPLE 11.1 ZHONG LIN-LIN, FIFTH-GRADE GIRL, CHUNTIAN PRIMARY SCHOOL, SHENZHEN

One time, our class was elected for square formation. That day, we were practicing in the badminton court. Because I did well on parade step, our teacher

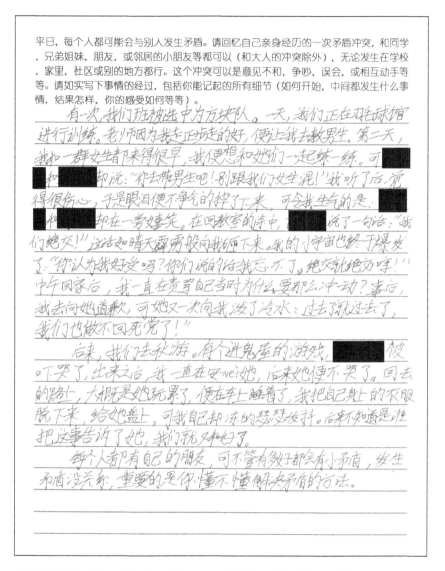

平日，每个人都可能会与别人发生矛盾。请回忆自己亲身经历的一次矛盾冲突，和同学，兄弟姐妹，朋友，或邻居的小朋友等都可以（和大人的冲突除外），无论发生在学校，家里，社区或别的地方都行。这个冲突可以是意见不和，争吵，误会，或相互动手等等。请如实写下事情的经过，包括你能记起的所有细节（如何开始，中间都发生什么事情，结果怎样，你的感受如何等等）。

EXAMPLE 11.1 Zhong Lin-Lin, fifth-grade girl, ChunTian Primary School, Shenzhen

asked me to teach the boys. The next day, I came early with other girls, so I wanted to practice with them. But Guo Liang-Liang and Lu Gui-Cheng said, "you go lead the boys! Don't join our girls!" After hearing this, I felt sad, tears came from my eyes, But what made me angry was: Gao Liang-Liang and Lu Gui-Cheng were laughing on the side. On the way back to classroom, Guo Liang-Liang said, "we break up!" This hit me like a thunder out of a clear sky. I couldn't take this anymore, "you think I'm happy? I'll never forget what you said. Break up is fine!" After getting back at noon, I blamed myself for being impulsive. After this, I reached her for apology, But she ignored me: let the past be the past, we would never be best friends again! Then, we went to the fall outing. There was a ghost house game, Guo Liang-Liang cried because of the fear. After coming out, I comforted her, and then she stopped crying. On the way back, she was probably tired, fell in sleep in the car, I took out my jacket, covered her up, but I was freezing. Someone told her this shortly after, and we made up. Everyone has friends, but no matter how close the relationship is there must be conflicts, It is okay to have conflicts, the most important thing is to know how to solve conflicts.

Landscape of Action

In the first box in Figure 11.1, we see how practice in story-making entails practice in noticing and organizing the features of narrative that Bruner (1990) called the landscape of action. There are two important components of this practice. First, we remember that narratives are provoked when something out-of-the-ordinary happens. The culturally expected experiences of everyday life are the background, against which a narrator upstages the problem that must be resolved or explained. Zhong Lin-Lin marks the exceptionality of the events she describes

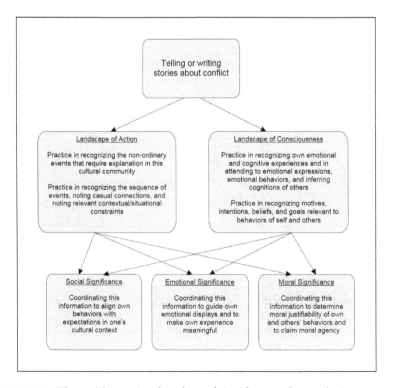

FIGURE 11.1 The social, emotional, and moral significance of story-sharing

in her very first sentences, telling us that her assignment to work with the boys happened "one time." When her friend suggested a break-up, Zhong Lin-Lin reports that the experience was so unexpected, so non-canonical, that it "hit me like a thunder out of a clear sky." It is difficult to estimate the importance of the ability to see ordinariness and exceptionality in the same way as the other members of one's cultural community see it. Bruner (1990) held this to be an important part of what we mean by 'common sense.' Getting our expectations for the way things unfold in alignment with the expectations of the people around us is key to becoming a 'cultural native' (Ochs & Schieffelin, 1984). Part of what Lin-Lin has to figure out to make sense of her experience is what made this "one day" different. Narrative form directs her focus to this matter. "Once upon a time" is a classic beginning for many of the tales told to children. "Once upon a midnight dreary." "I was walking in the park one day, in the merry, merry month of May." In classical literature, in popular song, and in everyday stories, we show children that they can begin their story by establishing the background context that gives rise to the 'trouble' that makes a story. If an author or a storyteller fails to establish this context, or misjudges the extent to which the context will be shared by the audience, then the story will be incoherent. Getting better and better at making stories entails getting better and better aligned with the cultural community in which the story is shared.

The second feature of the landscape of action box in Figure 11.1 directs our attention to the importance of an unfolding sequence of events that will constitute the chaotic influx of experience as a story. Zhong Lin-Lin creates a story by selecting nine events over at least three days (there may have been days in between), and her story marks time and place at every transition. She begins with the 'one day' when her assignment to help the boys set the stage for her conflict. "The next day," we learn, the precipitating rejection that is the subject of Zhong Lin-Lin's story happened. She describes what was said, and then moves her reader in time to understand what she experienced "after hearing this." An even more serious rejection ("we break up") is marked for time and place: "on the way back." The first move toward reconciliation happens "after getting back at noon," when Zhong Lin-Lin reflects on her own behavior. "After this" self-recrimination, Zhong Lin-Lin reports about her efforts to apologize, which were rebuffed. The next act in Zhong Lin-Lin's story happens when the class attended the fall outing. "After coming out" of the ghost house, Zhong Lin-Lin is able to comfort her friend/antagonist, Guo Liang-Liang. We get another scene change to "on the way back," and Zhong Lin-Lin recounts her act of kindness. "After that" someone told Guo Liang-Liang about Zhong Lin-Lin's caring behavior and reconciliation occurred. The ability to select these nine events from the flow of experiences that constitute human phenomenology, from the host of interactions Zhong Lin-Lin would have experienced during these days, to link these nine together to make a coherent story – this is a quintessential narrative skill. A child with less narrative practice would not be able to make a clear and meaningful connection between the relevant events that connected her teacher's decision to let Zhong Lin-Lin instruct the boys to her sacrificial gesture of kindness.

Landscape of Consciousness

In the second box in Figure 11.1, we see how practice in story-making entails practice in noticing and organizing the features of narrative that Bruner (1990) called the landscape of consciousness. Here too, we recognize two important components of the psychological mindedness required to enrich a story with the landscape of consciousness: attention to the interior experience of self and other, and the recognition of motives and reasons for human behavior. In many cultural traditions, and in all of the cultural communities from which we collected data, stories are likely to report about the interior life of the actors. Zhong Lin-Lin's story would hardly make sense at all without her reports of her own emotional, cognitive, and perceptual states ("sad," "angry," "couldn't take it," "happy," "never forget," "freezing"), her reports of Guo Liang-Liang's emotional, cognitive, and perceptual behaviors ("laughing," "think," "crying," "falling asleep"), and her inferences about Guo Liang-Liang's emotional and perceptual states ("ignored," "fear," "comforted," "probably tired").

Hundreds of research studies have investigated questions about how and when children come to hold the theory that other people have thoughts and emotions (Wellman, 2011). The assumption of other minds, referred to as 'theory of mind,' is critical to many other developing cognitive and social skills (Imuta, Henry, Slaughter, Selcuk, & Ruffman, 2016), and a vast theory-of-mind literature has shown that children's understanding of epistemic and volitional mental states is influenced, in part, by conversations with parents, siblings, and peers, in which mental and emotional states become the focus of attention (Hughes & Devine, 2015). This research has inspired training programs to promote children's theory-of-mind skills during middle childhood by involving them in conversations about mental states (Bianco, Devine, Hughes, & Banerjee, 2014). Such training may be advantageous for some children, but we believe that most children 'pick up' common-sense theories about beliefs and emotions – not because they are given explicit training, but because their lives are rich with stories. The stories children hear and the stories they tell orient them to the role of their own interior lives in motivating their own behavior, and invite them to imagine the internal states of other actors.

As difficult as it may be to recognize emotions and thoughts, the second component of a landscape of consciousness is arguably more difficult (and more culturally specific). Narrative practice will direct children's attention to the relevance of motives, reasons, and goals in explaining human behavior. Everyone on our research team resonated with Zhu Ying-Ke's lament that "people are so complex. Could it be?" quoted at the beginning of this chapter. The ability to discern our own motives is difficult and the ability to posit a plausible motive for the behavior of others can seem impossible. Zhong Lin-Lin's story makes a clear causal link between her own skill in parade step and her teacher's decision to assign her to teach the boys. Then, she allows the reader to make a link between this assignment and her classmates' rejection – but Zhong Lin-Lin does not explicitly impute jealousy or other motives to Guo Liang-Liang and Lu Gui-Cheng. She reports her own motive ("I wanted to practice") and she explains the reason for her own anger ("Guo Liang-Liang and Lu Gui-Cheng were laughing"), and although she makes explicit links between emotional states and behaviors in her friend (she cried "because of the fear" and she fell asleep because she was "probably tired"), Zhong Lin-Lin does not suggest motivations for the behaviors of her friends.

Learning to impute motivations to self and others is a significant component of the acquisition of what Bruner (1990) called a folk psychology. Understanding the internal states that explain human behavior has been a primary goal of psychologists since the inception of the discipline (James, 1890), and each of the grand theories that has guided research has included a theory of motivation. A compelling argument made by Nisbett and Wilson (1977), however, convinced many researchers to turn more attention to the attributions that ordinary people make about the causes of human behavior than on what 'actually' motivates us. When families believe that success is caused by innate talent, their children's school performance and interest in learning suffers in comparison to children from families who believe success is caused by hard work and persistence (Dweck, 2006). In many cultural communities, individuals who believe that they control their own fate enjoy higher scores on many measures of well-being than do those who believe that external forces cause them to do the things they do (Ryan & Deci, 2000). Social, developmental, and educational psychologists in recent decades have found that many outcomes are influenced by people's beliefs about human motivation, and cultural psychologists and anthropologists have repeatedly shown that such beliefs vary greatly both within and between cultural communities (Triandis, 1994).

How do children 'pick up' this feature of a folk psychology? How do they learn what the other people they interact with believe about why people behave the way they do and about what counts as an explanation? As sixth-grader Ying-Ke lamented, "People are so complex!" Instruction in interpreting human motivation is not required by the 'Common Core' learning standards we reviewed in Chapter 10. Around family dinner tables, in Sunday School or other religious education settings, in formal and informal gatherings, we rarely give children lectures that explicate our theories of human motivation. What we do is tell stories. Sometimes people are motivated by greed – and we tell children stories about a king named Midas who wanted gold too much. Sometimes people are motivated by curiosity, and we give children a whole series of books about a curious monkey named George. Children begin to figure out what makes people do things by listening to stories.

Then, almost as soon as we start telling such stories to children, we also start asking children to tell their own stories – to explain their own behavior in narrative accounts. "Why are you fighting with your sister?" "Why did you fail your math test?" "Why didn't you come when I called you?" These questions are tricky. Some answers could get you out of trouble, but some will get people mad at you. Some answers will get you out of trouble if you give them to your teacher but not if you give them to your mother. Children need a lot of practice with a lot of stories about a lot of conflict situations to get this down. And if it is not difficult enough to figure out what might work in the way of reporting one's own motives, narrative form and attention to the landscape of consciousness in a good story encourages inferences about the motives of *other* people as well as motives of the self.

Across our samples we found more reports of own motives than of others' motives, and we found grade-related increases in the tendency to include reports of motives in children's stories. The most common motive reports were descriptions of goal states using the word 'want' or 'trying to,' in such locutions as "I wanted to practice with them." The second most common motive reported was retaliation, as in "someone hit me I hit them back." More complex motives were often implied, but not explicitly stated. We see this in Zhong Lin-Lin's story, where the reader may recognize jealousy as the motive for excluding Zhong Lin-Lin, but we cannot tell whether she understands this. Maybe Zhong Lin-Lin's kindness to Guo Liang-Liang was motivated by her remorse for her own behavior ("I blamed myself for being impulsive"), or by her desire to recover the relationship ("the most important thing is to know how to solve conflicts"). She declines to give us an explicit motivation statement. What is clear to us in Zhong Lin-Lin's story and in hundreds of other stories is that coming to understand what counts as an explanation for human behavior is hard work – and that it is work that children undertake as they create narrative accounts of their conflicts.

The Social Significance of Story-Sharing

Figure 11.1 also suggests three important consequences of the skills children practice when they tell or write stories about their own experience. In the Social Significance box, we suggest that children coordinate their developing narrative skills in ways that help them align their own motives and goals, their own thoughts and emotions with the needs and desires of others. Harry Stack Sullivan (1953) proposed more than sixty years ago that the drive for intimacy with peers that emerges during middle childhood motivates children to engage in this difficult work of matching their own needs and desires with those of others to form satisfying reciprocal relationships. This is a project that inevitably leads to conflict, and we are convinced that Piaget (1932/65) was on to something so many years ago when he argued that it is through conflicts with peers, those classmates and playmates of equal status, that children are granted the opportunity to negotiate rules for behavior. If they ultimately are to interact in peaceful and enjoyable ways, they must use these conflicts

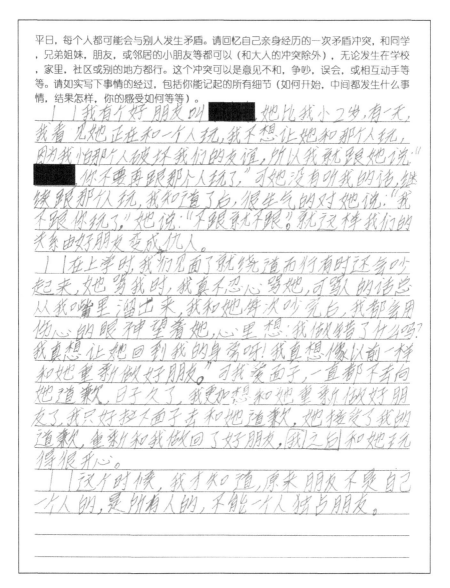

平日，每个人都可能会与别人发生矛盾。请回忆自己亲身经历的一次矛盾冲突，和同学，兄弟姐妹，朋友，或邻居的小朋友等都可以（和大人的冲突除外），无论发生在学校，家里，社区或别的地方都行。这个冲突可以是意见不和，争吵，误会，或相互动手等等。请如实写下事情的经过，包括你能记起的所有细节（如何开始，中间都发生什么事情，结果怎样，你的感受如何等等）。

我有个好朋友叫█████，她比我小2岁，有一天，我看见她正在和一个人玩，我不想让她和那个人玩，因为我怕那个人破坏我们的友谊，所以我就跟她说："█████你不要再跟那个人玩了。"可她没有听我的话，继续跟那人玩，我知道了后，很生气的对她说："我不跟你玩了。"她说："不跟就不跟。"就这样我们的关系由好朋友变成仇人。

在上学时，我们见面了就绕道而行有时还争吵起来，她骂我时，我真不忍心骂她，可骂她的话总从我嘴里溜出来，我和她每次吵完后，我都会用伤心的眼神望着她，心里想：我做错了什么吗？我真想让她回到我的身旁呀！我真想像以前一样和她重新做好朋友。可我爱面子，一直都不肯向她道歉。日子久了，我更加想和她重新做好朋友了，我只好抛下面子去和她道歉，她接受了我的道歉，重新和我做回了好朋友，我之后和她玩得很开心。

这个时候，我才知道，原来朋友不是自己一个人的，是所有人的，不能一个人独占朋友。

EXAMPLE 11.2   Zhen Chun-Hua, fifth-grade girl, ChunTian Primary School, Shenzhen

as opportunities to practice their emerging narrative skills. Conflict resolution is fundamentally interpersonal and it cannot be achieved simply through training with hypothetical vignettes or as a result of lecturing and moralizing by authority figures. It happens primarily when children are given opportunities to narrate the real, lived, and inevitable struggles of childhood. Consider Example 11.2.

EXAMPLE 11.2 ZHEN CHUN-HUA, FIFTH-GRADE GIRL, CHUNTIAN PRIMARY SCHOOL, SHENZHEN

I have a good friend named Lin Fan-Fan, she is two years younger than me, One day, I saw her playing with someone, I didn't want her to play that person, Because I was afraid that person would intervene in our friendship, So I told her, "Lin Fan-Fan, don't play with that person," But she didn't listen to me, she kept playing with that person, After I knew it, I told her angrily, "I don't want to play with you anymore," She said, "do whatever you like." Because of this our relationship went from friends to enemies. When going to school, we avoided seeing each other on the way to school, and sometimes we argued, When she called me names, I didn't have the intention to insult her back, but I couldn't help insulting her, After we argued, I always looked at her sadly, I thought: did I do something wrong? I really wanted her back to my side! I wanted to be friend with her like before. But I didn't want to lose my reputation, I didn't go apologize to her, After a while, I wanted to be friend with her again even more, So I had to go apologize to her, she accepted my apology, And we became good friends again. After that she and I had good time playing. That moment, I knew, a friend not only belongs to me, but to other people, We can't take friends as our property.

Zhen Chun-Hua describes one of the primary friendship troubles we discussed in Chapter 3: to what extent should friendship be an exclusive relationship ("We can't take friends as our property")? She describes two of the major forms of social aggression discussed in Chapter 4: rejection ("I don't want to play with you anymore") and name-calling. Chun-Hua's difficulty in deciding to apologize to Fan-Fan is complicated by the need to protect her reputation, and this echoes the experiences recounted by many children whose need for intimate friendship conflicted with a need to maintain social standing. (Recall Isabel's anguish in Example 3.14.) Chun-Hua's story is similar to dozens of others in Memphis and Orlando whose stories helped us see how much work children do to figure out how to maintain satisfying social relationships.

The coordination of landscape of action and landscape of consciousness information is critical to social development and as children get better and better at this, they are preparing to become full-fledged participants in their various cultural communities (Ochs & Schieffelin, 1984). We reported in Chapter 10 that children who wrote narratives that were more coherent and more attentive to a landscape of consciousness had better peer relationships. We found the development of narrative skills to be especially advantageous for children who tended to be disliked or victimized (Davidson, Walton, Kansal, & Cohen, 2016). We want to discuss two reasons why this may have worked. First, better story-makers may have better peer relations because they are better at conflict management (Davidson, Walton, & Cohen, 2013; Walton, Harris, &

Davidson, 2009). Zhong Lin-Lin reminds us, as Piaget (1932/65) did, that conflict between friends is inevitable. The ability to tell one's side of the story, to explain one's own behavior, and to recount the sequence of events that made one's behavior reasonable may be critical to resolving conflict without violence and without the abandonment of relationships. This is at the heart of peer mediation programs, in which children are encouraged to resolve disagreements by listening to and understanding one another's stories about what happened (Powell, Muir-McClain, & Halasyamani, 1995; Burrell, Zirbel, & Allen, 2003). Children who can create narratives that coordinate landscape of action information (presenting a clear chronology and establishing the appropriate context) with landscape of consciousness information (reporting relevant thoughts, emotions, and motives) have the skills they need to make their behaviors understandable to their peers in conflict-threatening situations. These skills help them preserve relationships.

A second reason why narrative skill predicts peer success may be related to the fact that story-making and story-sharing is a primary form of entertainment and an important cultural practice in a wide variety of contexts (Goodwin & Kyratzis, 2011; Miller & Goodnow, 1995). The social activity in which people tell stories to other people about past events, events that typically involved other people, exercises cultural knowledge and social intelligence. Engel (2015) argued convincingly that the cultural practice we sometimes derisively label as 'gossip' is a natural training ground for the development of psychologists and novelists and for ordinary people whose curiosity orients them to the lives of other humans. Personal narratives nurture a curiosity about other people – about the ways that others' experiences are similar to and different from our own. Indeed, sharing vivid stories with detailed attention to characters' thoughts, motives, and actions may also invite our listeners to experience those events with us, just as reading descriptive fiction does (Mar, Oatley, Hirsch, Dela Paz, & Peterson, 2006). This interest in others motivates the development of human relationships, and ultimately the development of human culture. This, we believe, is why children who developed strong narrative skills in one academic year set themselves up to be more preferred as a playmate by their classmates the following year (Davidson, Walton, Kansal, & Cohen, 2016).

The Emotional Significance of Story-Sharing

The Emotional Significance box of Figure 11.1 draws a connection between narrative practice and emotional competence. Amy Halberstadt and colleagues proposed a compelling theoretical model of affective social competence, which respects the complexity of emotion socialization (Halberstadt, Denham, & Dunsmore, 2001). To form agreeable relationships and take a valued place in their communities, children must simultaneously learn to (1) experience their own emotional reactions, accept them, and modulate their intensity, (2) communicate their own feelings effectively by bringing their emotion displays in alignment with cultural expectations, and (3) recognize others' communication of feelings and interpret those correctly. Halberstadt's model underlines the way development in each of these three areas entails increasing awareness of one's own and others' emotions, increasing the ability to use language to identify emotions, increasing alignment with cultural expectation for emotion communication, and increasing the ability to regulate emotional experience. We see evidence that the sharing of stories is critical to these developmental accomplishments, and both of the above stories illustrate this. Zhong Lin-Lin's story in Example 11.1 is typical in that it was provoked by her own emotional discomfort. She reports both her experience of sadness ("After hearing this I felt sad") and her behavioral display of that feeling ("tears came from my eyes."). She doesn't claim agency or control over this emotion display – the tears just came. She uses the counterfactual 'but' to contrast her sadness (caused by the rejection) with her anger (caused by being laughed at). When her friend proposes a break-up, Zhong Lin-Lin reports her own loss of control ("I couldn't take it anymore") and she agrees to a break-up. From this point on, Zhong Lin-Lin's story is about her effort to understand her own emotional reactions ("I blamed myself for being impulsive") and her efforts to recover her relationship, primarily by helping Guo Liang-Liang manage her fear of the ghost house and by alleviating her discomfort by covering her with her own jacket. In Example 11.2, we see similar evidence of the narrative nature of emotion competence. Zhen Chun-Hua reports about her own fear ("I was afraid that person would intervene in our friendship") and her own expressions of anger and of sadness ("I told her angrily," "I looked at her sadly"). In many ways the story turns on Zhen Chun-Hua's struggle to regulate her anger ("I didn't have the intention to insult her back, but I couldn't help insulting her") and to manage her competing desires to recover the friendship and maintain her reputation ("I wanted to be friend with her like before. But I didn't want to lose my reputation").

Susan Engel (1995) described the 'cooling' power of stories about difficult emotional experiences. When they tell about situations that provoked strong emotions, children can take some control over those feelings – re-experiencing sadness, anger, regret, compassion, and physical discomfort, as Zhong Lin-Lin and Zhen Chun-Hua did, but re-experiencing it in a context that gives authorial control. Narrating emotional experience gives children an opportunity to examine their own emotion communication alongside the emotion communication of others. This reflection on the experiencing self is a critical feature of narrative and is critical to all three of Halberstadt's components of emotional competence. Narrative helps children adapt and modulate their own emotional experience, examine and evaluate the effectiveness of their emotional communication, and make inferences about the emotional lives of others.

The Moral Significance of Story-Sharing

Finally, we see in the Moral Significance box in Figure 11.1 a connection between narrative practice and moral development. Indeed the tendency of children to use their accounts of conflict situations to claim their own moral authority is probably the most striking feature of our data. Story-sharing is quintessentially a moral activity for three reasons: the first pertains to the landscape of action, the second to the landscape of consciousness, and the third to the way those two get coordinated to create agency.

Bruner (1990) argued that narratives always take a moral stance. This is first a consequence of a fundamental property of story-telling related to the landscape of action: We tell stories when something report-worthy happens – something unexpected in a cultural context. As it turns out, these report-worthy events are rarely morally neutral. The first moral analysis a child must do when making a story is in selecting, from among all the things that happen, those that warrant reporting and explaining. They must consider what features of the cultural context give meaning to their own and others' behaviors. Zhen Chun-Hua's story reports about how her own expectation for exclusiveness from a friend is challenged. She describes a moral struggle, played out in a conflict between friends, that was the focus of many stories discussed in Chapter 3 about the obligations of friendship. Members of a cultural community come to agree with one another about the expectations and obligations of social life – but it is a fragile and regularly challenged agreement. The project of establishing which behaviors will be backgrounded and which will be featured in the stories shared is at the heart of the creation, the re-creation, and the transformation of this moral order.

Attention to the landscape of action will get children attuned to what is culturally canonical in their communities, but we have seen that good stories also attend to the landscape of consciousness, and this attention is at the heart of perspective-taking. Piaget (1932/65) observed a shift in children's moral judgment in the early elementary school years, from an exclusive focus on the consequences of misbehavior to a recognition that the intentions of the actor matter, and this observation stimulated hundreds of studies about children's ability to infer motives and their inclination to do so (Malti & Ongley, 2014). In Piaget's theory of moral development, children's newfound ability to imagine the point of view of others propels them into new moral sensibilities and is the hallmark of a change from early to middle childhood. Malti and Ongley (2014) review research and theory disputing the timing of this shift and the abruptness of it, but no one doubts the importance of perspective-taking to moral judgment. Bruner (1990) made a powerful argument that it is in the human practice of sharing stories that we are able to consider others' points of view. Children identify with characters in the stories that are told to them and thus refine their ability to see the world from the perspective of others. When we invite children to tell their own stories, they have an opportunity to invite others in to glimpse the world as they see it. Our examination of children's stories about their own conflict supports a growing body of research demonstrating the importance of narrative practice to moral development in middle childhood (Dray et al., 2009; Wainryb et al., 2005).

A third reason why stories are so critical to moral development has to do with the author's power to position the self as a certain type of character in the story. Moral agency, the responsibility we take for our own actions, and the responsibility we ascribe to others is a narrative accomplishment. The very grammar of a personal narrative will usually put the author in the subject position. When Zhen Chun-Hua makes the simple report "I told her," she positions herself as the agent of the telling and she takes responsibility for the consequences ("Because of this our relationship went from friends to enemies"). When she is the agent of an unacceptable behavior, she finds a way to mitigate her own responsibility by denying intentionality ("I didn't have the intention to insult her back, but I couldn't help insulting her"). Throughout this book we have seen dozens of ways that children position themselves in their own stories. Daria, in the Introduction (and in Example 11.3 in this chapter), positioned herself as "a big bad wolf" (who "got into boiling hot water"). Samuel, in Chapter 3, positioned himself as "a really awesome friend." In Chapter 7, Warren positioned himself as "the better man" because of his willingness to apologize, but Vincent positioned himself as "emotionless," like a famous boxer. Sometimes children made themselves the object in their own stories, claiming a victim role (e.g., "he always spreaded rumors about me"), but even when they did this, they were likely to claim agency by the end of the story ("I stood up for my self and he never spreaded any rumors again"). The establishment of agency entails justifying and critiquing the behavior of others and the self.

In our Memphis and Orlando samples, we found age-related increases in the tendency of children to use their narratives to critique their own behavior. Even among our third-graders it was common for children to justify their own behavior and critique the behavior of an antagonist. By the time they entered the sixth grade, however, their moral analysis tended to be more nuanced, and they were more likely to include self-critique and to take at least partial responsibility for the trouble that provoked their stories. In Shenzhen, we did not find this grade-related shift. Indeed, we found self-critique to be pervasive among even the youngest authors. "Did I do something wrong?" Chun-Hua asks herself. "I blamed myself for being impulsive," we hear from Lin-Lin. This tendency of the Shenzhen children to focus on self-critique and self-improvement is consistent with the curriculum standards that guide their weekly moral class (Chinese Department of Education, 2011). It is also consistent with research examining narratives shared in family settings with preschoolers (Miller &

Fung, 2012). At least among Chinese families in Hong Kong, Taiwan, and among Chinese Americans (where these matters have been studied), it is normative for narratives shared with children to be clearly didactic, and for children to be encouraged to find and admit to their own failings (Fung & Chen, 2011; Miller, Fung, & Mintz, 1996; Miller, Wiley, Fung, & Liang, 1997). Jin Li, in a thoughtful comparison of guiding educational principles in the US and China, argued that this emphasis is pervasive in China and in much of Asia, influenced by Confucian principles. In this cultural context, it is not surprising to see them exhort their readers, as one fifth-grader did, to "admit your faults, it is the key to reconciliation." In many ways it is more surprising to find that our U.S. children came to do this as well. In a cultural context in which their parents and teachers are likely to be more concerned with protecting children's self-esteem than with cultivating self-critique (Miller & Fung, 2012), we nevertheless found that when children were asked to write about their own conflicts, they came to subject their own behavior to moral critique. This, we believe, is a very good reason to encourage narrative accounts of conflict.

The three mechanisms we have described so far explain a relationship we saw between narrative and the moral development of individual authors. We believe, however, that the moral significance of narrative operates as much at the level of the cultural community as at the level of the individual. A moral order emerges in the classroom as children engage in the practice of sharing stories. When we encourage all children to share narrative accounts of their experience, we invite those on the margins and those in the center of the peer network to evaluate and challenge existing peer norms, values, and behaviors. This has the potential to transform a classroom into a place where acceptance and compassion are expected, so that acts of cruelty or exclusion will be recognized as needing explanation. Story-sharing is critical to the transmission of moral values because it is the primary way we bring children into the moral discourse of their cultural communities.

Making Stories/Molding the Future

Bruner (1986) described two features of human intellect that are realized in narrative: reflexivity and subjunctivity. Reflexivity describes our capacity to turn our thought in upon itself, and this accounts for our tendency to alter our interpretation and behavior in the present in light of our past and to alter our interpretation and memory of the past in light of our present. Children used their stories to contrast a former self with a present self, and in so doing they organized a plan for their own development. Notice how this worked in Daria's story, repeated from Example 0.1 in the Introduction of this book, presented here as Example 11.3.

EXAMPLE 11.3   DARIA, FIFTH-GRADE GIRL, MAGNOLIA SPRINGS ELEMENTARY, ORLANDO

"I'll kick you in your face talk to me that way"! I was yelling my head of to this stuck up no good girl. Who thougt she was the big bad wolf all of this day at the day cares playgound. She walked and she talked and she got knocked right in the face by the bigger wolf in town me! But it all started when she told my bff that I was useing her an that she needed not be my friend any more then the whole day care spreded the romer and she stop being my friend and. Told me what that toe jam said So I confronted her about it then she went bleasick! And acted like she was going to hit me but of stad of her hitting me I pounched her and made her nose bleed then I looked at my fit and realied what I had just done. Then I realy wasent the cool Kid in day care and to think I would had even done it over not having to just ask to tell the troth to my X bff then doing what I did. And at the end of it all I was the one who got in the boialing hot water with my mom and the towlets mother. But that is the old me and now I look back and say wow I did something So mean and sien then I have not been in nother fit! And that was 4 years ago!

Daria is a fifth-grader as she writes this story about the last fight she was in, "And that was 4 years ago!" She has construed this conflict as a turning point in her own life history. She recounts being surprised by her own violence ("then I looked at my fit and realied what I had just done"). She reports that this prompted a re-consideration of the kind of person she was ("Then I realy wasent the cool Kid in day care"). The current Daria is able to "look back" on "the old me" and to evaluate that person ("wow I did something So mean"), and to claim a more peaceable current identity ("and sien then I have not been in nother fit!"). When we give children the power of narrative, we give them authority to author their own development, the authority to take a cultural, epistemological, and moral stance as they describe the world and their relationship to it. This is a powerful tool to put in the hands of a child. It cultivates the reflexivity that allows her to create a history from which she and her community cannot be excluded.

The presentation of the self as a moral actor in one's own story is only part of the moral work narrators do. The story-maker *as author* can claim the power to evaluate what has transpired and this is related to Bruner's second feature of thought that is realized in narrative – the ability to think about possible worlds, to consider what might be or what could have been – to think in the subjunctive case. Daria imagines what response she might have made: "and to think I would had even done it over not having to just ask to tell the troth to my X bff then doing what I did." This ability to think about how things might have turned out, to contrast what was imagined or intended with what actually happened, is a critical feature of moral analysis. It is also the kind of thinking that motivates cultural change. The world our children create will be different from the world we offer them, because they have this power to imagine possibilities.

We have seen above, and throughout this book, how narrative practices are beneficial to children, facilitating social, emotional, and moral development. But, truth be told, our reasons for sustaining weekly KidsTalk sessions for the past twenty-five years have at least as much to do with the benefits to grown-ups as the benefits to the children who participate. The developmental psychology students who spend thirty minutes a week in a circle with six children telling about their own lives leave their class with a keener understanding of social, emotional, and moral development than they would have gotten had they only read theory and research on the topics. The theory and research we cover in class comes alive for them in their weekly KidsTalk sessions, and the examples they bring back to class enrich our discussions. In Chapter 2, we talked about the development of a research team as an interpretive community, and a critical part of that development was the experience we all had regularly with children the same age as those whose stories we studied. A practice of inviting children to tell us about their experience is obviously beneficial to those adults whose academic or professional interests are focused on childhood. Beyond that, we would encourage listening to children's stories by anyone who has an interest in the future that the next generation will construct.

We believe that many adults recognize that 'out of the mouths of babes' come, at times, insightful and important nuggets of truth and wisdom, but if they pay attention to children's stories at all, most adults do so because they find them sweet, cute, or entertaining. Our hunch (and fear) is that most people don't recognize how necessary a story-sharing culture is for children's social, emotional, and moral development and especially for their ability to resolve conflicts peacefully. We hope that our work and the findings we present in it from our two decades of research on conflict narratives begin to convince people of just how crucial story-sharing is. A big part of our belief that narrative about conflict, in particular, is so important comes from the fact that conflict is inevitable, and children, indeed all people, must learn how to make sense of it. If children are not granted opportunities to talk about and take a moral stance regarding their painful experience with rejection or harassment on the playground, how could we expect them to begin to process, discuss, and make moral sense out of the tragic shooting of their aunt in a nightclub in Orlando, or the mowing down by a truck on a festive holiday night of their next-door neighbor in Nice, or the shooting by a police officer of an African American cafeteria worker in their school who was pulled over for a broken taillight in St. Paul? We do not expect most children to experience this level of traumatic violence, but the reality is that some children will. The hope that has grown with our work these past eighteen years is that when children are part of cultural communities that value story-sharing, they will acquire and practice the important social, emotional, and moral skills necessary for interpreting and responding to difficult, and at times utterly tragic, events. These skills are what allow children to become change agents locally and globally.

Our children are becoming citizens as they participate in elementary school classrooms. We want them to know their histories and to understand the political, economic, and legal systems that organize life in their communities. We want them to learn to enjoy fully the art, music, and literature of their own and other cultures. We want them to experience and satisfy their curiosity about the natural and human-made environments, and to know how to use the technologies that will allow them to advance our understanding in these areas. We want them to know how to take care of themselves, to manage conflicts with others, and to maintain satisfying relationships. All of these educational goals, we believe, are enhanced by a robust narrative practice that encourages the sharing of both oral and written stories about personal experiences.

If they are to become fully participating citizens in a complex global society, children need to know how to story their own experience and how to listen to the stories of others. If our children learn to write persuasive essays that use evidence to make a clear argument for one policy or another, but do not learn to listen with open hearts to the stories of their fellow citizens or to produce the narrative account of how they came to hold this position on this issue, we can expect the polemics that have been described as 'culture wars.' On the other hand, if our children grow up in classrooms where they resolve conflicts by coming to understand each other's stories – classrooms that nurture the development of empathy and help children see others' perspectives, classrooms where every child has a voice in establishing a moral order, they will be prepared to play their role in creating neighborhoods and larger communities where their own children will be able to flourish.

References

Bianco, F., Devine, R. T., Hughes, C., & Banerjee, R. (2014). Promoting theory of mind during middle childhood: A training program. *Journal of Experimental Child Psychology*, *126*, 52–67.

Bruner, J. S. (1986). *Actual minds possible worlds*. Cambridge, MA: Harvard University Press.

Bruner, J. S. (1990). *Acts of meaning*. Cambridge, MA: Harvard University Press.

Burrell, N. A., Zirbel, C. S., & Allen, M. (2003). Evaluating peer mediation outcomes in educational settings: A meta-analytic review. In B. M. Gayle, R. W. Preiss, N. Burrell, & M. Allen (Eds.), *Classroom communication and instructional processes: Advances through meta-analysis* (pp. 113–26). New York, NY: Routledge.

Chinese Department of Education. (2011). *Moral education curriculum standards* (Zhang Hui Trans.). Beijing, China: Chinese Department of Education.

Davidson, A. J., Walton, M. D., & Cohen, R. (2013). Patterns of conflict experience that emerge in peer reports and personal narratives during middle childhood. *Journal of Applied Developmental Science*, *17*(3), 109–22.

Davidson, A. J., Walton, M. D., Kansal, B., & Cohen, R. (2016). Narrative skills predict peer adjustment across elementary school years. *Social Development*.

Dray, A. J., Selman, R. L., & Schultz, L. H. (2009). Communicating with intent: A study of social awareness and children's writing. *Journal of Applied Developmental Psychology*, *30*, 116–28.

Dweck, C. (2006). *Mindset: The new psychology of success.* New York, NY: Random House.

Engel, S. (1995). *The stories children tell: Making sense of the narratives of childhood.* New York, NY: W. H. Freeman and Company.

Engel, S. (2015). *The hungry mind: The origins of curiosity in childhood.* Cambridge, MA: Harvard University Press.

Fung, H., & Chen, E. C.-H. (2011). Across time and beyond skin: Self and transgression in the everyday socialization of shame among Taiwanese preschool children. *Social Development, 10,* 419–37.

Goodwin, M. H., & Kyratzis, A. (2011). Peer language socialization. In A. Duranti, E. Ochs, & B. B. Schieffelin (Eds.), *The handbook of language socialization* (pp. 365–90). Cambridge, MA: Blackwell.

Halberstadt, A. G., Denham, S. A., & Dunsmore, J. C. (2001). Affective social competence. *Social Development, 10,* 79–119. doi:10.1111/1467-9507.0015.

Hughes, C., & Devine, R. T. (2015). A social perspective on theory of mind. In M. E. Lamb (Ed.), *Handbook of child psychology* (7th ed.) (Vol. 3, pp. 564–609). Hoboken, NJ: John Wiley.

Imuta, K., Henry, J. D., Slaughter, V., Selcuk, B., & Ruffman, T. (2016). Theory of mind and prosocial behavior in childhood: A meta-analytic review. *Developmental Psychology, 52*(8), 1192–1205.

James, W. (1890). *Principles of psychology.* New York, NY: Holt.

Malti, T., & Ongley, S. F. (2014). The development of moral emotions and moral reasoning. In M. Killen, J. G. Smetana, M. Killen, & J. G. Smetana (Eds.), *Handbook of moral development* (2nd ed.) (pp. 163–83). New York, NY: Psychology Press.

Mar, R. A., Oatley, K., Hirsh, J., Dela Paz, J., & Peterson, J. B. (2006). Bookworms versus nerds: Exposure to fiction versus non-fiction, divergent associations with social ability, and the simulation of fictional social worlds. *Journal of Research in Personality, 40*(5), 694–712.

Miller, P., Fung, H., & Mintz, J. (1996). Self-construction through narrative practices: A Chinese and American comparison of early socialization. *Ethos, 24*(2), 237–80.

Miller, P. J., Wiley, A. R., Fung, H., & Liang, C. H. (1997). Personal storytelling as a medium of socialization in Chinese and American families. *Child Development, 68*(3), 557–68.

Miller, P. J., & Fung, H. (2012). How socialization happens on the ground: Narrative practices as alternate socializing pathways in Taiwanese and European-American families: I. Introduction. *Monographs of the Society for Research in Child Development, 77*(1), 1–14.

Miller, P. J., & Goodnow, J. J. (1995). Cultural practices: Toward an integration of culture and development. *New Directions for Child and Adolescent Development,* 5–16. doi:10.1002/cd.23219956703.

Nisbett, R. E., & Wilson, T. D. (1977). Telling more than we can know: Verbal reports on mental processes. *Psychological Review, 84*(3), 231.

Ochs, E., & Schieffelin, B. B. (1984). Language acquisition and socialization: Three developmental stories. In R. A. Shweder & R. A. LeVine (Eds.), *Culture theory essays on mind, self, and emotion* (pp. 276–320). Cambridge, MA: Cambridge University Press.

Piaget, J. (1932/65). *The moral judgment of the child.* New York, NY: Free Press.

Powell, K. E., Muir-McClain, L., & Halasyamani, L. (1995). A review of selected school-based conflict resolution and peer mediation projects. *Journal of School Health, 65*(10), 426.

Ryan, R. M., & Deci, E. L. (2000). Self-determination theory and the facilitation of intrinsic motivation, social development, and well-being. *American Psychologist, 55*(1), 68–78.

Sullivan, H. S. (1953). *The interpersonal theory of psychiatry*. New York, NY: Norton.

Triandis, H. C. (1994). *Culture and social behavior*. New York, NY: McGraw-Hill.

Wainryb, C., Brehl, B., & Matwin, S. (2005). Being hurt and hurting others: Children's narrative accounts and moral judgments of their own interpersonal conflicts. *Monographs of the Society for Research in Child Development, 70*(Serial No. 281).

Walton, M. D., Harris, A. R., & Davidson, A. J. (2009). "It makes me a man from the beating I took": Gender and aggression in children's narratives about conflict. *Sex Roles, 61*, 383–98.

Wellman, H. M. (2011). Developing a theory of mind. *The Wiley-Blackwell handbook of childhood cognitive development, 2*, 258–84.

APPENDIX A

Description of Corpora

I. Winterton, Fall 1996

A. Participants. All third- to fifth-grade students (approximately half female) present on the data collection day participated in the study (n = 345). Children attended a midtown public elementary school in Memphis, Tennessee. Sixty percent of the children were eligible for free lunch and breakfast at school, and school-wide achievement in reading and math at the time of data collection was just below the 50th percentile nationwide. Seventy-nine percent of the students were African American, 20% were European American, with 1% other ethnicities.

B. Collection procedures. Stories were collected as part of a study of conflict resolution interventions. Stories were written in class and were collected by the classroom teachers who told the children that their stories would go to the researchers at the nearby college. Children were quite familiar with the college because college students were on their campus daily, participating in volunteer projects.

   1. Prompt: "Write a story about something that happened to you."

C. Transcription procedures. The stories were transcribed by undergraduate researchers who preserved the children's spelling and punctuation, dividing sentences based on the child's punctuation, or, in its absence, on the transcriber's judgment of subject-predicate units. Each story was checked by two additional coders, and differences in segmenting decisions were resolved by the research team. All person and place names were changed and were substituted with names that preserved as much social information in the name as possible (i.e., ethnicity, formality, length).

II. Connors Elementary School, Fall 1998, Spring 1999, Spring 2000

A. Participants. All fourth- to sixth-grade students (approximately half female) present on data collection days participated in the study (n = 179). Children attended a public elementary school in an economically depressed neighborhood where 87.6% of students were eligible for free lunch and breakfast at school. Students tested at the 37th percentile on standardized tests of reading and math skills. At the time of data collection, several blocks of the surrounding public housing had recently been demolished and in a poll taken the following year, 71% of the adult residents in the surrounding neighborhood felt it unsafe to walk outside. Ninety-seven percent of the students were African American.

B. Collection procedures. Narratives were collected as part of a school-board-mandated character education program. All children at the school participated in the program. On three occasions (in the fall and spring of one academic year, and again in the spring of the next year) classroom teachers read the prompt and gave children 30 minutes of class time to write their stories. They were told that their stories would be given to the researchers and that their teachers would not read them. Children were familiar with the researchers, who were regularly implementing other curriculum activities in their classes.

1. Prompt: Write a story about a conflict that really happened to you. Think about an argument, a fight, or some kind of misunderstanding. Write everything you can remember about what happened from the beginning to the end.

C. Transcription procedures. The stories were transcribed by undergraduate researchers who preserved the children's spelling and punctuation, dividing sentences based on the child's punctuation, or, in its absence, on the transcriber's judgment of subject-predicate units. Each story was checked by two additional coders, and differences in segmenting decisions were resolved by the research team. All person and place names were changed and were substituted with names that preserved as much social information in the name as possible (i.e., ethnicity, formality, length).

III. Ironwood Elementary School, Fall 1998, Spring 1999, Spring 2000

A. Participants. All fourth- to sixth-grade students (approximately half female) present on data collection days participated in the study (n = 351). The children attended a public magnet school in a central-city neighborhood in Memphis. 51% of the children were eligible for free lunch at school. Sixty-five percent were African American, 30% were European American, 5% were other ethnicities (primarily Asian or mixed).

B. Collection procedures. Narratives were collected as part of a school-board-mandated character education program. All children at the school participated in the narrative program. On three occasions (in the fall and spring of one academic year, and again in the spring of the next year) classroom teachers read the prompt and gave children 30 minutes of class time to write their stories. They were told that their stories would be given to the researchers and that their teachers would not read them. Children were familiar with the researchers, who were implementing other curriculum activities in their classes.

    1. Prompt: Write a story about a conflict that really happened to you. Think about an argument, a fight, or some kind of misunderstanding. Write everything you can remember about what happened from the beginning to the end.

C. Transcription procedures. The stories were transcribed by undergraduate researchers who preserved the children's spelling and punctuation, dividing sentences based on the child's punctuation, or, in its absence, on the transcriber's judgment of subject-predicate units. Each story was checked by two additional readers, and differences in segmenting decisions were resolved by the research team. All person and place names were changed and were substituted with names that preserved as much social information in the name as possible (i.e., ethnicity, formality, length).

IV. Community Wellness: Wellness Facility, Summer and Fall 2006

A. Participants. These stories were collected from 68 children ranging in age from 5 to 13 with 53 females and 13 males. All child-authors were participating in a program known as KidsTalk (described in Appendix F) through the Child Life program at an inner-city health and wellness center in Memphis, which strives to provide comprehensive and affordable medical care for families who are not receiving insurance but are employed. Children attended the program while their parents were participating in a health or wellness activity or class provided by the center, so opportunity to participate was based largely on the parent's schedule. Eighty-seven percent of the children who participated in this program were African American, 7% European American, and over 68% of them came from families who fall more than 200% below the federal poverty line. Participation frequencies in the KidsTalk program varied among the children, ranging from 13 children who each took part in one session to one child who participated in 27 sessions.

B. Collection and transcription procedures. Stories were collected over a period of nine months by undergraduate research team members. An average session consisted of up to six children and two or three adult facilitators. First, one of the adults would pose a prompt for the session and would encourage the children to "tell everything that happened from the beginning to the end." The children were first allowed to share their personal narratives with the group, and turn-taking was designated by passing around a "talking stick." After the story-telling portion was completed, each child would then go to a computer with a facilitator who would type as he or she dictated the story previously shared. The story was then read back to the child, and he or she was allowed to make any edits to make sure it was just as he or she wanted it. Before data analysis, all person and place names were changed and were substituted with names that preserved as much social information in the name as possible (i.e., ethnicity, formality, length).

1.   Prompts:

 a)   Tell a story about something that happened to you at Community Wellness.
 b)   Tell a true story about a time you felt really good about yourself.
 c)   Tell a true story about a time when you didn't feel good about yourself.
 d)   Tell a true story about a time when someone was doing something dangerous.
 e)   Tell a true story about something that happened at recess.
 f)   Tell a true story about a time when you helped take care of someone younger than you.
 g)   Tell a true story about something that happened while you were watching TV.
 h)   Tell a true story about a time you went on a field trip.
 i)   Tell a true story about something that happened while you were playing outside.
 j)   Tell a true story about a conflict that really happened to you. Tell about an argument, a fight or a misunderstanding.
 k)   Tell a true story about a time you made up with someone after an argument or fight.
 l)   Tell a true story about a time you were lonely.
 m) Tell a true story about a time when something didn't turn out the way you wanted it to.
 n)   Tell a true story about a time there was a fight.
 o)   Tell a true story about a time someone hurt you.
 p)   Tell a true story about a time you made something.
 q)   Tell a true story about something that happened when you did something for the first time.
 r)   Tell a true story about something that happened when you were at a sleepover.

s) Tell a true story about something that happened when someone was mean.
t) Tell a true story about a time there was a fight.
u) Tell a true story about a time you were home alone.
v) Tell a story that really happened about a time when you hurt someone.
w) Tell a true story about something that happened when you got someone in trouble.
x) Tell a true story about a time you got in trouble.
y) Tell a true story about something that happened when someone was blamed for something they didn't do. Tell a story about a time when you cheered someone up.
z) Tell a true story about something that happened at school.
aa) Tell a true story about a time when you got hurt.
bb) Tell a true story about something that happened when you were at the doctor or dentist.
cc) Tell a true story about a time when you did something that was not healthy.
dd) Tell a true story about a time you saw someone doing something unhealthy.
ee) Tell a true story about a time when you got a surprise.
ff) Tell a true story about something that happened on a trip.
gg) Tell a true story about a time when someone wouldn't share.
hh) Tell a true story about a time you visited relatives.
ii) Tell a true story about a time when a big change happened in your life.
jj) Tell a true story about time when you got lost.
kk) Tell a true story about a time when you felt thankful.
ll) Tell a true story about something that happened when you were visiting relatives.

V. College Elementary, Spring 2010, Spring 2011

A. Participants. All third- to fifth-grade students (approximately half female) present on the data collection days participated in the study (n = 364). The children attended a highly research-focused public school located on a university campus in Memphis, Tennessee, and all were participants in a longitudinal study of peer interactions conducted at the university. The school predominantly served middle-class children (fewer than 20% eligible for free or reduced lunches), from mostly non-Hispanic white (63.6%) and African American (26.8%) families.

B. Collection procedures. Stories were collected by the Peer Interaction Group, researchers at the University of Memphis, and the Narrative Development Research Team at Rhodes College. On six occasions in the 2010 school year, and four in 2011, children were brought in by their teacher to the school library, where the study was conducted. In the first two sessions of each academic year, children completed self-report and peer nomination surveys. In each of the remaining sessions, held approximately one month apart, children were asked to write a true story for half an hour in response to the prompts below.

1. Prompts Spring 2010:

   a) Write a story about a conflict with a classmate that really happened to you.
   b) Write a story about something that happened on the playground.
   c) Write a true story about a time someone did not show respect.
   d) Write a true story about a time when a friend did not act like a friend.

2. Prompts Spring 2011:

   a) Write a story about a conflict with a classmate that really happened to you.
   b) Write a true story about a time you were angry.

C. Transcription procedures. The stories were transcribed by undergraduate researchers who preserved the children's spelling and punctuation, dividing sentences based on the child's punctuation, or, in its absence, on the transcriber's judgment of subject-predicate units. Each story was checked by two additional readers, and differences in segmenting decisions were resolved by the research team. All person and place names were changed and were substituted with names that preserved as much social information in the name as possible (i.e., ethnicity, formality, length).

VI. Magnolia Spring Elementary School, Orlando, Fall 2009, Spring 2010

A. Participants. All third- to fifth-grade students (42.5% female) present on the data collection days participated in the study (n = 183). These students attended a public elementary school that served many children living in low-income neighborhoods, including approximately 20% who lived in a nearby homeless shelter. Eighty-two percent of students at the school qualified for free or reduced lunch. The school was rich in ethnic diversity, with 36.5% of participants African American, 31.5% European American, 18.8% Hispanic, 2.8% Asian, 0.6% Indian, and 7.7% multi-racial.

B. Collection procedures. Researchers from Rollins College traveled to each classroom two times in the fall and two times in the spring to collect data. They told the children they were interested in learning what it was like "to be a kid in your school." For the first visit of the fall and spring semesters, children wrote personal narratives about their experiences with peer conflict in response to the prompt below. Each participant had 30 minutes to write. A researcher then read the story back to the child and allowed him or her to make any edits. During the second visit, participants completed a survey regarding their own and others' social-emotional and academic behavior. Teachers also answered survey questions about the students' social and academic behavior for each semester.

    1) Prompt: Write a story about a conflict that really happened to you. Think about an argument, a fight, or some kind of misunderstanding. Write everything you can remember about what happened from the beginning to the end.

C. Transcription procedures. The stories were transcribed by undergraduate researchers who preserved the children's spelling and punctuation, dividing sentences based on the child's punctuation, or, in its absence, on the transcriber's judgment of subject-predicate units. Each story was checked by two additional coders, and differences in segmenting decisions were resolved by the research team. All person and place names were changed and were substituted with names that preserved as much social information in the name as possible (i.e., ethnicity, formality, length).

VII. ChunTian Primary School, Shenzhen, China, Spring 2012

A. Participants. All 152 children present in one fourth-, one fifth-, and one sixth-grade class (45.4% female) on the data collection day participated in the study. The school principal selected one class at each grade based on students' and teachers' available schedule on the day of data collection. These students attended a public elementary school that served middle-class children, mostly Han Chinese. Many of the families had moved from villages or smaller cities only one generation back, so that most regularly visited families in more rural settings.

B. Collection procedures. The researcher (a Shenzhen native) was introduced to the children and explained to them the purpose of our research and invited questions about our work. Children were given 30 minutes to write in response to the prompt below. They were Mandarin speakers and wrote in Chinese.

    1) Prompt: (Written for the children in Chinese) Write a story about a conflict that really happened to you. Think about an argument, a fight, or some kind of misunderstanding. Write everything you can remember about what happened from the beginning to the end.

C. Transcription procedures. The stories were typed into an electronic file in Chinese. Unlike the U.S. stories, these stories did not include grammatical or punctuation errors. (The children had carefully used white-out to correct any errors they might have made.) Stories were coded in Chinese by native speakers, but translations were made for the purposes of illustration and to facilitate discussion on the research team. Stories that were selected for close readings and interpretive analysis were translated by two researchers for whom Mandarin was their first language. Discrepancies were discussed with a third Mandarin speaker. Names were changed with an effort to select similarly common names.

VIII. FLASH Summer Day Camp, Memphis, TN, Summer 2014

A. Participants. Stories were collected from 27 first- to sixth-graders (approximately half female) who attended a summer day camp that provided recreational and educational activities, including games and sports, cooking and crafts, science and computer activities. Children came from professional families, 81% European American, 7% African American, and 12% mixed or other ethnicities. Most of the children attended a private church-related elementary school. Children attended camp for different periods of time, with some coming for only one week, some for all four weeks. Number of times children participated ranged from 2 to 20.

B. Collection procedures. The KidsTalk program (described in Appendix F) was held every day at summer camp for four weeks. These sessions were incorporated into ordinary camp activities and were an option for any child who wished to participate. Six or seven children gathered in a circle with a researcher and shared stories in response to the prompts below. Sessions averaged 40 minutes and were audio-recorded.

1. Prompts:

   a) Tell a true story about something that happened on a field trip.
   b) Tell a true story about a time you tried something new.
   c) Tell a true story about a time you or someone else got in trouble.
   d) Tell a true story about a time you or someone else did something dangerous.
   e) Tell a true story about a conflict you had with a friend. Tell about an argument, a fight or a misunderstanding.
   f) Tell a true story about a time you made something.
   g) Tell a true story about a time you helped someone.
   h) Tell a true story about a time you felt scared.
   i) Tell a true story about a big change that happened in your life.
   j) Tell a true story about a time you got lost.

k) Tell a true story about a time something happened that was not fair.
l) Tell a true story about a time you felt embarrassed.
m) Tell a true story about a time you felt proud.
n) Tell a true story about a time you felt left out.
o) Tell a true story about a time you got a surprise.
p) Tell a story about a time someone was mean to you.
q) Tell a true story about something that happened on the 4th of July.
r) Tell a true story about a time someone cheated.
s) Tell a true story about a time you visited relatives.
t) Tell a true story about a time you cheered someone up.
u) Tell a true story about a time you broke something.
v) Tell a true story about a time you fixed something.
w) Tell a true story about a time you helped someone younger than you.
x) Tell a true story about a time you got hurt or hurt someone else.
y) Tell a true story about a time you felt angry.
z) Tell a true story about a time you felt happy.
aa) Tell a true story about a time you felt thankful.
bb) Tell a true story about a time you felt unthankful.

C. Transcription. Audio recordings were made of each session, and the recordings were silenced for those children whose parents did not give consent. In addition, whenever a child's name (present or absent from the session) was mentioned, the recording was edited to silence the name. All audio sessions were later transcribed by a professional transcription company. Person and place names were changed and were substituted with names that preserved as much social information in the name as possible (i.e., ethnicity, formality, length).

APPENDIX B

Moral Voice Coding Manual

I. Overview

Our goal in this coding is to identify the author's evaluative stance. Children may have a clear and strong moral voice, explicitly critiquing people or behaviors and telling the reader which behaviors were morally justified. Sometimes an author may make explicit positive evaluations of some behavior, but may be vague or unclear about a moral critique. The author may critique or justify the behavior of another character, but be completely silent about the moral significance of his or her own actions. The coding we undertake here will allow us to examine:

a.   absent, implicit, and explicit moral evaluations
b.   positive and negative evaluations
c.   self and other evaluations.

II. Coding Process

Begin coding by reading the entire story through, just listening for the child's meanings. If you are uncertain about what the child means in parts of the story, re-read and try to discern what he or she is trying to say before you go on to code. In four subsequent readings of the story, code each of the four variables described below: justification of self, critique of self, justification of other, and critique of other. Do not try to code all four variables at once. Read the story again for each variable.

It is imperative to have coding instructions in front of you the whole time you are coding, and to refer to them often. It is surprisingly easy to miss whole categories of events, especially those that are relatively rare. When they haven't shown up in several stories, coders will sometimes stop looking for them. The only way to avoid this is to be regularly looking at the coding manual. As a rule of thumb, never code more than ten stories without re-reading the category descriptions.

Coding is not an activity that you can do when you are sleepy or distracted. Take regular breaks, and monitor your ability to stay alert. Thanks for being conscientious and thoughtful about this important part of the research effort!

III. Explicitness Rating

Coders will give each story four explicitness ratings, one for each of the four variables described below (*Justification of the Self, Critique of the Self, Justification of the Other, Critique of the Other*). Make each rating on a three-point scale:

> 0 = the author shows no evidence of making any evaluation.
> 1 = the author does not make an explicit evaluative statement, but the story implies an evaluative tone.
> 2 = the author makes at least one explicit evaluative statement in the story.

In each of the four categories for coding moral voice, record the highest level of explicitness of moral evaluation present at any point in the story.

IV. Moral Voice Variables

A. Justification of the Self

This category concerns the moral voice that is used to justify the author's own behavior or reasoning, or to positively evaluate the self.

> Explicitness = 2
>
> Explicit moral expressions include the use of deontic auxiliaries (e.g. should, ought, supposed to), judgments of right and good, and words and actions of truth, honesty, loyalty, fairness, compassion, and so on. Code as explicit stories in which the author describes learning a lesson or when he or she provides a moral summary of the story. If the child evaluates a 'former self' negatively, but reports a change of heart or claims to have learned a lesson, this will count as explicit justification of the self.
>
> Examples: "I didn't touch her because I'm not supposed to hit girls."
>
>   "That day I learned that friends don't belong to you."

Explicitness = 1

There seems to be a moral voice used to justify or positively evaluate the self, but it is not explicitly expressed. This happens when the author gives reason for his or her own behavior, but does not clearly evaluate the reason. Include references to retaliation as a reason, where the child seems to assume that the reader will recognize retaliation as justification.

Examples: "I didn't want to fight because I had on a dress."

"he hit me, so I hit him back".

Explicitness = 0

There is no place in the narrative where the author makes or implies any positive evaluation of self.

B. Critique of the Self

This category concerns whether the author recognized or acknowledged her/his own fault or wrongdoing at any point in the story.

Explicitness = 2

The story contains an explicit moral voice expressed to critique or negatively evaluate the self. Explicit expressions included acknowledgment of own fault or wrong, judgments of the author about the self as wrong, stupid, or bad. It also included apologies, admissions of guilt, and recognition of own mistakes. Deontic auxiliaries (should, ought to, etc.) are often markers of explicit evaluation.

Examples: "I felt so so bad hitting him and I apologized".

"I think I should not have hit him because brother is still too young."

Explicitness = 1

There seems to be a moral voice used to critique or negatively evaluate the self, but it is not explicitly expressed. The author reports a behavior, seeming to recognize that the reader will evaluate it negatively, although the author does not explicitly do so.

Example: "then I didn't walk away. I kept yelling at him."

(Note that if the author had said "I should have walked away," this would be rated as explicit.)

Explicitness = 0

There is no place in the narrative where the author makes or implies any negative evaluation of self.

C. Justification of the Other

This category concerns the moral voice used by the author to evaluate another character positively or to justify another's actions or words.

Explicitness = 2

Explicit moral expressions include the use of deontic auxiliaries (e.g. should, ought, supposed to), judgments of right and good, and words and actions of truth, honesty, loyalty, fairness, and compassion.

Example: "I admit, she didn't do anything wrong."

"She was being a really good friend."

Explicitness = 1

There seems to be a moral voice used to justify or positively evaluate another character, but it is not explicitly expressed. This happens when the author gives a reason for behavior, but does not clearly evaluate the reason. Include references to retaliation as a reason, where the child seems to assume that the reader will recognize retaliation as justification.

Examples: "He thought I called his sister a name."

"I pushed him, so he pushed me."

Explicitness = 0

There is no place in the narrative where the author makes or implies any positive evaluation of another character in the story.

D. Critique of the Other

This category concerns whether the author accused another character of fault or wrongdoing or negatively evaluated another character at any point in the story. Listen for a voice of moral indignation.

Explicitness = 2

The story contains an explicit moral voice expressed to critique or negatively evaluate another character in the story. Explicit expressions included accusations of guilt and the use of morally charged words to describe another's behavior or character (e.g., cheat, lie, mean, stupid, wrong, etc.). Use of deontic auxiliaries (should have, ought to) are indicators of explicit critique.

Examples: "He hit the girl, my mother taught me never to hit a girl."

"She's supposed to be my best friend. Friends don't act like that."

Explicitness = 1

There seems to be a moral voice used to critique or negatively evaluate another character, but it is not explicitly expressed. The author reports a behavior, seeming to recognize that the reader will evaluate it negatively, although the author does not explicitly do so.

Example: "My best friend wanted to play with my other friend."

"He dropped my stuff on the floor and walked away."

Explicitness = 0

There is no place in the narrative where the author makes or implies any negative evaluation or critique of any other character.

APPENDIX C

Psychological Mindedness Coding Manual

I. Overview

Our goal in this coding is to identify all occasions in which the children give attention to the internal states of themselves or of other actors in their stories. This is a feature of narrative that Bruner (1990) called the landscape of consciousness. We will count occasions in which children report or infer emotions, thoughts, motives, and psychological traits of the self or of other characters in their stories.

II. Coding Process

Begin coding by reading the entire story through just listening for the child's meanings. If you are uncertain about what the child means in parts of the story, re-read and try to discern what he or she is trying to say before you go on to code. This coding will require four passes through the data, one for each of the four variables described below: motives, mental states, emotional states, traits. Do not try to code all four variables at once.

It is imperative to have coding instructions in front of you the whole time you are coding, and to refer to them often. It is surprisingly easy to miss whole categories of events, especially those that are relatively rare. When they haven't shown up in several stories, coders will sometimes stop looking for them. The only way to avoid this is to be regularly looking at the coding manual. As a rule of thumb, never code more than ten stories without re-reading the category descriptions.

Coding is not an activity that you can do when you are sleepy or distracted. Take regular breaks, and monitor your ability to stay alert. Thanks for being conscientious and thoughtful about this important part of the research effort!

III. Count Variables

Each of the four variables below is a count, and the unit of analysis for this count is the subject-predicate unit. The stories have been segmented into these units and lines are numbered. In each line of the story, check to see whether there are instances of the variable. We will count the number of lines in the story that contain the variable. Therefore, the score for each variable will range from zero to the total number of lines in the story. If a line includes more than one instance of the same variable, it will advance the count for that variable by one. For example, if the child writes "I was sad and happy at the same time," this will count as one instance of a report of own emotions, not two. If the child said, "Even though she was sad, I was happy," this will count as one instance of own and one instance of others' emotion. If the child said "I was mad, mad, mad, mad, mad," this will advance the 'own emotion' count by only one.

If there are no instances of the variable in the story, enter a zero. However, if the child does not write a story, leave the variable blank for that ID number. Blanks must be distinguished from zeros.

IV. Counting Motive, Intentions, and Reasons

As you read the story through again, ask yourself about the author's attention to the motives and intentions of the actors in the story. Does this author recognize that the reader will want to know why the protagonists acted as they did?

As you go through line by line, note the presence of:

a. reports of own motives, intentions, or reasons, [note: Sometimes the author will report about her own motive in the voice of another character, as in "She said I did it on purpose." This *will* count as motive-self – even if the author goes on to dispute its veracity.];
b. reports of any other characters' motives, intentions, or reasons;
c. reports of motives, intentions, or reasons made in the first-person plural (attributed to both self and other). ⸂We⸃

Watch for the following categories of motivations/intentions/reasons:

A. Any report that attributes effort toward a goal or desire for an outcome.

1) reports of desiring, wanting, wishing, hoping for;
2) reports of trying to, going for, seeking, looking for;
3) DO NOT CODE "going to" or "getting" as motivation, unless it fits in the "in order to" rule described in section B4 below.

B. Reports of reasons or causes for behaviors or actions of characters.

1) If the child explains what the character is doing the behavior "FOR," this will count. For example, in story 2232, the author describes spying

on girls "for fun." This mention of "for fun" clearly shows the author's motivation for the particular behavior.

2) Pay attention to any use of 'because.' This will usually flag an occasion in which the author is attempting to explain something that has happened.

- If the author gives a reason for the behavior of the self or of any characters, this will count. For example, "We jumped over the fence because our ball went back there" provides a motive for jumping the fence, and will be coded as motive-we.
- If the author uses because to explain something that cannot be attributed as a reason or motive of any character in the story, this will not count. For example, "I fell on the sidewalk because it was slippery" provides an explanation for the fall, but not a reason of any actor, so it will not count.
- This may be tricky, because "The teacher wouldn't let us have recess because it was raining" *will count* because the rain is posited as a reason for the teacher's behavior. However, "We couldn't go to recess because it was raining" would *not* count because the reason cannot be attributed to the teacher.

3) Pay attention to any use of the word 'so.' Sometimes this word is used to mark an explanation or a reason, as in "I was bored / so I took a walk." This *would count* as motive-self because boredom is posited as the reason for the walking. Sometimes, however, children use 'so' just to signal what happens next, without imputing causality.

- "I got out my notebook and pencil / so I found out that we were supposed to do page 20 / so I did it." In this example the first occasion of 'so' will *not count*, but the second *will count* as an instance of motive-self.
- Sometimes it is not clear whether the child means 'so then' (with no causal intent) or 'so therefore' (imputing causality). If it is reasonable to interpret the 'so' as 'so therefore,' count the instance of 'so' as a motive/reason.

4) Pay special attention to the use of infinitives. With each use of an infinitive, ask whether the child's meaning can be paraphrased by inserting the words "in order to." If this works, then the infinitive should count as an instance of a reason.

- For example, "I went inside to get a bandaid" and "I left to play soccer" *will count* because the child went or left in order to get a bandaid or to play soccer – the intent to get a bandaid was the reason for going.
- "I started to go inside," or "I had to play dominos," or "she told me not to get dirty" *would not count*. In all of those cases, the insertion of 'in order to' does not preserve the meaning.

C. Reports of NOT having a reason, or of not knowing why someone did something count any time the author explicitly notes the absence of a motive or reason, or a failure to understand the reason for someone's behavior (E.g., "I have no idea why I did it.").

- Do not count reports of not knowing unless they pertain to the behavior or actions of characters in the story. "I don't know why it keeps on raining every day," *would not* count.

D. Reports of intention that may overlap with our moral concerns coding.

1) Doing something 'on purpose' or 'accidentally.'
2) DO NOT count 'making a mistake' (e.g. "I made a mistake on the homework"). Unlike 'accident,' which signals a lack of intention, 'mistake' usually signals that the behavior or outcome was recognized as wrong, not that it was performed unintentionally.
3) Code meaning or not meaning something (or not really meaning). Be careful with this, because it will only count when it refers to the intention of a person. We would not count "scarlet means bright red," but we would count "She meant to say scarlet, not scarret." We *will* count "She really means it," or "I meant to give it back."
4) Code reports that a character was 'just kidding' or 'not serious' or 'only joking.' Expressions such as these indicate that the character did not intend a literal meaning of the act; it indicates a playful motive.

joking

- Be careful with these words, because they will NOT count if they are used to report or describe a behavior or activity, not to describe a motive. "We were joking around in math class" would not count.

E. Code any use of the word motive, goal, reason, intention.

V. Coding Reports of Emotional States

As you read the story through again, ask yourself about the author's attention to the emotions of the characters in the story. Does the author report what he or she and other characters were feeling as the story unfolds?

As you go through line by line, note the presence of:

a. reports of own emotions [note: Sometimes the author will report about an emotion and will deny experiencing it (e.g., "I was not even scared."), or will report about another character's imputing emotion to the self (e.g., "she thought I was mad at her") This *will* count as emotion-self.];
b. reports of any other character's emotions;
c. reports of emotions made in the first-person plural (attributed to both self and other).

Watch for the following categories of emotion reports:

A. Reports about emotions

1) emotional states (sad, happy, mad, etc.);

2) emotional traits (shy, proud, etc.);

3) DO NOT CODE emotional behaviors (crying, laughing, stomping one's foot, etc.);

4) DO NOT CODE interpersonal behaviors, even though they may imply emotion – examples include: "making up, becoming friends/enemies, apologizing, blaming, agreeing, disagreeing";

5) count such reports as "I'm sorry," "We got over it," "He cooled off," which describe states, but do not count "She apologized," which is a report of a behavior;

6) count reports of behaviors that are defined by their effect on emotional states (e.g. "They were bugging me"). Note that in this case it is the author who experiences the emotion, even though another character is the subject of the verb 'bugging.'

VI. Coding Reports About Mental States

As you read the story through again, ask yourself about the author's attention to the cognitive experiences of the characters in the story. Does the author report what he or she and other characters were thinking as the story unfolds?

As you go through line by line, note the presence of:

a. reports of own mental states [note: Sometimes the author will report about mental states attributed to self by another character (e.g., "She said I don't know my times tables"). This *will* count as own mental state, even if the author goes on to deny it.];

b. reports of any other character's mental states;

c. reports of mental states made in the first-person plural (attributed to both self and other).

Watch for the following categories of mental state reports:

A. Reports about mental processes

1. Include thinking, guessing, wondering, remembering, knowing, believing, imagining, pretending, 'getting it,' searching, looking, etc.

2. School work – DO NOT COUNT general instances of school work such as "I was doing math," "I was working" ...

3. Do code instances of school work if the author is describing mental processes (e.g. solving, finding out, searching for, looking for, etc.).

4. Count mental states or abilities (confusion, seriousness, being smart or stupid, being 'good at math,' for instance).

5. Count decision-making processes (e.g. choosing, deciding, etc.).

6. Do NOT count reports of perceptual states (seeing, hearing.) This is tricky, because 'I see' will count if it means 'I understand.' Listening and watching will count because they are reports about attentional states, whereas seeing and hearing are reports only of perceptual states.

APPENDIX D

Authorial Voice Coding Manual

I. Overview

In our effort to code these stories *as stories*, we will consider several features of the child's writing, starting with global assessments of the story, and then moving to counts of individual features.

II. Coding Process

This coding will require several passes through the data, with the three rating variables assessed in the first pass, and the three sets of count variables assessed in three subsequent passes.

It is imperative to have coding instructions in front of you the whole time you are coding, and to refer to them often. It is surprisingly easy to miss whole categories of events, especially those that are relatively rare. When they haven't shown up in several stories, coders will sometimes stop looking for them. The only way to avoid this is to be regularly looking at the coding manual. As a rule of thumb, never code more than ten stories without re-reading the category descriptions.

Coding is not an activity that you can do when you are sleepy or distracted. Take regular breaks, and monitor your ability to stay alert. Thanks for being conscientious and thoughtful about this important part of the research effort!

III. Ratings of Literary Skills and Authorial Voice

Each story will be given three ratings, each on a three-point scale, with a 3 indicating the strongest narrative skill. If the child did not provide a story, leave the code blank (do not code as a 0). Read each story three times, once for each rating.

A. Clarity

Clarity refers to the ease with which the writing can be understood. We recognize that this understanding is culture bound, and that readers immersed in different narrative traditions would find different stories clear. For our purposes, we will take a stance that is consistent with the academic and educational aims of the schools the children attend. From this perspective, there are two primary contributors to clarity: sequentiality (clarity of plot structure) and issues of common ground (knowledge shared between the author and reader). A story that is high in clarity is focused and coherent, without irrelevant digressions, and the events in the story follow a logical sequence (note that this may not be the same as a chronological sequence; the author may begin the story in the middle of the action and then move back to the beginning, but the sequence in which the events occurred remains clear). The author provides all of the information necessary for you to comprehend the story. After reading the story once, you understand what happened. On the other hand, a story that is low in clarity is difficult to follow, and the order of events may seem scrambled. The author may make mistaken assumptions about the reader's knowledge (for example, using pronouns without explaining to whom they refer), requiring the reader to re-read in order to understand the events described. Rate the story according to the following criteria. Try not to make your ratings based on the child's mastery of writing conventions. Even if words are misspelled and punctuation is not used in standard ways, if you can understand the story, rate it accordingly. CLARITY

1 = This author did not express the story clearly. The story does not include enough information; that is, there are serious problems of common ground. Connections between events or ideas may be confusing or absent altogether. Though you may be able to understand the overall gist of the story, parts of it remain unclear after multiple readings.

2 = This author did an adequate job of expressing the story clearly. There may be a few digressions, and occasional problems of common ground. However, you can easily understand the majority of the story.

3 = This author expressed the story very clearly. The connections between ideas/events make sense, and all of the necessary information is included (there are no major problems of common ground). After reading the story once, you have a very clear understanding of what happened.

B. Conventions

This rating assesses the correct use of conventions of writing, namely grammar, punctuation, capitalization, and spelling. When assigning a rating, consider the number of errors relative to the length and complexity of the story. If the author appears to flout conventions for stylistic effect (e.g., using all capital letters for emphasis or using incomplete sentences to add drama) do not consider these to be errors. Rate the story according to the following criteria:

Conventions

1 = This story contains numerous errors in spelling, grammar, punctuation, and capitalization relative to the length and complexity of the story. There are errors in almost every line.

2 = This story contains some errors in spelling, grammar, punctuation, and capitalization relative to the length and complexity of the story. Several lines in the story may contain errors. The grammar and punctuation is generally simplistic.

3 = This story contains few errors in spelling, grammar, punctuation, and capitalization relative to the length and complexity of the story, and the author uses more sophisticated forms of grammar and punctuation. The author uses these conventions to guide the reader through the text, and they contribute to the clarity and style of the writing.

C. Expressiveness

Expressiveness refers to an author's ability to tell an engaging story with individual flavor, a distinct writing style. As you read a story with a strong expressive voice, you get a sense of the person behind the words and feel as if you can almost hear the child speaking to you. Elements of tone, such as humor or irony, may contribute to expressiveness. In addition, it is often marked by creative use of language, such as similes and metaphors (e.g., "He ran at me like a bull, with fury in his eyes") or by the use of vocabulary that is advanced or atypical for the author's grade level (e.g., "I thought I would perish" rather than "I thought I would die"). Rate the story according to the following criteria:

Expressiveness

1 = This story is straightforward, with minimal evidence of creativity. The author seems indifferent, uninvolved, or distanced from the audience. The writing comes across as monotone rather than expressive.

2 = This story is mostly straightforward, but there are some instances of creativity and expressiveness. The writer's voice may seem to come through for a few lines, then fade away.

3 = This story is expressive, and the author's voice comes through clearly throughout the story. The writing displays a unique personal style, and the reader feels a strong interaction with the writer.

IV. Counts of Literary Features

Complete the ratings of all the stories in the data set before coming back to code the count variables. The first two variables below (metanarrative comments and emphasis markers) can be coded in a second pass through the data.

The reported speech variables can be coded in a third pass and Cultural Voice in a final pass.

A. Metanarrative Comments *code in a 2nd pass of the story*

Sometimes an author demonstrates an awareness of the self as a story-teller. These are often asides that move out of the story time and into the telling time to address the reader directly or to comment on the writing process. Count the number of lines (subject-predicate units) in the story that include any of these types of metanarrative comments. If the child did not provide a story, leave a blank. Code as a 0 only if the child wrote a story that included no instances of metanarrative comments.

1. The author addresses the reader directly. All uses of a second-person pronoun will be metanarrative.

   Examples: "you know what happened then?"
             "So like I told you he kept on bothering me"

2. The author comments on the story itself.

   Examples: "so on I go with my story."
             "Well that's my story and it's all 100% true!"

3. The author makes an aside or parenthetical comment.

   Examples: "By the way, this didn't happen at Magnolia Springs."
             "(the teacher still doesn't know, so don't tell her.)"

4. The author poses a rhetorical question.

   Example: "Who could believe it?"
             "Did I mention we where in 2nd grade"

5. The author labels parts of the narrative.

   Example: "The End. Non-fiction"
             "Here's the next part of my story."

B. Emphasis Markers *2nd pass*

Emphasis markers are literary devices that direct the reader to pay special attention to particular parts of the story. We will count two types of emphasis markers: intensifiers and orthographic attentional devices. Count the number of lines (subject-predicate units) in the story that include any of these types of metanarrative comments. If the child did not provide a story, leave a blank. Code as a 0 only if the child wrote a story that included no instances of emphasis markers.

1. Intensifiers are words or phrases that express extremity or exceptionality. They occur when the author quantifies an adjective or adverb to increase or decrease the intensity of the statement.

    Examples: "it was *pretty* dumb,"
    "my eyes get watery because I get *way too* mad".

2. Orthographic attentional devices are orthographic features that the author uses to emphasize their thoughts, actions, or emotions. This includes the use of purposefully misspelled words; one or more exclamation points; repeated words; and use of all capital letters.

    Examples: "I got *sooo* mad"
    "It is still going on today!!"
    "he talks about my mother *very very* wrong"
    "*YOUR NOT MY FRIND ANYMORE!*"

C. Reported Speech 3rd pass

The incorporation of dialogue in a story is a critical part of the achievement of authorial voice. In a third pass through the data, identify all occasions in which the author talks about speech of any type. This coding can best be accomplished if the story is read aloud. Even when the children do not use quotation punctuation marks, the inclusion of multiple voices in their stories can often be detected when read aloud. Count the number of subject-predicate lines that contain reports of speech (not the number of individual quotes). We will count the six types of talk-about-talk described below.

1. Direct Quotation. Although our authors do not always include appropriate quotation punctuation, direct quotation can be identified because the verb tense and any deictic pronouns are consistent with the time and place of the reported speech event, not with the time of the story writing.

    Examples: "So he asked me why are you getting an attitude?"
    "The next day she said don't even look at me."

2. Indirect Quotation. Here authors transposed the report of speech into the narrator's own voice so that the tense and pronouns were consistent with the time of the story writing rather than the occasion of the actual speech (that is, the author has moved to the telling time rather than the story time).

    Examples: "So he asked me why I was getting an attitude."
    "The next day she said not to even look at her."

3. Mixed Quotation. Children sometimes reported speech in a form in which the tense was consistent with the time of the original speech but pronouns were consistent with the narrative voice or vice versa.

> Examples: "So he asked me why am I getting an attitude."
> "The next day she said don't even look at her" [where context makes it clear that 'her' referred to the speaker, not the author.]

4. Putative Voicing. Some of the speech reported in the stories will not fall clearly into any of the three categories above, either because the voicing is disputed or the case is subjunctive. In these instances, the narrator was speculating about whether the reported speech content was actually voiced or was speculative about who said it. These include reports about what should have been said, what one was told to say, or what one may say in the future.

> Examples: "She should tell her to quit that stuff."
> "But if I did say it she didn't have no busy putting my name in it."

5. Reported Speech Act. Authors sometimes labeled a speech act (e.g., asked, yelled at, phoned) or a discourse form (e.g., argued, had a conversation, talked it out) without revealing specific content. This category includes glosses that reported about speech without telling the reader what was said – only that it was said.

> Examples: "He said something real mean."
> "I told her the whole story."
> "We discuss things out and we both apolijize."

6. Report of non-speech. Count any occasions in which the author makes a note of the fact that speech did not happen. Reports of non-speech indicated that the author or an actor in the story expected speech to happen, or that the author anticipated that his or her reader would expect speech at this point in the story.

> Examples: "I didn't say NOTHING to him."
> "We didn't speak to each other for a while."

As you classify each report of speech into one of the above categories, indicate for each whose speech was reported, in one of four categories:

a. self ("I sad that was not fair.");
b. other child, multiple other children, or self and other children ("They all told the teacher he sprong on me." "We decided to tell the principal.");
c. adult ("My mom said we don't need to be fighting like little boys.");
d. generalized other ("Everyone says I'm the best dancer.").

In one final read of the story, look for instances in which the author embedded speech acts within speech acts. These are complex sentences that enclose one speech event within another. For example, the line "So I told Shamira to tell her to stop telling lies" is triply embedded. The reported speech act 'telling lies' is embedded in the putative speech by Shamira who may tell her to stop, which is embedded in the indirect speech act by the author who told Shamira what to tell. Count the number of lines in the story that include embedded reports of speech.

D. Cultural Voice

Once the above coding is completed for the entire data set, begin a new pass through the data to code cultural voice. Again, this coding requires reading each story aloud. Again, we will count the number of lines in the story that include evidence of this variable.

With this coding we hope to capture a facet of narrative voice by counting the colloquial or idiomatic expressions in each story. These are instances in which the author incorporates linguistic expressions or turns of phrase whose meaning is not captured in a literal translation. The use of such expressions is evidence of the child's integration in a cultural community, and of the child's skill at appropriating language for his or her own purposes.

What makes this coding difficult is the fact that pushed to the limits of our logic, we see that language is virtually never literal, and that abstraction, by its very nature, is metaphorical. Any use of language entails an appropriation of a cultural toolkit and is evidence of the integration into a cultural community. Our task is to distinguish a subset of non-literal language we want to designate as idiomatic or colloquial. We will approach this task by asking whether the expression the child uses could be used to identify him or her as part of a particular cultural community, looking specifically for the following five kinds of expressions:

1. Language that identifies the child as a member of a school or educational community.

    a) This will include all expressions that have special meaning in a school setting, such as being sent to the principal or sent to the office, getting suspended, telling the teacher, copying off someone's paper, taking names. Note that some of these expressions may be quite literal (e.g., going to the principal's office, putting my name on the board), but the intended meaning is not captured in the literal understanding, and it is the school context that gives the expressions the extra meanings associated with punishment or with reward.

    b) We will also include expressions that are especially common in a school setting, so as to be a regular part of school life, such as 'getting in' or 'standing in line.' Putting something in ABC order or 'raising our hands' are other examples of expressions that describe school-identified (if not school-exclusive) behaviors.

   c)   We are especially eager to include occasions in which the child appropriates the voice of the teacher or school authority by using specific and identifiable vocabulary of curriculum. For example, we know that 'she gave me an I-message' is part of a violence-prevention curriculum. If a child says, 'I used my walking feet,' and we know that there is a sign on the auditorium door that says "Please use your walking feet," we would count this.

2.   Language that identifies the child as part of a regional language community. Examples of this are, 'y'all' in the Southern US or 'yous guys' in parts of the US Northeast. Ethnic or social class groups might be identified by expressions such as 'honey chile' or 'down yonder.' Recognizing these requires that your own ear is attuned to such language variations.

3.   Language that places the child in a 'generation' or that identifies the author with popular culture, street culture, an 'in group' or peer group.

   a)   Expressions that identify the author as a child or that would usually only be used by a child or spoken to a child should count here because they identify the author with an age group. These might include 'saying a bad word,' 'calling names,' 'getting a whooping,' or 'being a baby.'

   b)   We want to count expressions that could be read as the author's claim to be 'street-savvy' or 'cool.' Many of these would be recognized as 'slang' because they would not be used by someone trying to be proper or by someone who was not an insider. Examples of this kind of language are 'She's too cool for school,' 'he thinks he's all that,' 'he got a beat down,' 'she got an attitude with me,' 'checking his family,' or 'dissing me.' The use of the verb 'to like' for quotation or for emphasis would count here, as in 'I was like, really mad' or 'I was like no way.'

   c)   Count any expression that you recognize as a quotation of popular culture (TV, movies, lyrics). Examples of these are "so that's my final answer" or "he got three thumbs up" or "she's bad to the bone."

4.   Language that claims cultural authority or identifies the author with a broader cultural context.

   This would include quotations from classical culture (e.g., the Bible, Shakespeare, Aesop) or the use of the language of jurisprudence or liturgy (e.g., 'the truth and nothing but the truth' or 'till death do us part').

5.   Common idioms and metaphors that are recognizable by most members of the larger culture, but would not be easily translatable.

   Examples of these are, 'kicked the bucket,' 'got on his high horse.' We believe that these show the child's willingness and ability to appropriate culture in a way that the use of more literal language does not. They differ from the above items (1 to 4) in that they do not seem to belong to a specific cultural community or source of cultural authority. They do seem to show, however, that the child is claiming a cultural/literary/discursive tradition in a notable way.

Our task is to count those items while NOT counting the following.

a. We will not count conventional metaphors that are so culturally common that most people do not recognize them as metaphorical at all. We will exclude most orientational metaphors (making up, working it out, getting through it) and possession or acquisition metaphors (getting sick of it, taking a break, getting back at, having a go at). These are certainly metaphorical and colloquial, but they are so common in the language that they do not serve to identify the child with a cultural community.

b. Similarly, we will exclude common colloquial expressions that are easy to translate, and do not have culturally specific roots. For example, 'here we go again,' 'once in a while,' 'the rest of the day.' The difference between colloqui-alisms we count in item 5 above and those we do not count may be discerned by imagining a second-language learner trying to make sense of it. You can see that 'once in a while,' or 'ever so often' would cause less puzzlement than 'once in a blue moon.' The latter would count for us; the two former expres-sions would not.

For each line, code as a 1 if a colloquial or idiomatic expression is present, or as a 0 if it is not present. If a line appears to contain more than one colloquialism or idiomatic expression, we will count it only once. However, if an author uses the same expression multiple times on different lines of the story, we will count it each time it occurs. If the child did not write a story, leave the variable blank for that ID number rather than entering a 0.

Here are coding procedures that will support reliability.

a. Code only when rested and alert.

b. Re-read the coding manual each time you sit down to code, and re-read it after each 15 stories coded.

c. Read the stories out loud. Colloquialisms (and other indicators of 'voice') are more easily recognized when voiced than when read silently.

d. Ask yourself the following questions about each line of the story:

- Is this 'school language'?
- Is this regional language?
- Does the language suggest an ethnic group or any clear cultural community?
- Is this 'street talk' or language of 'the hood'?
- Does the use of this expression communicate 'I'm cool' or 'I'm an insider'?
- Does the use of this expression constitute a claim to cultural authority?
- Can you identify this expression as a quotation or a reasonable effort at quotation of any popular or classical source?

e.   If all of the above answers are 'no,' but the expression still seems as though it may be countable, then do the following:

- Parse the phrase. If its meaning is perfectly obvious to anyone who knows the vocabulary of the component parts, it will not usually count as colloquial. The expressions we want to identify are those that would generally trip up a second-language learner. They would have to learn them separately as expressions, or they would have to figure them out from context because the words themselves would not reveal the meaning or would suggest a different meaning than that intended.

- Ask yourself who would use this expression. If you can identify a particular cultural community in which this expression is common or with which this expression is identified, then we do want to count it. If almost any speaker of English is likely to say this, it is less likely to be one of the phrases we want to count.

APPENDIX E

KidsTalk Prompts

KidsTalk Twofer Prompts (Paired Prompts)

1) Tell a true story about a time you won.
2) Tell a true story about a time you lost.
3) Tell a true story about a time you lost something.
4) Tell a true story about a time you found something.
5) Tell a true story about a time you got a surprise.
6) Tell a true story about a time you gave someone a surprise.
7) Tell a true story about a time someone hurt your feelings.
8) Tell a true story about a time you hurt someone else's feelings.
9) Tell a true story about a time you made something for someone.
10) Tell a true story about a time someone made something for you.
11) Tell a true story about a time you got in trouble.
12) Tell a true story about a time someone else got in trouble.
13) Tell a true story about a time someone was mean to you.
14) Tell a true story about a time you were mean to someone.
15) Tell a true story about a time someone was nice to you.
16) Tell a true story about a time you were nice to someone.
17) Tell a true story about a time someone was disrespectful.
18) Tell a true story about a time someone was respectful.
19) Tell a true story about a time you felt included.
20) Tell a true story about a time you felt left out.
21) Tell a true story about a time you made someone feel welcomed.
22) Tell a true story about a time someone made you feel welcomed.
23) Tell a true story about a time you felt good about yourself.
24) Tell a true story about a time you did not feel good about yourself.
25) Tell a true story about a time you felt happy.

26) Tell a true story about a time you felt sad.
27) Tell a true story about a time you felt smart.
28) Tell a true story about a time you felt dumb.
29) Tell a true story about a time you felt proud.
30) Tell a true story about a time you felt embarrassed.
31) Tell a true story about a time you broke something.
32) Tell a true story about a time you fixed something.
33) Tell a true story about a time someone did you a favor.
34) Tell a true story about a time you did someone a favor.
35) Tell a true story about a time you accomplished a goal.
36) Tell a true story about a time you did not accomplish your goal.
37) Tell a true story about a time you turned out to be right.
38) Tell a true story about a time you turned out to be wrong.
39) Tell a true story about a time someone did not agree with you.
40) Tell a true story about a time you did not agree with someone.
41) Tell a true story about a time you were loyal to a friend.
42) Tell a true story about a time a friend was loyal to you.
43) Tell a true story about a time you stood up for someone.
44) Tell a true story about a time someone stood up for you.
45) Tell a true story about a time you told a lie.
46) Tell a true story about a time you told the truth.
47) Tell a true story about a time you lost your temper.
48) Tell a true story about a time you controlled your temper.

Feeling Prompts

49) Tell a true story about a time you felt thankful.
50) Tell a true story about a time you felt grumpy.
51) Tell a true story about a time you cheered someone up.
52) Tell a true story about a time you felt curious.
53) Tell a true story about a time you felt lonely.
54) Tell a true story about a time you felt angry.
55) Tell a true story about a time you felt scared.
56) Tell a true story about a time you felt excited.
57) Tell a true story about a time you felt jealous.
58) Tell a true story about a time you felt loved.

Personal Health, Safety, and Well-Being Prompts

59) Tell a true story about a time you got lost.
60) Tell a true story about a time you got hurt.
61) Tell a true story about a time someone did something dangerous.
62) Tell a true story about a time something bad or scary happened with an animal.

63) Tell a true story about a time you were home alone.
64) Tell a true story about a time you did something unhealthy.
65) Tell a true story about something you did on the weekend to get moving.

Personal Development, Character Prompts

66) Tell a true story about a big change that happened in your life.
67) Tell a true story about something that happened when you were little.
68) Tell a true story about a time something didn't turn out how you wanted.
69) Tell a true story about a time you tried something new.
70) Tell a true story about a time you did something brave.
71) Tell a true story about a time you discovered something.
72) Tell a true story about a time you learned something new.
73) Tell a true story about a time you were precise or accurate.
74) Tell a true story about a time you were responsible.
75) Tell a true story about a time you took care of a pet or another animal.
76) Tell a true story about a time you cleaned things up or organized something.
77) Tell a true story about a time you helped take care of the Earth.
78) Tell a true story about a time you had to do something that you did not want to do.
79) Tell a true story about a time you did your best.
80) Tell a true story about a time you changed your mind about something.
81) Tell a true story about a time you did something silly or goofy.

Relationships/Relationship Problems Prompts

82) Tell a true story about a time you made a friend.
83) Tell a true story about a time a friend didn't act like a friend.
84) Tell a true story about something you did with a best friend.
85) Tell a true story about a conflict that really happened to you.
86) Tell a true story about an argument you had.
87) Tell a true story about a misunderstanding you had with someone.
88) Tell a true story about a time something happened that was not fair.
89) Tell a true story about a time there was a fight.
90) Tell a true story about a time someone wouldn't share.
91) Tell a true story about a time someone was blamed for something they didn't do.
92) Tell a true story about a time you made up after a fight or argument.
93) Tell a true story about a time someone cheated.
94) Tell a true story about a time you gave someone a present.
95) Tell a true story about a time you helped someone.
96) Tell a true story about a time you helped someone in your family.
97) Tell a true story about a time you helped someone younger than you.

98) Tell a true story about a time you helped someone you didn't know.
99) Tell a true story about a time you asked for help.
100) Tell a true story about a time you visited relatives.
101) Tell a true story about a time you felt homesick.
102) Tell a true story about a time when you met someone new.
103) Tell a true story about a time you taught someone else how to do something.
104) Tell a true story about something you did on the weekend with your family.
105) Tell a true story about a time you made someone smile or laugh.
106) Tell a true story about your favorite teacher.

Context (Where It Happened/What You Did) Prompts

107) Tell a true story about a time you planted something.
108) Tell a true story about a time you made something in the kitchen.
109) Tell a true story about a time you made something.
110) Tell a true story about something that happened on the playground.
111) Tell a true story about something that happened at the dentist.
112) Tell a true story about something that happened at the doctor.
113) Tell a true story about something that happened on the 4th of July.
114) Tell a true story about something that happened on Halloween.
115) Tell a true story about something that happened on a trip.
116) Tell a true story about something that happened at school.
117) Tell a true story about something that happened at recess.
118) Tell a true story about something that happened on a field trip.
119) Tell a true story about something that happened at a sleepover.
120) Tell a true story about something that happened while you were playing outside.
121) Tell a true story about a time you went to a new place.
122) Tell a true story about something you did with a pet.
123) Tell a true story about a time you celebrated something.
124) Tell a true story about something that happened on your birthday.
125) Tell a true story about something that happened when you were playing a sport.
126) Tell a true story about something that happened on when you were playing a game.
127) Tell a true story about something that happened during the summer vacation.
128) Tell a true story about your favorite thing you have ever done at the Community Wellness Center.
129) Tell a true story about a time you were in a very beautiful place.

APPENDIX F

Instructions for KidsTalk Facilitators

KidsTalk is a program designed to promote children's natural tendencies to talk about their experiences. Story-sharing is important to moral development, to emotion regulation, to the developing sense of self, and to the establishment and maintenance of relationships. The ability to share personal stories is a precursor to literacy skills and has been shown to be critical to our ability to cope with adversity. We are seeking to encourage the story-sharing practices and to create an atmosphere in which children know that their own stories are valued by others. All we really do when we facilitate KidsTalk sessions is listen to kids talk about their lives, responding naturally, and giving minimal instruction. Here are a few guidelines.

- A group of five to eight children should sit in a circle with one or two adult facilitators. Groups may be composed of same-aged or mixed-age children. We have most successfully run KidsTalk sessions with children between ages seven and twelve.
- Open each session by reviewing names and welcoming each child (each child should be spoken to by name, and should get full eye contact!). Tell the children that we are there because we love sharing stories with each other about things that really happened, and we really want to hear everyone's stories. Remind them about being good listeners, and introduce an object that will serve as a 'story stick.' The person holding the story stick gets everyone's full attention.
- Introduce the topic for the day, and invite someone to tell about something that happened to them that relates to the topic. Use the expression "tell about something that happened to you" rather than "tell a story about

a time when" because some children think that "tell a story" is a request for fiction.

- If the children are shy, you may need to get things started (especially in the first few sessions) by telling a story of your own. If you do this, be sure to make your story short and simple. You don't want to intimidate the children by telling a story that is nothing like a story they might be able to share.
- Let the children volunteer, but make sure everyone gets a chance to tell a story. Some children may need to be encouraged. Try not to give the floor to the same child twice until each child has had a turn.
- Although you should try to react naturally to the story, you should not make corrections or suggestions. Even if you know that the child has told the story in a confusing way or has said something that is not correct, don't challenge the child's story.
- You MAY ask questions if the story is not clear or not elaborated at all. This may especially be needed in the first couple of sessions. Initially the children may not include the basic elements in their story, and may need to be prompted with, "And then what happened?" or "So what did you do next?" Over sessions, they'll get better at constructing narratives, and will not need such prompting.
- Listen intently, and make it clear to all the children that you are giving your attention fully to the child who is telling a story. Model good listening behavior: this will make it more likely that the children will listen to each other. Show normal (not exaggerated) emotional responses – surprise, concern, laughter, sadness, relief.

Suggestions for Common KidsTalk Problems

- We want the children to listen to each other, but we want to do as little correcting as possible. Here are some strategies for getting the children to listen.

  - Sometimes, when a child is not paying attention, if you make exaggerated gestures of your OWN attention to the storyteller that will prompt better listening. (Lean forward toward the speaker, gaze with intent interest, turn your head, as if trying to hear better.)
  - If a child is being disruptive while another child is talking, try first to intervene without saying anything, maybe by putting your hand on the child's chair.
  - If you need to say something to quiet a child, first just say "Listen!" not as if you are correcting the child, but as if the storyteller is saying something you just don't want anyone to miss.

- ○ If you have to say more than this to get a child to stop talking, try "Remember the rule about stepping on each other's words," but try to say it in a non-judgmental, non-threatening way.
- ○ If a lot of children are distracted, or you are having difficulty getting the circle to settle, introduce a 'listening posture,' and encourage the children to 'listen with their whole bodies.' You may get everyone to kneel and sit on their heels, then switch for the next story to sitting cross-legged. You may suggest a hand position – the idea is to involve the body in a way that can help the children focus.
- ○ Remember to compliment the children who are listening well.

- Sometimes a child's story goes on too long. This happens especially with children who need more attention than they are getting. Sometimes it just happens because the child does not have the narrative skills to end the story.

  - ○ You may have to interrupt the story and gently take the story stick back. Try to find a time when it seems as though the story could be coming to an end. You could say, "Thank you for that story!"
  - ○ If the child resists giving up the story stick, just say "We have to make sure we have time for everyone to share stories."
  - ○ If you have a child who you know is inclined to keep the floor too long, give the floor first to another child and, when that child has finished, say, "Thanks for that story. It had a beginning, middle, and an end!" Sometimes, this will be enough to help the long-winded child understand the need to end the story.

- Sometimes a child speaks so softly or so quickly that you cannot understand what he or she is saying.

  - ○ If this is a problem, you can begin the KidsTalk session with a brief instruction about using our 'audience voice.' Demonstrate an inside voice, an outside voice, and an audience voice. Pass the story stick around, and let each child say, "My name is ____, and this is my audience voice."

- Sometimes the children in the circle will fall into a 'copy-cat' routine, in which each story will be nearly identical to the other stories. This may be especially troubling if the story they are copying is off-topic or is inappropriate in some way.

  - ○ When you see this happening, take a turn telling a story yourself. This can interrupt the copying, and this can get the children back to the topic of the day.

- We don't want to interrupt the stories or correct stories, but sometimes it may be necessary to do so. On these occasions, try to be as gentle as possible in taking the story stick from the child:

  - If a child tells a story about a seriously disturbing matter, such as family violence that may require intervention, you may need to say, "Oh, ＿＿, this sounds like an important story you need to tell to a special grown-up. Let's talk about this as soon as KidsTalk is over." Then take the stick and immediately tell a story of your own, so that the other children's attention will move to your story rather than to the troubling story. Follow up with the child, in accordance with our procedures. If you have not been able to stop the story before the other children might have been upset, then you should discuss the matter right away with other staff, and please report as soon as is feasible to the Director or Counselor.

  - If a child should tell a story that is provoking strong emotion, for example a story about a death of a grandparent or a pet, you may want to use a similar strategy as above, depending on your best judgment about the child's ability to resolve the matter. Story-sharing is one of our best ways of coping with and regulating strong emotion, so you do not necessarily want to intervene to stop a child from telling a sad story. You will have to be sensitive, however, to the possibility that a child could bring up emotions he or she is unable to regulate. Use your best judgment, always being attentive both to the emotions expressed by the story-teller and to those expressed by the listening children.

  - We want KidsTalk stories to be personal narratives. Interrupt the story-teller if he or she begins to recount a movie or TV show. Just say – "Hold on a minute! KidsTalk is for stories about things that really happened to you. Think for a minute more and you'll remember a time when . . . [re-state the prompt]" – then give the story stick to someone else or tell a short story yourself while the child is thinking.

- Any time a KidsTalk session has been difficult for any reason, discuss the session afterward with your professor, your supervisor, or the designated staff person.

APPENDIX G

The Reader's Toolkit: A Text-to-Self Exercise to Facilitate Learning

Whitney Chatterjee, a teacher and reading interventionist in Charleston, South Carolina, developed *The Reader's Toolkit* (2016), a set of tools (given to each child in a 'toolkit') that make advanced reading skills, such as drawing inferences and applying prior knowledge to learning in independent reading, concrete and applicable for young readers. For example, during classroom reading exercises, when students make a text-to-self connection, they pull out a paper clip with their picture glued to it from their toolkit and attach it to the page where they made a connection. Students then share their personal story with the rest of the class. Just as they know that a paper clip attaches one piece of paper to another, they come to realize that their own personal stories attach to those of the characters or the information in a book. This simple but powerful activity keeps children engaged by using a tangible object and it draws them into a narrative community by giving them the opportunity to share (and to listen to) personal stories that are related to course material. (See all examples of reading tools in the tables below.)

TOOLS FOR DECODING WORDS:		
hippo		Use the hippo to memorize sight words that don't follow the rules.
pencil		Use the pencil to mark the vowels and circle the digraphs in order to decode challenging words.
band-aid		Use the band-aid to cover up the prefix or suffix of a word andsound it out in parts.

magnifying glass		Use the magnifying glass to look for clues in the pictures.
scissors and highlighter		Use the scissors to cut out a word that you can't seem to read. Use the highlighter to highlight clues that will help you understand what the word might mean.

TOOLS FOR READING FLUENTLY:		
running shoes		Use the running shoes to get a running start after you decode a challenging word.
stop sign		Use the stop sign to remember to stop at the end of every sentence as you read.
microphone		Use the microphone to read fluently with expression and inflection.

TOOLS FOR UNDERSTANDING IDEAS:		
picture frame and hammer		Use the picture frame to create a picture in your mind of what is happening in the story. Use the hammer to hang all of your pictures up in your gallery.
file folder		Use the file folder to record important details from the story. Give the folder a label that indicates the main idea of the story.
paper clip		Use the paper clip to attach what you already know to what you are reading about.
ruler		Use the ruler to stop along the way and measure where you are in the story and how well you can retell it.
tape measure		Use the tape measure to reach ahead in the story and predict what might happen next.
brain		Use your brain to leave think-prints as you use the tools to gather clues and understand ideas from the story that the author didn't even write down!

INDEX